Teachers Engaged in Research

Inquiry Into Mathematics Classrooms, Grades 3–5

a volume in
Teachers Engaged in Research

Series Editor
Denise S. Mewborn
University of Georgia

Teachers Engaged in Research

Inquiry Into Mathematics Classrooms, Grades 3–5

edited by
Cynthia W. Langrall
Illinois State University

INFORMATION AGE
PUBLISHING

Greenwich, Connecticut • www.infoagepub.com

Library of Congress Cataloging-in-Publication Data

Teachers engaged in research : inquiry into mathematics classrooms, grades
3-5 / edited by Cynthia W. Langrall.
    p. cm. – (Teachers engaged in research)
 Includes bibliographical references.
 ISBN 1-59311-497-4 (pbk.) – ISBN 1-59311-498-2 (hardcover)
 1. Mathematics–Study and teaching (Elementary) 2. Elemental school
teaching–Research. I. Title: Inquiry into mathematics classrooms, grades
3-5. II. Langral, Cynthia W. III. Series.
 QA11.2.T42 2006
 372.7–dc22

                     2006007052

Printed in the United States of America

LIST OF CONTRIBUTORS

Barbara Adams	Des Moines Public Schools
Judy Atcheson	Zippel Elementary School, Presque Isle, Maine
Marilyn Cochran-Smith	Boston College
Tammy Covi	Rochester Elementary School, Rochester, Illinois
Cynthia Langrall	Illinois State University
Cheryl A. Lubinski	Illinois State University
Christina Nugent	Dubuque Community School District, Dubuque, Iowa
Eileen Phillips	Vancouver School Board, B.C., Canada
Laurel D. Puchner	Southern Illinois University Edwardsville
Nadene Ratcliffe	Tri-Valley Elemntary School, Downs, Illinois
Gwen Scheibel	Millstadt Consolodated School, Millstadt, Illinois
Jennifer Segebart	Johnston Community School District, Johnston, Iowa
Janet Sharp	Montana State University
June Soares	Fowler and Letourneau Elementary Schools, Fall River, Massachusetts
Meghan B. Steinmeyer	University of Wisconsin Milwaukee
Ann R. Taylor	Southern Illinois University Edwardsville
Keri Valentine	Clarke County School District, Athens, Georgia
Janet Warfield	Illinois State University
Dorothy Y. White	University of Georgia
Vicki Zack	St. George's School, Montreal, Quebec, Canada

CONTENTS

SERIES FOREWORD

Marilyn Cochran-Smith
Boston College

This series, *Teachers Engaged in Research: Inquiry Into Mathematics Classrooms*, represents a remarkable accomplishment. In four books, one each devoted to teaching and learning mathematics at different grade level groupings (Pre-K–2, 3–5, 6–8, and 9–12), ninety-some authors and co-authors write about their work as professional mathematics educators. Across grade levels, topics, professional development contexts, schools, school districts, and even nations, the chapters in these four books attest to the enormous complexity of teaching mathematics well and to the power of inquiry as a way of understanding and managing that complexity.

In a certain sense, of course, the education community already knows that doing a good job of teaching mathematics is demanding—and all too infrequent—and that it requires deep and multiple layers of knowledge about subject matter, learners, pedagogy, and contexts. Nearly two decades of ground-breaking research in cognition and mathematics education has told us a great deal about this. But the books in this series are quite different from most of what has come before. These four books tell us about teaching and learning mathematics from the inside—from the perspectives of school-based teacher researchers who have carefully studied the commonplaces of mathematics teaching and learning, such as the whole

Teachers Engaged in Research
Inquiry in Mathematics Classrooms, Grades 3–5, pages ix–xx

class lesson, the small group activity, the math problem, the worksheet where the student shows his or her work, the class discussion about solutions and answers, and the teacher development activity. Taking these and other commonplaces of mathematics teaching and learning as sites for inquiry, the multiple authors of the chapters in these four books offer richly textured and refreshingly insightful insider accounts of mathematics teaching and learning. Reflecting on the contrasts that sometimes exist between teachers' intentions and the realities of classroom life, the chapters depict teachers in the process of considering and reconsidering the strategies and materials they use. Drawing on students' work and classroom discourse, the chapters show us what it looks like as teachers strive to make sense of and capitalize on their students' reasoning processes, even when they don't end up with traditional right answers. Staying close to the data of practice, the chapters raise old and new questions about how students—and teachers—learn to think and work mathematically. In short, this remarkable quartet of books reveals what it really means—over time and in the context of different classrooms and schools—for mathematics teachers to engage in inquiry. The goal of all this inquiry is nothing short of a culture shift in the teaching of mathematics—the creation of classroom learning environments where the focus is deep understanding of mathematical concepts, practical application of skills, and problem solving.

These four books provide much-needed and rich detail from the inside about the particulars of mathematics teaching and learning across a remarkably broad range of contexts, grade levels, and curricular areas. In addition, the books tell us a great deal about teachers' and pupils' learning over time (and the reciprocal relationships of the two) as well as the social, intellectual and organizational contexts that support their learning. Undoubtedly teachers and teacher educators will find these books illuminating and will readily see how the authors' successes and the struggles resonate with their own. If this were the only contribution this series made, it would be an important and worthwhile effort. But this series does much more. The books in this series also make an important contribution to the broader education community. Taken together as a whole, the chapters in these four books have the potential to inform mathematics education research, practice and policy in ways that reach far beyond the walls of the classrooms where the work was originally done.

TAKING AN INQUIRY STANCE

This series of books shows brilliantly and in rich and vivid detail what it means for teachers to take an inquiry stance on teaching and learning mathematics in K-12 classrooms over the professional lifespan. "Inquiry stance" is a concept that my colleague, Susan Lytle, and I have written about over the last decade and a half. It grew out of the dialectic of our simultaneous work as teacher educators involved in day-to-day, year-to-year participation in teacher learning communities, on the one hand, and as researchers engaged in theorizing the relationships of inquiry, knowledge, and practice, on the other. In our descriptions of inquiry as stance, we have repeatedly emphasized its distinction from "inquiry as project." By inquiry project (as opposed to stance), we refer to things like the classroom study that is the required culminating activity during the student teaching semester in a preservice program where inquiry is not integral and not infused throughout, or, the day-long workshop on teacher research or action research that is part of a catalog of professional development options for experienced teachers rather than a coherent part of teacher learning over the lifespan.

Teacher research or inquiry *projects* are discrete and bounded activities, often carried out on a one-time or occasional basis. In contrast, as we have suggested (Cochran-Smith & Lytle, 1999), when inquiry is a *stance*, it extends across the entire professional lifespan, and it represents a world view or a way of knowing about teaching and learning rather than a professional project:

> In everyday language, "stance" is used to describe body postures, particularly with regard to the position of the feet, as in sports or dance, and also to describe political positions, particularly their consistency (or the lack thereof) over time. In the discourse of qualitative research, "stance" is used to make visible and problematic the various perspectives through which researchers frame their questions, observations, and interpretations of data. In our work, we offer the term *inquiry as stance* to describe the positions teachers and others who work together in inquiry communities take toward knowledge and its relationships to practice. We use the metaphor of stance to suggest both orientational and positional ideas, to carry allusions to the physical placing of the body as well as to intellectual activities and perspectives over time. In this sense, the metaphor is intended to capture the ways we stand, the ways we see, and the lenses we see through. Teaching is a complex activity that occurs within webs of social, historical, cultural and political significance. Across the life span an inquiry stance provides a kind of grounding within the changing cultures of school reform and competing political agendas.

> *Inquiry as stance* is distinct from the more common notion of inquiry as time-bounded project or activity within a teacher education course or professional development workshop. Taking an inquiry stance

means teachers and student teachers working within inquiry communities to generate local knowledge, envision and theorize their practice, and interpret and interrogate the theory and research of others. Fundamental to this notion is the idea that the work of inquiry communities is both social and political—that is, it involves making problematic the current arrangements of schooling, the ways knowledge is constructed, evaluated, and used, and teachers' individual and collective roles in bringing about change. To use *inquiry as stance* as a construct for understanding teacher learning in communities, we believe that we need a richer conception of knowledge than that allowed by the traditional formal knowledge-practical knowledge distinction, a richer conception of practice than that suggested in the aphorism that practice is practical, a richer conception of learning across the professional life span than that implied by concepts of expertise that differentiate expert teachers from novices, and a rich conception of the cultures of communities as connected to larger educational purposes and contexts . (pp. 288–289)

Developing and sustaining an inquiry stance on teaching, learning and schooling is a life-long and constant pursuit for beginning teachers, experienced teachers, and teacher educators alike. A central aspect of taking an inquiry stance is recognizing that learning to teach is a process that is never completed but is instead an ongoing endeavor. The bottom-line purpose of taking an inquiry stance, however, is not teachers' development for its own sake (although this is an important and valuable goal), but teachers' learning in the service of enriched learning opportunities for Pre-K–12 students.

The chapters in these four books vividly explicate the work of Pre-K–12 teacher researchers who engage in inquiry to transform their teaching practice, expand the mathematical knowledge and skill of their students, and ultimately to enhance their students' life chances in the world. Across the 50 chapters in these books, the serious intellectual work of mathematics teaching is revealed again and again as are the passion teachers have for their work (and their students) and the complexity of the knowledge teachers must have to support students' emerging mathematical development.

INQUIRY INTO TEACHING AND LEARNING IN MATHEMATICS

Over the last two decades, various forms of practitioner inquiry, such as teacher research, action research, and collaborative inquiry, have become commonplace in preservice teacher preparation programs as well as in professional development projects and school reform efforts of various kinds. Although there are many variations and often different underlying assumptions among these, the use of inquiry has generally reflected a move away from transmission models of teacher training and retraining wherein teachers are expected to implement specific practices developed by others. The move has been toward a concept of teacher learning as a life-long process of both posing and answering questions appropriate to local contexts, working within learning communities to construct and solve problems, and making all of the aspects of the work of teaching possible sites for inquiry.

As this series of books demonstrates so clearly, an inquiry stances is quite compatible with the professional standards for teaching and learning mathematics that have emerged since the mid 1980s. In fact, in a number of the chapters in these books, the explicit purpose of the researchers is to study the implementation and effectiveness of standards-driven mathematics teaching and learning. The chapters concentrate on a wide range of mathematics topics, for example: concepts of number, addition and subtraction, algebraic thinking, linear measurement, geometric patterns and shapes, classification and sorting, mathematical proofs, multiplicative reasoning, division of fractions, data analysis and probability, volume, and the concept of limit. The chapters also examine what happens in terms of students' learning and classroom culture when various strategies and teaching methods are introduced: bringing in new models and representations of mathematical concepts and operations, teaching with problems, using writing in mathematics instruction, having students share their solution strategies, supporting students' own development of the algorithms for various mathematical operations, encouraging students to work in small groups and other collaborative arrangements, including role play in one's repertoire of mathematics teaching strategies, and integrating multiple opportunities for students to participate in hands-on technology and to work with technology-rich problems. Taken as a group, the chapters in these four volumes illustrate the power of an inquiry stance to widen and deepen teachers' knowledge of the subject matter of mathematics at the same time that this stance also enhances teachers' understanding of the learning processes of their students. Both of these—deeper knowledge of mathematics and richer understandings of learners and learning—are essential ingredients in teaching mathematics consistent with today's high standards.

Some of the chapters in these four volumes are written by single authors. These chronicle the ongoing efforts of teachers to understand what is going on in their classrooms so they can build on the knowledge and experiences students bring at the same time that they expand students' knowledge and skill. It is not at all surprising, however, that many of the chapters are co-authored, and even the single-authored chapters often reflect teachers' experiences as part of larger learning communities. Inquiry and community go hand in hand. The inquiries reported in these volumes feature collaborations among teachers and a whole array of colleagues, including fellow teachers, teacher study groups, teacher educators, university-based researchers, professional development facilitators, curriculum materials developers, research and development center researchers, and directors of large-scale professional development projects.

Across the chapters, there is a fascinating range of collaborative relationships between and among the teacher researchers and the subjects/objects of their inquiries: two teachers who collaborate to expand their own knowledge of mathematical content, the teacher researcher who is the subject of another researcher's study, the school-based teacher researcher and the university-based researcher who form a research partnership, the teacher who collaborates with a former teacher currently engaged in graduate study, pairs and small groups of teachers who work together to implement school-wide change in how mathematics is taught, teachers who team up to examine whether and how standards for mathematics teaching and learning are being implemented in their classrooms, teachers who engage in inquiry as part of their participation in large-scale professional development projects, the teacher who is part of a team that developed a set of professional development materials, a pair of teachers who collaborate with a university-based research and development group, a group of teachers who develop an inquiry process as a way to induct new teachers into their school, two teachers who inquire together about pedagogy and practice in one teacher's classroom, and teachers who form research groups and partnerships to work with teacher educators and student teachers. Almost by definition, practitioner inquiry is a collegial process that both occurs within, and stems from, the collaborations of learning communities. What all of these collaborations have in common is the assumption that teacher learning is an across-the-professional-lifespan process that is never "finished" even though teachers have years of experience. The chapters make clear that learning from and about teaching through inquiry is important for beginning and experienced teachers, and the intellectual work required to teach mathematics well is ongoing.

The inquiries that are described in these four books attest loudly and clearly to the power of questions in teachers' and students' learning. These inquiries defy the norm that is common to some schools where the competent teacher is assumed to be self-sufficient and certain and where asking questions is considered inappropriate for all but the most inexperienced teachers. Similarly, the chapters in these four books challenge the myth that good teachers rarely have questions they cannot answer about their own practices or about their students' learning. To the contrary, although the teachers in these four books are without question competent and may indeed be self-sufficient and sometimes certain, they are remarkable for their questions. Teachers who are researchers continuously pose problems, identify discrepancies between theory and practice, and challenge common routines. They continuously ask critical questions about teaching and learning and they do not flinch from self-critical reflection: Are the students really understanding what the teacher is teaching? What is the right move to make at various points in time to foster students' learning? How does the teacher know this? Are new curricular materials and teaching strategies actually supporting students' learning? How do students' mathematical ideas change over time? What is the evidence of students' growth and development? How can theory guide practice? How can practice add to, even alter, theory? These teachers ask questions not because they are failing, but because they—and their students—are learning. They count on their collaborators for alternative perspectives about their work and alternative interpretations of what is going on. In researching and writing about their work, they make explicit and visible to others both the decisions that they make on an ongoing basis and the intellectual processes that are the backdrop for those decisions. Going public with questions, seeking help from colleagues, and opening up one's practice to the scrutiny of outsiders may well go against the norms of appropriate teaching behaviors in some schools and school districts. But, as the chapters in this series of books make exquisitely clear, these are the very activities that lead to enriched learning opportunities and expanded knowledge for both students and teachers.

In this current era of accountability, there is heavy emphasis on evidence-based education and great faith in the power of data and research to improve educational practice. The chapters in the four books in this series illustrate what it looks like when mathematics teaching and learning are informed by research and evidence. In some of the chapters, for example, teacher researchers explicitly examine what happens when they attempt to implement research-based theories and teaching strategies into classroom practice. In these instances, as in others, practice is driven by research and evidence in several ways. Teacher researchers study the work of other researchers, treating this work as generative and illuminating, rather than regarding it as prescriptive and limiting. They reflect continuously about how others' research can (and should) inform their curricular, instructional, and assessment decisions about teaching mathematics. They also examine what consequences these decisions have for students' learning by collecting and analyzing a wide array of classroom data—from young children's visual representations of mathematical concepts and operations to classroom discussions about students' differing solutions to math problems to pre- and post-tests of students' mathematical knowledge and skill to interviews with students about their understandings to students' scores on standardized achievement tests.

In many of the chapters, teachers explicitly ask what it is that students know, what evidence there is that students have this knowledge and that it is growing and developing, and how this evidence can be used to guide their decisions about what to do next, with whom, and under what conditions. Braided together with these lines of inquiry about students' learning are questions about teachers' own ways of thinking about mathematics knowledge and skill. It is interesting that in many of the inquiries described in these four books, it is difficult to separate process from product or to sort out instruction from assessment. In fact, many of the chapters reveal that the distinctions often made between instruction and assessment and between process and product are false dichotomies. When mathematics teaching is guided by an inquiry stance and when teachers make decisions based on the data of practice, assessment of students' knowledge and skill is ongoing and is embedded into instruction, and the products of students' learning are inseparable from their learning and reasoning processes.

Finally, in some of the chapters in this quartet of books, teacher researchers and their colleagues use the processes of inquiry to examine issues of equity and social justice in mathematics teaching and learning. For example, one teacher problematizes commonly used phrases and ideas in mathematics education such as "success," particularly for those who have been previously unsuccessful in mathematics. Another explores connections between culture and mathematics by interviewing students. A trio of teachers examines the mathematical understandings of their students with disabilities, while another teacher chronicles his efforts to construct mathematics problems and projects that focus on social justice. Each of these educators values and draws heavily on the data of students' own voices and perspectives; each works to empower students as active agents in their own learning. These examples are a very important part of the collection of inquiries in this book series. When scholars write about teaching and teacher education for social justice, mathematics is the subject matter area least often included in the discussion. When teachers share examples of teaching for social justice in their own schools and classrooms, mathematics is often the area they have the most difficulty incorporating. When student teachers plan lessons and units related to equity and diversity, mathematics is often the subject area for which they cannot imagine any connection. The chapters in these books that specifically focus on equity and social justice make it clear that these issues readily apply to mathematics teaching and learning. But even in the many chapters for which these issues are not the explicit focus, it is clear that the teachers' intention is to empower all students—even (and especially) those groups least well served by the current educational system—with greater mathematical acuity and agency.

THE VALUE OF TEACHERS' INQUIRIES INTO MATHEMATICS TEACHING AND LEARNING

There is no question that engaging in inquiry about teaching and learning mathematics is an important (and often an extremely powerful) form of professional development that enhances teachers' knowledge, skill and understandings. This is clear in chapter after chapter in the four volumes of this series. The authors themselves describe the process of engaging in self-critical systematic inquiry as transformative and professionally life-changing. They persuasively document how their classroom practices and their ways of thinking about mathematical knowing changed over time. They combine rich and multiple data sources to demonstrate growth in their students' knowledge and skill. Undoubtedly many Pre-K–12 teachers and school- and university-based teacher educators will find the inquiries collected in these four volumes extraordinarily helpful in furthering their own work. The questions raised by the teacher researchers (often in collaboration with university-based colleagues and others) will resonate deeply with the questions and issues of other educators striving to teach mathematics well by fostering conceptual understandings of big mathematical ideas, reliable but imaginative problem solving strategies, and solid mathematical know-how about practical applications to everyday problems. The teacher researchers whose work is represented in these volumes have made their questions and uncertainties about mathematics teaching explicit and public. In doing so, they have offered their own learning as grist for the learning and development of other teachers, teacher educators, and researchers. This is a major contribution of the series.

Few readers of the volumes in this series will debate the conclusion that systematically researching one's own work as a mathematics educator is a valuable activity for teacher researchers themselves, for their students in Pre-K–12 schools and classrooms, and for other Pre-K–12 teachers and teacher educators who are interested in the same issues. But some readers will raise questions about whether or not there is value to this kind of inquiry that carries beyond the participants involved in the local context or that extends outside the Pre-K–12 teaching/teacher education community. After all, the argument of some skeptics might go, for the most part the inquiries about mathematics teaching and learning that are included in this series were prompted by the questions of individual teachers or by small local groups of practitioners working in collaboration. With a few exceptions, these inquiries were conducted in the context of a single classroom, course,

school, or program. Almost by definition then, the skeptics might say, few of
the inquiries in these four volumes can hold up to traditional research criteria
for transferability and application of findings to other populations and contexts (especially if conceptualized as the identification of causes and
effects). For this reason, the skeptics might conclude, the kind of work
included in this series is nothing more than good professional development for individuals in local communities, which may be of interest to
other teacher educators and professional developers.

Putting aside for the moment that good professional development is
essential in mathematics education (not to mention, hard to come by), the
skeptics' line of argument, as outlined in the paragraph above, is both
short-sighted and uninformed. The inquiries that are part of the *Teachers
Engaged in Research: Inquiry Into Mathematics Classrooms* series are valuable
and valid well beyond the borders of the local communities where the work
was done, and the criteria for evaluating traditional research are not so
appropriate here. With many forms of practitioner inquiry, appropriate
conceptions of value and validity are more akin to the idea of "trustworthiness" that has been forwarded by some scholars as a way to evaluate the
results of qualitative research. From Mishler's (1990) perspective, for
example, the concept of validation ought to replace the notion of validity.
Validation is the extent to which a particular research community, which
works from "tacit understandings of actual, situated practices of a field of
inquiry" (Lyons and LaBoskey, 2002, p. 19), can rely on the concepts,
methods, and inferences of an inquiry for their own theoretical and conceptual work. Following this line of reasoning, validation rests on concrete examples (or "exemplars") of actual practices presented in enough
detail so that the relevant community of practitioner researchers can
judge the trustworthiness and usefulness of the observations and analyses
of an inquiry.

Many of the inquiries in these four books offer what may be thought of
as exemplars of teaching and learning mathematics that are consistent
with current professional standards in mathematics education. Part of what
distinguishes the inquiries of the teacher researchers in these four books
from those of outside researchers who rely on similar forms of data collection is that in addition to documenting students' learning, teacher
researchers have the opportunity and the access to systematically document their own teaching and learning as well. They can document their
own thinking, planning, and evaluation processes as well as their questions, interpretive frameworks, changes in views over time, issues they see
as dilemmas, and themes that recur. Teacher researchers are able to analyze the links as well as the disconnects between teaching and learning that
are not readily accessible to researchers based outside the contexts of practice. Systematic examination and analysis of students' learning juxtaposed

and interwoven with systematic examination of the practitioners' intentions, reactions, decisions, and interpretations make for incredibly detailed and complex analyses—or exemplars—of mathematics teaching and learning.

With rich examples, the teacher researchers in these books demonstrate how they came to understand their students' reasoning processes and thus learned to intervene more adeptly with the right question, the right comment, a new problem, or silent acknowledgement and support. Braiding insightful reflections on pedagogy with perceptive analyses of their students' understandings, the authors in these four books make explicit and visible the kinds of thinking and decision making that are usually implicit and invisible in studies of mathematics teaching. Although they are usually invisible, however, these ways of thinking and making teaching decisions are essential ingredients for teaching mathematics to today's high standards. I believe that a critical contribution of this series of books—a contribution that extends well beyond the obvious benefits to the participants themselves—is the set of exemplars that cuts across grade levels and mathematics topics. What makes this series unique is that the exemplars in this book do not emerge from the work of university-based researchers who have used the classroom as a site for research and for the demonstration of theory-based pedagogy. Rather the trustworthiness—or validation—of the exemplars in these four books derives from the fact that they were conducted by school-based teacher researchers who shouldered the full responsibilities of classroom teaching while also striving to construct appropriate curriculum, develop rich teaching problems and strategies, and theorize their practice by connecting it to larger philosophical, curricular, and pedagogical ideas.

This series of books makes a remarkable contribution to what we know about mathematics teaching and learning and about the processes of learning to teach over time. Readers will be thoroughly engaged.

REFERENCES

Cochran-Smith, M., & Lytle, S. L. (1999). Relationship of knowledge and practice: Teacher learning in communities. In A. Iran-Nejad & C. Pearson (Eds.), *Review of research in education* (Vol. 24, pp. 249–306). Washington, DC: American Educational Research Association.

Lyons, N., & LaBoskey, V. K. (Eds.). (2002). *Narrative inquiry in practice: Advancing the knowledge of teaching.* New York: Teachers College Press.

Mishler, E. (1990). Validation in inquiry-guided research: The role of exemplars in narrative studies. *Harvard Educational Review, 60*(4), 415–442.

CHAPTER 1

INTRODUCTION TO THE 3–5 VOLUME

Cynthia W. Langrall[1]
Illinois State University

What is a teacher's role in research? Certainly teachers have been the *impetus* of research studies throughout the history of educational research. They also have been referred to as *consumers* of research. It is unusual, however, for teachers to be considered *producers* of research. Yet it is not unusual for teachers to be engaged in inquiry. In fact, some would consider this a fair description of what it means to teach. The difference is that for most teachers, the process as well as the product of their inquiry is tacit. It may not be well defined in terms of specific research questions or systematic in terms of data collection and analysis. Furthermore, their work may not be presented to colleagues for discussion and review or disseminated for publication. Those scholarly activities are not part of the culture of teaching in most school systems in North America.

But that may be changing, as demonstrated by the chapters in this volume. Teachers are becoming engaged in research in a variety of ways and their voices are gaining presence in the mathematics education research community. The authors who contributed to this volume were involved in research through activities that included:

Teachers Engaged in Research
Inquiry Into Mathematics Classrooms, Grades 3–5, pages 1–12
Copyright © 2006 by Information Age Publishing
All rights of reproduction in any form reserved.

- reading and reflecting on research and other literature in the field,
- interpreting findings from the research literature to influence their instructional practice,
- participating in study groups with their colleagues,
- generating research questions for themselves and others to investigate,
- participating in research studies and professional development projects led by other researchers, and
- designing and implementing their own studies and sharing their findings with others.

The authors' involvement in these research activities had a profound impact on their conceptions of teaching and learning, and prompted changes in their instructional practice. Such direct impact on practice is one of the many benefits of research that emanates from the classroom and that is conducted by teachers themselves. By sharing the teacher research in this volume, we hope to broaden its impact beyond the authors' classrooms and schools to the wider mathematics education community.

HOW THIS VOLUME CAME TO BE

History of the Series

The idea for the *Teachers Engaged in Research* series arose from efforts by the Research Advisory Committee (RAC) of the National Council of Teachers of Mathematics (NCTM) to expand traditional conceptions of research in mathematics to include practitioner inquiry and the research questions that are of interest to practitioners. Beginning in the late 1990s, the RAC made a concerted effort to recognize teachers as producers (and not just consumers) of research. To this end, NCTM sponsored a Working Conference on Teacher Research in Mathematics Education in Albuquerque, NM in 2001. The goal of this conference was to articulate a list of issues that should be considered in developing a framework for teacher research in mathematics education. This conference led to a grant proposal that would have brought together participants from the conference for a writing workshop with the goal of producing a publication similar to this one. For a variety of reasons, that project did not come to fruition.

The RAC turned its attention to including teacher researchers as participants–both attendees and speakers–at the Research Presession that precedes the annual NCTM meeting. Also, there was ongoing dialogue in the RAC about a publication that would highlight practitioner inquiry. Simultaneously, the RAC and the Educational Materials Committee (EMC) decided that it was time to issue an update of the *Handbook of Research on Mathematics Teaching and Learning* (Grouws, 1992). Unbeknownst to many, the series titled *Research into Practice* edited by Sigrid Wagner was originally conceived by the EMC as a "companion" to the handbook. The *Research into Practice* series featured chapters co-authored by university-based researchers and classroom teachers and reflected a view of teachers as consumers of research—an accurate reflection of the field at the time. When the RAC and EMC discussed the update of the handbook and its companion, the companion was recast to reflect a view of teachers as producers of research. The *Handbook of Research on Mathematics Teaching and Learning, 2nd Edition* (Lester, in preparation) documents a portion of the knowledge base available in mathematics education; the four volumes of the *Teachers Engaged in Research* series fill a gap in that knowledge base by focusing on the research contributions of classroom teachers, thus allowing a different set of voices to be heard.

The goal of this series is to use teachers' accounts of classroom inquiry to make public and explicit the processes of doing research in classrooms. Teaching is a complex, multi-faceted task, and this complexity often is not captured in research articles. Our goal is to illuminate this complexity. Research that is done in classrooms by and with teachers is necessarily messy, and our stance is that the ways in which this is so should be articulated, not hidden.

Identifying Authors

Using the participants of the Albuquerque conference as a starting point, the editorial board for the series generated a list of teachers, projects, and university faculty who we knew had been engaged in classroom research themselves or might know of others who had. Through personal contacts with these individuals, and those they led us to, we compiled a list of potential authors, the nature of their work, and relevant background information. For each volume, we attempted to generate a set of potential authors and topics that would span aspects of the *Principles and Standards for School Mathematics* (NCTM, 2000), such as the content standards, process standards, and principles. We also tried to find a set of pieces that would span various roles that teachers might play in research—principal researcher, co-researcher, research participant, and consumer of research. We then invited authors for specific chapters in accordance with the categories outlined above. Authors were specifically asked to highlight the following aspects of their work in their manuscripts:

- mathematical content and processes that were addressed (using the *Principles and Standards* document as a guide)
- demographic data on school/student population/community (as it pertains to the research)
- the authors' role in the research and what the experience was like for them
- data sources for the work (incorporated into the narrative as appropriate, e.g,. interview transcripts, student work, teacher reflections, summary of a class session)
- explanation of data analysis process (How did the authors make sense of their data?)
- articles that influenced their work (rather than a full literature review, references to work that may have sparked their curiosity, helped them think of data collection methods, contrasted their findings, or was helpful in another way)
- implications (How did this influence the authors' subsequent teaching? What might others take away from this study?)

We particularly stressed the need for the manuscripts to reflect disciplined inquiry and for claims to be based on evidence.

The Review Process

The editorial board took great care with the review process in an effort to be respectful of the varied experiences the authors had with writing for publication. Initial outlines and drafts were reviewed and commented on by the volume editor to ensure that the general flavor of the manuscript met the goals for the series. For the grades 3–5 volume, more polished drafts were reviewed by two reviewers—one teacher and one university teacher educator.[2] To the extent possible, we solicited reviewers who had experience with teacher inquiry. We asked reviewers to be sensitive to the fact that the authors were making themselves vulnerable by sharing their research with a wider audience, and we reminded them that the type of research reflected in the manuscripts might be different than research that is traditionally reported in journal articles. Thus, we asked the reviewers to approach their task from a mentoring frame of mind, striving to both support the authors and strengthen the manuscript.

The timeline from first draft to final publication of this series was a long one, and I commend the authors in this volume for their patience and willingness to engage in the challenging and arduous process of writing for publication. I have developed great respect for the ways in which they, as teacher researchers, have documented, analyzed, and shared their experiences integrating inquiry with teaching.

WHAT WE LEARN FROM THIS RESEARCH

Through the chapters in this volume we learn about the questions that capture the attention of teachers, the methodologies they use to gather data, and the ways in which they make sense of what they find. Some of the research findings could be considered preliminary, others confirmatory, and some may be groundbreaking. In all cases, they provide fodder for further thinking and discussion about critical aspects of mathematics education.

Barbara Adams and Janet Sharp (Chapter 2) tackle the issue of why a teacher would (or should) engage in classroom research. They detail the process of developing a research question and designing a study motivated by a problem of practice and informed by the research literature. Although Adams and Sharp provide a summary of their findings about how Grade 5 students developed algorithms for dividing fractions, an important focus of the chapter pertains to their personal and professional growth as a result of their collaboration. As readers, we learn how the teaching practices of both teacher (Adams) and academic (Sharp) were influenced by the research and the value each of these perspectives brought to the research collaborative. We also gain insights into the common, everyday challenges that can be expected when conducting teacher research.

The research presented by Tammy Covi, Nadene Ratcliffe, Cheryl Lubinski, and Janet Warfield (Chapter 3) is another example of collaboration between teacher educators at the school and university levels. It stemmed from a conjecture that many students fail to rely on reasoning when solving mathematics problems. These authors designed a study to test their conjecture by examining a wide range of students' solutions to a nonroutine problem. They provide the reader a detailed description of the framing of their research questions and their methods of investigation. The finding that few students in their study exhibited a reasoned approach to solving the problem prompted the authors to consider implications for instruction. Their work underscores the importance of obtaining evidence to test one's conjectures and using evidence to guide practice. This chapter also shows the generative nature of research in that the investigation of a general pedagogical problem has pointed the way to further research through its implications for classroom practice.

Rather than conducting her own research, June Soares (Chapter 4) participated in a professional development project that encouraged teachers to incorporate into practice the findings of research about algebraic reasoning. Soares discovered that although the children in her class exhibited many of the same misconceptions highlighted in the research, they also had the capacity to reason algebraically when given the opportunity to extend their thinking. Her first-hand account illustrates the power of research to influence practice when teachers are introduced to new ways of thinking about learning and teaching and encouraged to test those new ideas in their classrooms. Instrumental to her professional growth were the opportunities to dialog about the research and her students' understanding with experts in the field and other teachers in the project, as well as to participate directly in the research being conducted in her classroom.

Judy Atcheson (Chapter 5) reports on the research she conducted, in part, as a result of her participation in the Albuquerque Conference on Teacher Research in Mathematics Education. Working with the instructor and students of a university mathematics methods class, Atcheson designed, implemented, and assessed an instructional unit aimed at developing students' multiplicative reasoning. The collaboration allowed for richer data sources and analyses than might have been possible had she worked alone. Additionally, the preservice teachers gained experience delving deeply into students' thinking and examining the practice of teaching "in the moment." Atcheson's engagement in the research process acted as a form of professional development that has influenced her teaching beyond the context of the multiplication unit.

Eileen Phillips (Chapter 6) explores the role of writing in mathematics learning. Her research was prompted by her dissatisfaction with the quality of students' writing and belief that, from a student's perspective, much of the writing being called for in mathematics was not sufficiently justified. Thus, she sought to explore ways that writing could be incorporated into instruction genuinely and with mathematical purpose. In describing her work as a teacher researcher, Phillips makes an important distinction between *usual* teaching practice and *researched* teaching practice in terms of the degree of reflection in which she engages and the records that she keeps. She also contrasts her work as a teacher researcher with that of an "outside" researcher and reminds us of the affordances and constraints inherent in this dual position.

Christine Nugent (Chapter 7) and Jennifer Segebart (Chapter 8) were involved in a project designed to introduce teachers to action research and to help them make data-driven decisions about their instructional practice with the overarching goal of improving student achievement. Although they participated in different phases of the project, they both were involved in workshops and seminars to learn about current trends in mathematics education research and ways of implementing research ideas in the classroom. In examining their practice, they were encouraged to consider students' opportunity to learn and attitude toward mathematics. Both teachers drew from the research literature and used data from students' standardized achievement test scores to inform their work, albeit in different ways. Nugent took a qualitative stance in studying the effects of research-based changes in her approach to problem-solving instruction. Segebart's approach was more quantitative in nature as she studied the effects of an instructional unit on data and probability as well as general pedagogical changes she incorporated into her instructional practice. The investigations undertaken by Nugent and Segebart illustrate the personal, situated nature of action research and their work provides some insights into the first steps of teachers entering the arena of teacher research.

Meghan Steinmeyer (Chapter 9) describes how she seized the opportunity, provided by her participation in a professional development project, to study her own teaching. More specifically, she examined her role in, and the effectiveness of, the pedagogical practice of having students share their solution strategies for multi-digit subtraction. Steinmeyer was familiar with the research literature in this area and had developed a classroom practice of promoting student inquiry and teaching for understanding. Nevertheless, it was not until she took a reflective stance and closely examined her own teaching that she was able to fully appreciate the effects of her work and its contribution to the development of her students' understanding.

Keri Valentine and Dorothy White (Chapter 10) describe an action research project in which they investigated Valentine's use of questioning to teach probability. The impetus for the study was Valentine's interest in improving the effectiveness of her questioning and coming to "own" the ideas espoused in a teacher development project she had participated in with White. Again, we see the benefits of collaboration, which in this study–conducted in an inclusive classroom–also included a special education teacher. Valentine and White remind us that an inquiry approach to instruction can be beneficial for all students, even those experiencing learning difficulties.

The chapter by Ann Taylor, Laurel Puchner, and Gwen Scheibel (Chapter 11) is presented from two perspectives, essentially reporting a study within a study. One perspective is that of a teacher researcher (Scheibel) engaged in lesson study and the other is that of two university researchers (Taylor and Puchner) examining lesson study as a means of professional development. The lesson study process afforded Scheibel the opportunity to examine her instructional approach to problem solving. This had a profound effect on her own understanding of problem solving and how to teach it, and raised her expectations of students' abilities to solve problems. Taylor and Puchner's research findings describe and explain the depth of professional learning that was facilitated by the lesson study process.

In the final chapter, Vicki Zack (Chapter 12) shares a perspective of teacher research sharpened by 12 years of experience. The overarching aim of her work has been to study how learning is interactively accomplished; that is, how mathematical meaning is constructed and shared. She has pursued this systematically over the years by examining students' explanations, arguments, and notions of proof. Zack gives new meaning to the concept of *longitudinal* research as she returns to data that were collected years before and re-examines them in light of more recent work. In the process of conducting research to better understand her students' thinking she has deepened her own understanding of mathematics. Zack presents a thoughtful discussion about the rewards and challenges of teacher research and her closing remarks provide a poignant conclusion to this volume.

THEMES ACROSS THE RESEARCH

A number of commonalities or themes emerge when one looks across the body of research presented in this volume. The research can be characterized in two ways, as examining students' reasoning and problem solving and investigating aspects of instructional practice (with some studies specifically aimed at teacher questioning). Data sources commonly included video taped sessions, classroom observations, student work samples, teacher journals, and field notes. Thus for the most part, methods of analysis were qualitative in nature and involved coding transcripts, categorizing data, interpreting students' solution strategies and explanations, looking for trends and relationships among the data, and reflecting on what was found. Across the findings of these studies, several themes were evident and pertain to the importance of developing students' conceptual understanding along with procedural fluency, the benefits of engaging students in challenging problem-solving tasks and having them share their thinking, and the value of understanding and using students' thinking to inform instruction.

Perhaps the most important themes, however, are drawn from the teachers' perceptions of the benefits of engaging in research. Two in particular are noteworthy and related: the notion of teacher research as a form of professional development and the importance of collaboration. It is not surprising that many of the teachers reporting their work in this volume were introduced to, or given the opportunity to engage in research through their involvement in a professional development project. But it is also evident that the very act of conducting research resulted in the professional growth of every one of these teachers. What they learned about teaching and learning far exceeded the focus of their particular research questions. For some, the research validated their beliefs and instructional practices; for others it deepened or extended their understanding of mathematics, or raised their expectations of students' capabilities. And it is fair to say that for all, it increased their awareness of how students come to know and understand mathematics.

Does this imply that the answer to teacher professional development is to engage all teachers in classroom research? From a practical perspective, the answer is no. Research is a demanding enterprise for which teachers need time and support. The importance of collaboration to the success of the research reported in this volume is undeniable. Yet collaborations such as these with university teacher educators, mathematicians, and other teachers do not occur automatically. As you will see in the chapters that follow, they require great commitment from all involved and are built on trust and respect that is nurtured over time. Both school and university cultures need to support and value the type of collaborative work reported herein to make teacher research a viable professional development opportunity and to promote the contributions of teacher research to the field.

HOW THIS VOLUME MIGHT BE USED

This volume, and others in the *Teachers Engaged In Research* series, was written for teachers who have developed (or who are being encouraged to develop) an awareness of and commitment to teaching for understanding. The research findings presented in these chapters suggest instructional implications worthy of teachers' consideration. Often, authors have described instructional practices or raised issues that have the potential to broaden views of teaching and learning mathematics. Embedded in the chapters are interesting problems and tasks used in the authors' work that teachers could use in their own classrooms.

The volume could be particularly useful for teacher study groups, courses for preservice and inservice teachers, and professional development activities. A hallmark of good research is its connection to the extant literature in the field, and the authors of this volume have themselves drawn from the research literature to inform their work. The reference lists accompanying these chapters can be useful resources and should not be overlooked. Most importantly, this volume showcases the variety of ways teachers can become engaged in research and it is hoped that readers will recognize that teacher research can be accessible and potentially beneficial to their own work in the classroom.

This is not to suggest, however, that the volume is intended only for teachers. It could be an interesting, informative resource for other researchers, policy makers, school administrators, and teacher educators as well. In particular, the research presented in this volume provides an opportunity for those outside the classroom to gain insight into the kind of issues that matter to teachers, the ways in which those issues might be researched, and the contributions that research can make to the work of classroom teachers.

For the most part, what you are about to read are teachers' accounts of practice in which they have made public various aspects their teaching and their beliefs about teaching and learning. You might be tempted to examine their instructional approaches with a critical eye or to question the rigor of their research methods. And in fact, it is generally expected that published research stand up to such scrutiny. I encourage you, however, to also regard the work presented in this volume with respect (and perhaps even awe) and to champion the accomplishments of these teachers in studying and learning from their classroom practices and their students. They deserve no less for the risk they have taken in opening their research to public inspection. Learn from what they have presented. If you are a classroom teacher, let it inspire you to examine the questions of practice that interest or puzzle you. If you are a university teacher educator or researcher, let it be the impetus for you to engage in collaborative research with a classroom teacher.

NOTES

1   This chapter was written, in part, as a result of collaborative conversations with the editors of the other volumes of this series and the series editor. I wish to acknowledge the contributions of Joanna Masingila, Stephanie Smith, Laura Van Zoest, and Denise Mewborn. Also, I extend special thanks to Bea D'Ambrosio and Gini Stimpson, members of the editorial board, for their help in conceptualizing the nature and scope of this series and in identifying potential authors for each of the volumes.

2   A number of colleagues provided advice and input into the review process, as well as the editing of this volume. However, three people deserve special recognition for the careful reading and thoughtful reviews they provided to

the authors of these chapters: Molly Keogh, Robyn Ovrick, and Edward Mooney. I am grateful for their help and sincerely appreciate the time and energy they devoted to this work.

REFERENCES

Grouws, D. A. (Ed.). (1991). *Handbook of research on mathematics teaching and learning*. New York: Macmillan.

Lester, F. K. (Ed.) (in preparation). *Handbook of research on mathematics teaching and learning (2nd edition)*. Greenwich, CT: Infoage/NCTM.

National Council of Teachers of Mathematics. (2000). *Principles and standards for school mathematics*. Reston, VA: Author.

CHAPTER 2

THE IMPACT OF CLASSROOM RESEARCH ON STUDENT AND TEACHER LEARNING

Division of Fractions[1]

Barbara Adams
Des Moines Public Schools

Janet Sharp
Montana State University

My children settle into their seats for math by 8:15 am. But, I had arrived one and a half hours earlier to make copies, cut out some squares, organize the science display, and collect the books about heroes we would be studying that week. Then, my workday started with a 7:30 a.m. meeting of the academic achievement committee. The meeting ended with enough time only to make a quick check of email, reading several messages from parents as well as the daily school announcements. By 8:05, I position myself for hall duty and ten minutes later math begins.

Every day teachers organize their time and make the most of each minute in order to increase student learning. Why, then, would anyone

Teachers Engaged in Research
Inquiry Into Mathematics Classrooms, Grades 3–5, pages 13–32
Copyright © 2006 by Information Age Publishing
All rights of reproduction in any form reserved.

want to devote this prized instructional time to classroom research? What are the benefits of taking time to incorporate research into the daily life of a classroom? For us, a 5th grade teacher and a mathematics education professor, the quest to improve our understanding about students' thinking and impact our own teaching turned out to be worth the time. This chapter describes our project by focusing on reasons for our decisions, specifics of our project, and effects on our individual teaching practices at both school and collegiate levels. Along the way, we hope to reveal complexities in classroom research and to capture a useful description of resolving challenges as well as celebrating advantages of classroom research.

OUR RELATIONSHIP

We met during a collaborative four-year teacher development project connecting a university's faculty with teachers at an urban elementary school. The plan for school-wide growth included professional development for teachers and field experience for preservice elementary teachers. So, in our positions as classroom teacher (Adams) and university professor (Sharp), we valued one another as experts. This honest and mutual respect provided the foundation of our collaboration. Throughout the first two years of our relationship we guest taught in each other's classrooms, presented and attended program staff development, and evaluated Sharp's undergraduate students beginning with their early practicum-related courses and continuing to their later student teaching experiences in Adams' fifth-grade classroom. Since the time of the study we have both made career moves that modified our position responsibilities and geographic locations. Our new locations have changed the way we collaborate. Although our communication is now either written or discussed over the telephone, we continue to share what we learn from our students and colleagues.

GENESIS OF THE QUESTION

As we spent some of that treasured school-day time working together, we found ourselves discussing Michael, one of the preservice elementary teachers, who was troubled by fractions. He did not really understand them or find them useful. Although he could easily recall operation procedures, Michael had a difficult time helping students think conceptually about fractions. Despite this, we recognized he was making a conscious effort to carefully plan for and be upbeat in his instruction with 5th graders. *What was it about Michael's experiences that limited his fractional knowledge to the use of symbols and standard algorithms whereas 5th graders could represent fractions in a variety of ways?* Here we recognized our shared interest in understanding how young children learn fractional ideas and how those ideas transition into later grades. How were 5th grade students' typical fraction experiences different from middle school or even preservice elementary teachers' experiences? What instructional framework enabled 5th graders to construct knowledge about fractions? Did older students forget fraction knowledge because they seemed only to meet fractions during school? How could we know more about how 5th graders used their intuitive knowledge to make sense of fractions? What would make students remember algorithms later? For students who did remember fractions later, were they like Michael and limited in their understanding?

These questions reveal complex issues that can at first overwhelm educators because the questions appear unfocused. But, this is the nature of classroom research as we see it. Every piece of a child's learning experience is connected in a thick web and each strand of the web has an impact at some point. That is also one of the things making classroom research so hard. The prospect of isolating a single variable for replication in a lab setting not only does not appeal to us, but it is neither how classrooms work nor how children learn. That said we had to slow down and try to focus in on one cluster of things in order to find an appropriate first thing to study. We did not know how to immediately address Michael's awkwardness of fractions, but we did believe we could come to understand something about how fraction knowledge initially develops if we studied 5th graders' thinking. Typical 5th graders are on the precipice of studying fraction operations. We would start there too. In this round-about approach, we hoped to learn enough to modify our instruction in both college and elementary school.

Before we pinpointed our actual question, we needed to develop an understanding about when and how fraction knowledge develops. The National Council of Teachers of Mathematics (NCTM) (2000) suggests that by 5th grade students should have a conceptual understanding of fractions as parts of wholes, be able to recognize and find equivalent fractions, develop and use strategies to estimate computations involving fractions, and use visual models for addition and subtraction. We recognized these standards as combinations of procedural and conceptual knowledge. And, since procedural knowledge can grow from and along with conceptual knowledge (Carpenter, 1986), we wondered how our 5th graders would develop procedural knowledge of fractions that coincides with their understanding of whole numbers. We were swayed by Huinker's (1998) evidence that young students could develop algorithms from solving problems and kept in mind Kamii's (1985) insistence that students invent their own algorithms. When we found learning about abstract representations for fractions grows from problem contexts that are realistic to the children (Streefland, 1991), we knew we were well on our way to a meaningful question. In fact, the NCTM (2000) includes a comment about learning fractions in "situations relevant to students' experiences" (p. 148) as part of their standard for the 3–5 grade band. All of this information about the activities in which children should engage resonated with our instincts. Then, we read Mack (1990, 1995, 2001). She describes how students' existing informal knowledge about fractions influences learning. But, she also clarifies the role of the teacher as the ultimate piece of the puzzle, guiding questioning and carefully nurturing growth from each student's informal knowledge. This did not sound easy, but it was in harmony with our ideas about teaching. We were satisfied. We settled on an initial question.

Question: What sort of algorithm(s) would 5th graders invent for division of fractions if the learning was grounded in relevant contexts and students used their informal fraction knowledge and whole number knowledge to invent strategies for this operation?

We re-read the question several times, finding it long, wordy and overly-ripe with variables. So we tried to simplify it, rewriting to focus on fewer variables. But with each re-write, we recognized that, in some way, it no longer took into account the robustness of learning in classrooms. Classroom research requires an intricate question precisely because the ebb and flow of the classroom is taken into account. We retained our initial wording.

We settled on division of fractions because it is typically a 7th grade objective. We needed to concentrate on one thing and we knew it had to be a first experience for our students, or we would not be sure we were studying our instruction or the previous instruction of others. We believed our question would partially address why college students' recollections of fractions were limited to fraction operations without meaning. We also believed the question would help us find good ways to change our teaching. At the 5th grade level, we might better understand the role problem solving takes in developing fraction operation knowledge. At the collegiate level, we might better understand how studying children's work can help preservice elementary teachers experience situations in which they practice making the instructional decisions that will be required of them as teachers. By discussing 5th graders' efforts to solve division of fraction problems, preservice elementary teachers can become aware of how children approach new mathematical concepts and of how teachers might support growth in understanding. This became our first common bridge between collegiate education and classroom practice. We each wanted to discover more about how 5th grade learners develop algorithms for fraction division. However, we realized our collaboration would enrich not only our efforts to understand and implement ways to explore our question, but would also support our analysis of student work. We valued both an academic and a classroom teacher viewpoint about the data, which were authentic children's work. The best approach was a teaching experiment in the field.

ARTICLES THAT INFLUENCED OUR WORK

Reasons for Our Instructional Decisions

We anticipated our students would think about fractions using whole number and fraction concept knowledge. They knew a lot about whole numbers. We grew worried when we read how whole number interference (Behr, et.al., 1992) can cause students to misunderstand fraction operations because fractions do not appear to act exactly like whole numbers in algorithms. Then we read how Moss and Case (1999) pinpointed the problem causing 4th grade children to be so persuaded by whole number ideas. Students could not overcome whole number interference when taught only algorithms with symbols. We would focus on meaning for fraction division.

How is meaning developed? According to theorist Kieren (1988), children first know about fraction ideas from their personal lives. Rather than be troubled by this, Streefland (1991) asks teachers to capitalize on it, being mindful to place fraction experiences in realistic contexts building from there. We needed to find contexts that meant something to students. After checking textbooks for realistic problems, we grew tired of pizza and cooking recipes and supposed students would too. We paid attention to our own lives: cutting ribbon, scooping cereal, frosting portions of a cake, landscaping part of a yard, and storing portions of a pie.

We wondered about other aspects of writing good problems. We were thankful we read Pothier and Sawada's (1983) theory about the importance of ordering fractional amounts. Early experiences need denominators of powers of 2 (2, 4, 8, 16, …), middle experiences use other even denominators (6, 10, 12, …), and final experiences utilize odd denominators (3, 5, 7, 9, …). When we wrote our problems, we would not pick random fractions; we ordered them to reflect these stages.

We were not the only ones specifically interested in division of fractions. We remembered the invert and multiply algorithm from our own schooling and expected to read about it. But, several articles (Capps, 1962; Elashhab, 1978; McMeen, 1962; Kamii & Warrington, 1995; Warrington, 1997) opened our eyes to think about this operation with a different procedure. The common denominator algorithm is based on a familiar repeated-subtraction definition for division whereas the invert and multiply algorithm depends on division's inverse relationship with multiplication, an algebraic idea. But, even so, the common denominator algorithm is less commonly taught, due to complications associated with dealing with the remainder (Bray, 1963; Johnson 1965) at the end of the division process. (Table 2.1 shows procedures for the two algorithms.) If students were to build their own algorithms, the entire process would need to make sense, even the remainder. Still, we were encouraged. The subtractive definition of division would have meaning to our students and easily lend itself to our list of real-world situations. Our students knew how to rewrite fractions in improper form and could subtract fractions. This, together with students' prior knowledge about subtracting fractions, should be enough for students to solve problems and invent their own ways to operate. Kamii and Warrington (1995) assured us that students can do so while appropriately using whole number knowledge. We had the content figured out. Our next step was to think carefully about how the activity of the research project should take place within our classroom walls.

Both Kieren (1988) and Streefland (1991) explain that students must be nurtured toward developing representations using images, informal language and pictures as tools before they can use conventional language, or symbolic representations. We thought about discussion questions we might pose to move students from real-world experiences to pictures and to symbols. Kieren (1988) also prepared us not to be surprised when students flow back and forth between and among representations on their own. We would welcome this variety of representations.

Table 2.1.   Procedures of the Two Algorithms[2]

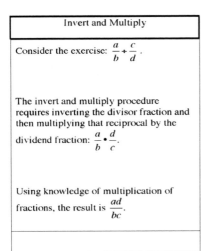

Invert and Multiply	Common Denominator
Consider the exercise: $\dfrac{a}{b} \div \dfrac{c}{d}$.	Consider the exercise: $\dfrac{a}{b} \div \dfrac{c}{d}$.
The invert and multiply procedure requires inverting the divisor fraction and then multiplying that reciprocal by the dividend fraction: $\dfrac{a}{b} \cdot \dfrac{d}{c}$.	The task is to determine how many times $\dfrac{c}{d}$ can be subtracted from $\dfrac{a}{b}$. Common denominators are required in order to complete the subtraction: $\dfrac{ad}{bd} \div \dfrac{bc}{bd}$.
Using knowledge of multiplication of fractions, the result is $\dfrac{ad}{bc}$.	The corresponding question is then: "How many times can bc go into ad? This is symbolized as $ad \div bc$ or $\dfrac{ad}{bc}$.
	(For a more thorough treatment of this algorithm, see Brickman, 1955.)

Securing Technical Assistance

Because teachers may feel they are not properly trained to conduct research (Zeichner & Noffke, 2001), they sometimes believe their research is less rigorous or not up to an acceptable standard (Borg, 1987) or that "research is something that only university faculty should do" (Fueyo & Koorland, 1997, p. 341). And frankly, some university researchers believe the same thing. In addition, from the teachers' point of view, theory may be something that is not seen as applicable to practice (Altrichter, Posch, & Somekh, 1993) whereas from the university researcher's point of view, events in one single classroom are no reason to modify theory. This separation between theory and practice can cloud both points of view. So, teachers often decide against conducting research in their classrooms and university researchers often conduct research as an "external observer," hoping to isolate small bits of information. However, if one believes education knowledge ought to be based on actual classroom activities, then research must be based on the hard work of classrooms' real teachers.

If classroom research can foster professional learning, then classroom teachers need both responsibility and support. The prospect of giving up valuable school-day time is daunting and ever the multi-taskers, teachers must see research results being worthwhile for their curriculum, professional development, and modification of instruction. By linking to a higher-education institution, teachers can strengthen their capacity for research and lessen their feelings of time pressures. In addition, many university researchers are extremely interested in how theories play out in one solitary classroom. In fact, they may believe theory should be modified until it plays out in every single classroom. The teaching experiment design allows the academic and the teacher to study children's thinking, putting theory and practice hand-in-hand. (We use terms coined by Zeichner & Noffke (2002), to describe ourselves. The academic is the university-based educator and the teacher is the P–12 educator. These terms clarify our research roles.) Such a collaborative effort requires and allows educators from school and college to reflect on individual teaching practices, while learning from each other.

SPECIFICS OF OUR PROJECT

Context

Our school consists of 3–5 grades and is partnered with a K–2 school in a different neighborhood. Our school building is in a mid-level socio-economic status neighborhood of primarily Caucasian residents and our partner building is located in a lower-level socio-economic status neighborhood of primarily African-American residents. The reasoning for this configuration was to allow children to attend their neighborhood's school during either the first half or the second half of their six years in elementary school, while developing cultural awareness without either neighborhood being bussed for the entirety of their schooling. The student body comprises 54% African-American and 46% Caucasian children. Sixty-six percent of the school population receives free or reduced lunch. Together the buildings serve approximately 600 children from a city of 600,000 in the mid-western United States.

Students in our classroom roughly reflected the ethnic demographic of the school. We taught 23 fifth grade mathematics students, 11 (48%) African-American children and 12 (52%) Caucasian children. Our children worked across a broad range of achievement levels, from low to high. Four of our students who struggled to grasp concepts and procedures received additional support in mathematics through Title I services. (Title I is a federally funded program designed to support students who require additional opportunities to learn.) We also had children who learned new ideas quickly and needed additional challenges.

Instruction

We knew our plan to use problem solving as a teaching method meant students would have to use pre-requisite knowledge to be successful. Our students knew whole number division and could subtract fractions. The problems would have to be solvable using those skills. We created 20 realistic problems for our students to solve and two worksheets with symbols only (for practice.) Along with each realistic problem, we had either a photograph of the information in the problem or physical items for students to manipulate. Students cut ribbon, poured orange juice, and partitioned pies. Figure 2.1 shows a sample of our problems.

The instruction followed the same general pattern for 10 days. We presented the realistic situations and made sure to clarify conditions. We allowed 4–7 minutes for children to individually solve each problem. We monitored

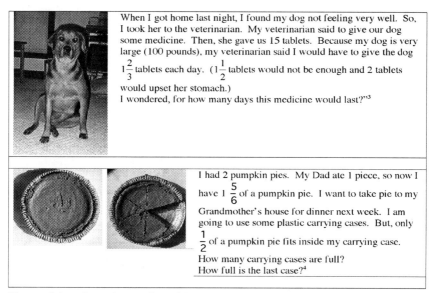

When I got home last night, I found my dog not feeling very well. So, I took her to the veterinarian. My veterinarian said to give our dog some medicine. Then, she gave us 15 tablets. Because my dog is very large (100 pounds), my veterinarian said I would have to give the dog $1\frac{2}{3}$ tablets each day. ($1\frac{1}{2}$ tablets would not be enough and 2 tablets would upset her stomach.)
I wondered, for how many days this medicine would last?"[3]

I had 2 pumpkin pies. My Dad ate 1 piece, so now I have $1\frac{5}{6}$ of a pumpkin pie. I want to take pie to my Grandmother's house for dinner next week. I am going to use some plastic carrying cases. But, only $\frac{1}{2}$ of a pumpkin pie fits inside my carrying case.
How many carrying cases are full?
How full is the last case?[4]

Figure 2.1.   Sample word problems.

their work, walking around the room so students could individually explain their reasoning and discuss strategies with us. We were delighted to see students fluidly using their existing fraction knowledge, rewriting in improper form, and correctly executing subtraction operations. To highlight different kinds of representations, giving equal balance to symbolic and pictorial representations, we selected student work to present to the class. As academic and teacher we team-taught, leading these discussions together. The student work helped our class recognize meaningful ways to record their thinking. As Kamii (1985) says, if children become convinced that another way is better, they will adopt it.

Data Collection and Analysis

The primary data source was students' solutions to the problems. We photocopied all daily work and returned original papers to the students with written comments about their thinking. In order to capture classroom discourse and reflect upon our own instruction we videotaped three of the lessons. It is our common practice to begin each new mathematical unit with a short pretest in order to make teaching decisions based on student needs. In this case, knowing that our 5th graders had no previous experiences with fraction division the pretest results were used to indicate growth when compared to posttest data.

Following each lesson we studied student solutions and looked for trends in student thinking about each problem. We made instructional decisions regarding the next day's lesson plan and selected problems that could build understanding. After the unit was complete, we looked for general trends in thinking for each student. As we sorted through all the student work we began to notice that we could: 1) look at students individually and recognize when general strategies appeared to become an algorithm, 2) group students according to how they solved problems and communicated their thinking, and 3) identify key problems that seemed to create "leaps" in thinking. During analysis, it was useful to support our findings with pre- and post-tests, daily field notes, and video records of classroom discussions.

RESULTS

Students tended to prefer to deal with problems in one of six basic ways:

- Developed common denominator algorithm with symbols, derived from pictures (n = 7)
- Demonstrated a common denominator-type algorithm with pictures (n = 6)
- Used technical symbols, supported with pictures, but no general procedure (n = 3)
- Showed conceptual understanding, no evidence of need for symbol algorithm (n = 2)
- Used technical symbols, but got incorrect answers (n = 2)
- Had Serious Holes in Mathematical Background and Could Not Engage (n = 3)

Two sustainable algorithms based on common denominators (one using pictures exclusively and the other including use of technical symbols) emerged among 13 of the students. Three students worked from symbols first and then attempted to support their symbolic work with pictures. Examples of some of these strategies are shown in Figure 2.2. We still think about how we might have nurtured students toward the invert and multiply algorithm, something no students invented. However students' algorithms did focus on and effectively use whole number division knowledge and fraction concept knowledge. For students who drew pictures, their work was impacted by the size of the denominators. Sure enough, problems with eighths were correctly solved more often than equivalent problems with sixths. For a complete description of our project, we invite you to read Sharp & Adams (2002).

Unexpected results came in the form of our personal growth in mathematics knowledge. With college degrees and years of teaching experience, we did not expect to learn as much math as we did. Subtle nuances about division, the meaning of the remainder as compared to the divisor, and the profound difference between repeated subtraction and fair sharing all were accentuated when dealing with fractions. The remainder needed to be compared to the divisor instead of the size of the original whole unit. For instance, applying the common denominator algorithm to $11/4 \div 5/4$ reduces it to $11 \div 5$ (since the denominators are equal). $11 \div 5$ results in 2 remainder 1. But the remainder of 1 is not indicative of an answer of 2 and ¼, rather, it indicates an answer of 2 and ⅕. The divisor (5) is now the unit of comparison, not the original size of the whole unit (fourths). In addition, the reason the common denominator algorithm worked as it did was due to the fact that a common denominator is necessary to subtract fractions.

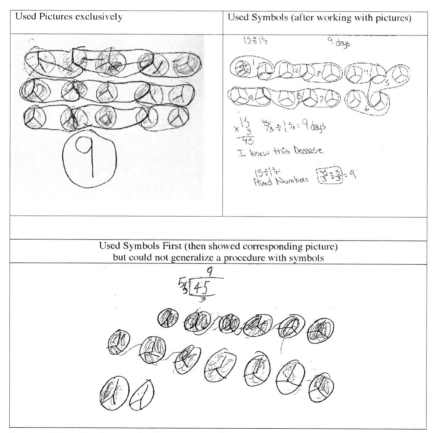

Figure 2.2.   Student solutions to the dog problem.

So it is equally necessary to repeatedly subtract fractions, which is repeated subtraction, one of the definitions of division. The fair-sharing definition of division did not emerge as meaningful to our students. Repeated subtraction, or measurement, is the process of division where a certain number of objects in a set are rearranged in such a way that the same amount is taken away from the set over and over. The number of take-aways is counted to determine the solution. Fair sharing, or partitive, is the process of division where a certain number of objects in a set are rearranged in such a way that the set is partitioned into a certain number of sets. The size of each set is counted to determine the solution.

Perhaps our experiences of successfully remembering the invert and multiply algorithm as being so different from Michael's memories had actually boxed us into one viewpoint. We came to appreciate that our existing division of fraction knowledge grew to put the common denominator method on equal footing with the invert and multiply method. In addition, our understanding of the invert and multiply method grew stronger, but we also became sensitive to the methods that now seemed harsh to us, for teaching about it.

EFFECTS OF THE RESEARCH ON
OUR TEACHING PRACTICES

One goal of this chapter is to illuminate roles we individually played in the research process. Another goal is to highlight the ways in which our collaboration influenced the work. To effectively consider our disparate contributions to the process, our individual perspectives are included as separate voices.

Teacher: At the 5th grade level, I now encourage a variety of possible strategies, knowing that students can develop a deeper understanding by connecting ideas as represented by their peers. Often in the process of discussion one strategy emerges as the most effective. As students begin to embrace an efficient strategy, they become more abstract in their thinking. In addition, I have learned to routinely engage my students in problem solving and consider situations that are meaningful to them. After watching my students remain focused on one problem for some length of time, I recognize the benefits of presenting them with challenging, meaningful mathematics.

Academic: At the college level, I now teach about fraction knowledge development as blossoming from learners' real worlds. This is a more robust appreciation of the complexities of fraction learning and instruction. It is important for college students to thoughtfully pose their own realistic word problems as they learn to teach math. It is equally important for them to study children's work, bringing authenticity to how learning theory effects teaching, by explaining the thinking behind children's work.

VALUE OF THE TEACHER

What perspective and insight does the teacher bring to classroom research? The teacher brings rich knowledge of each student's ability and the kind of individual support needed.

Teacher: Such was the case with our fifth-grader, Jerry. Jerry's level of abstract thinking along with his underdeveloped ability to communicate his reasoning led the academic to initially suspect the boy was simply guessing correctly. Knowing Jerry's ability to think logically and learn quickly helped me explain his success and consider ways to develop his reflective thinking. While it is true I was able to focus on particular students and describe their achievement in mathematics, I did not expect some children to understand fractional concepts as deeply as they did. Sadly, Kelly's sporadic school attendance throughout the school year had begun to affect my ability to fully aware of her level of understanding. I had spent most days throughout the year trying to get Kelly "caught up" following each absence. It was only through the time spent analyzing her work that I began to marvel at Kelly's ability to make sense of fractions while experiencing the social and educational effects of poor attendance. The advantage of stepping back and observing student learning also helped me to anticipate the needs of Billy, Demarco, and Andrea. As the mathematics became more challenging, they appeared to disconnect themselves from the group. I worked with those students privately so they could develop fractional concepts at their level of understanding.

VALUE OF THE ACADEMIC

What perspective and insight does the academic bring to the collaboration? The academic is immersed in educational research and theory.

Academic: Memories from my own classroom teaching of 7th and 8th graders guide my selection and interpretation of readings about how children learn. Not surprisingly then, research about fraction learning is particularly interesting because I witness my college students struggle with fractions in many of the same ways as my 8th graders. It was a quick matter to locate several relevant articles to share. I had even used some of the articles with my college students as part of communicating how instruction *should* look. It was essential to bring those visualizations to life as a part of our research. Many authors focused on establishing meaning for fraction knowledge, so we had the freedom and authority to challenge the district textbook. When the contexts were not meaningful, I suggested casting the book aside and writing our own problems. Whereas common sense or a gut feeling perhaps ought to have been enough support for the decision, I took increased comfort in the thought that both Kieren (1988) and Streefland (1991) would likely support decisions against beginning with problems that lacked purposefulness.

VALUE OF THE COLLABORATION

We drew from our respective fields of expertise to form a collaborative research team. While we each had our own value, there was value in the diversity of this collaboration itself. We did not expect to come to the project with identical knowledge and viewpoints nor depart from it without learning something new and useful.

We took delight whenever either of us learned something new. The teacher already knew how Jerry would respond to the problems. Yet, when the academic described her new knowledge about how children think, the teacher marveled anew at Jerry's responses to the problems, because she learned more about Jerry. Together, we developed a new awareness of how hard it is for children to communicate mathematical thinking. Somehow Jerry's inability to explain his thinking was not distressing to either of us anymore.

Our collaborative efforts would not have been as successful without mutual trust and respect for each other's expertise. Rather than judging the other person's lack of knowledge, we celebrated moments of new insights for us both. As an example, the academic already knew that ordering fractional denominators mattered. But, when the teacher agreed that this information coincided with her classroom experiences and hurriedly recalled memories of students being unable to solve a problem with thirds, the academic still learned something new. A classroom illustration brought theory to life.

Finally, we both had a vested interest in understanding the results. Between our concerns about our students like Michael and Jerry, this project was not a meaningless effort for either of us. We did not engage in it to earn external recognition through "publications" or "district recognition." We both wanted to know more about how students think about fraction division.

CHALLENGES OF CONDUCTING TEACHER RESEARCH

Time for Preparation, Instruction, Reflection, Analysis

Our students attended art class immediately following math time. We used that time for reflection because it was important to reflect immediately following math and because the academic had to leave shortly thereafter. Each day, we recorded individual reflections in our journals, which served as part of our data. We verbally revisited each day's classroom discourse to decide whether or not to make modifications for the next day. We assessed students' solutions. (This assessment was different from our trend analysis for the research. It gave feedback to the students.) This break in the day was also normally the teacher's planning period. So, for those two weeks, preparation for science, reading, language arts, and social studies had to occur early in the morning or after school.

For the academic, time expenditure manifested itself during the drive back and forth from the university to the school. Shuttling to and from the school building consumed 100 minutes each day and resulted in unsettling feelings of groundlessness. With two college classes to teach on Monday and Wednesday afternoons and team-teaching fifth graders every morning, the academic acutely felt a loss of time, just as the teacher had felt it. In addition, she felt mild disquiet moving back and forth from teaching children to teaching college students.

Curriculum issues

One of our first hesitations was the amount of time being set aside for teaching concepts not normally introduced in fifth grade. How would we explain to parents and other teachers this study was a worthwhile use of time, when the content was slightly beyond the fifth grade curriculum? Would we be able to adequately explain how such study might allow students to develop deeper understanding of fractions that would serve them later? Of greater concern, however, was the feeling that some students might be unsuccessful with this information. How would we deal with their frustration or confusion? We discussed our feelings and fears and reminded ourselves that we simply wanted to know how children thought when they knew the pre-requisite knowledge but did not bring any previous instructional baggage to the learning process. That said, we still wondered what we would do if students did not grasp the common denominator algorithm we expected.

Then we realized our actual fear was not really about students getting *that* algorithm. It was more about honoring another algorithm (invert and multiply) that we knew they would encounter later. Our efforts to understand how young children think would probably lead them to learn something different, and we needed to make sure what they had learned would not interfere with their understanding of the procedure to invert and multiply. Since we had not found a commercial textbook that specifically taught the common denominator method, what our children learned would not be a focal point of any curriculum they would encounter in the future.

Other Circumstances that Required Attention

Tasting the complexity of classroom research for the first time required our attention. Three stories illuminate realities of the classroom research environment. They are the kinds of things that can and should impact any research process as applied to classroom teaching.

Since our research focused on asking students to invent their own algorithms for division of fractions, we knew they needed to think about and practice solving problems outside class. This meant homework. And, at home, there are parents or guardians who have divided fractions in the past. One day, Nick abruptly switched from his nicely blossoming adding-up strategy to invert and multiply. We asked him to explain his thinking. He shrugged his shoulders and said, "That's just how Dad said to do it." For two days, Nick tried to invert and multiply, but he could never satisfy himself as to the reasoning behind it. So, he returned to his adding-up strategy that he had been in the process of inventing. We wished we had made a list of questions for parents to ask their children if the students needed additional support while solving problems at home, after all, parents had signed permission forms, they knew about the research.

One day, the academic arrived to find the classroom dark and empty. The principal had called a special assembly that coincided with our math time. There was nothing to be done at that point because the academic had other responsibilities back on campus immediately following her scheduled return. So, we lost a day of instruction and the children missed a day of math.

Thursday is band lesson day. Thankfully the teacher thought about this in advance and rescheduled the children's instrument lessons for the afternoons. Had those children been pulled from math for their band lessons, we would have been forced to re-teach those children in isolation from their classmates. We were keyed toward using classroom discussion for students to be able to refine their algorithms. In order to develop knowledge in a rich and copious way, they needed the social interaction of their classmates.

ADVANTAGES OF CONDUCTING TEACHER RESEARCH

We also noticed that we could use the collaboration to rely on our individual areas of expertise to save valuable time. For the academic, this experience was a chance to put into practice theoretical views about how students construct meaning of the division of fractions. For the teacher, this became a rare opportunity to step back and listen to students communicate their individual mathematical understanding and development. Moreover, this shared interest in the students' discourse caused us both to focus on the students' needs first, rather than our own personal gain. We cannot imagine how the professional growth that resulted from that shared concern could have been achieved any other way. Because we individually became re-attuned to the realities of classroom teaching and systematic in wondering about classroom practice, we both improved ourselves professionally.

Several other advantages of classroom research emerged. Both of us focused our mental energy on each part of the research process. We tried to anticipate snares and pitfalls so students would come out with new knowledge. We believe our results are more authentic than research that is posed and conducted by an outside source with little or no classroom teacher input. By conducting research that we knew mattered, the children also took it all seriously. They sensed our efforts to be thoughtful about problems and noticed how carefully we listened to them explain their thinking. The entire classroom atmosphere was academic, not trivial or novel.

When the students are part of the research in a meaningful way, they engage in a manner that is somehow different. About half way through our project, Katie stayed to talk at the end of math time. She turned in her work and asked, "Are you learning enough? Do you think you know what you needed to find out about us?" She smiled when we assured her we indeed had learned a lot and that we knew just exactly how hard she had been working to help us.

SUMMARY

Perhaps knowing how we worked together to conduct research and knowing that the outcomes of that research actually impacted our instruction will encourage other teachers and researchers to implement classroom research. For us, the project was not an ending. It was a beginning. Since so many fifth graders constructed a useful way of dealing with division of fraction, we better understand how to use a wealth of realistic problems when teaching about fractions in both college and school. Fifth graders are expected to build fraction knowledge on whole number experiences and use appropriate fraction knowledge to support this growth. Preservice elementary teachers now encounter theory through analysis of multiple examples of children's work. They address practical issues, like lesson planning, by applying learning theory. We have since worked in a 7th grade classroom to further study development of fraction concepts and operations. We invite teacher and academic alike to begin classroom research. For us, it has been an extremely important experience in our professional lives.

NOTES

1. This research was conducted, in part, as a result of support from the Exxon Education Foundation.
2. This table is reprinted with kind permission from the *Journal of Educational Research*, Heldref Publishers (Sharp & Adams, 2002).
3. This problem is reprinted with kind permission from the National Council of Teachers of Mathematics (Sharp, Garofalo, & Adams, 2002).
4. This problem is reprinted with kind permission from Allyn & Bacon Publishing (Sharp & Hoiberg, 2005).

REFERENCES

Altrichter, H., Posch P., & Somekh, B. (1993). *An introduction to the methods of action research*. London: Routledge.

Borg, W. R. (1987). *Applying Educational Research* (2nd ed.). New York, NY: Longman.

Borko, H., Eisenhart, M., Brown, C. A., Underhill, R. G., Jones, D., & Agard, P. C. (1992). Learning to tach hard mathematics: Do novice teachers and their instructors give up too easily? *Journal for Research in Mathematics Education, 23,* 194-222.

Behr, M., Harel, G., Post,T., & Lesh, R. (1992). Rational number, ratio, and proportion. In D. A. Grouws (Ed.), *Handbook of research on mathematics teaching and learning* (pp. 296-333). New York, NY: Macmillan.

Bray, J. C. (1963). To invert or not to invert. *The Arithmetic Teacher, 10,* 274-276.

Brickman, B. (1955). More rationalizing division of fractions. *The Arithmetic Teacher, 2,* 25-26.

Capps, L. R. (1962). Division of fractions. *The Arithmetic Teacher, 9,* 10-16.

Carpenter, T. P. (1991). Conceptual knowledge as a foundation for procedural knowledge. In J Hiebert (Ed.), *Conceptual and procedural knowledge: The case of mathematics* (pp. 113 – 132). Hillsdale, NJ: Lawrence Erlbaum Associates.

Elashhab, G. A. (1978). Division of fractions - Discovery and verification. *School Science and Mathematics, 78,* 159-162.

Fueyo, V., & Koorland, M. (1997). Teacher as Researcher: A Synonym for Professionalism. *Journal of Teacher Education, 48*(5), 336-344.

Johnson, H. (1985). Division with fractions – Levels of meaning." *The Arithmetic Teacher, 12,* 362 - 368.Huinker, D. (1998). Letting fraction algorithms emerge through problem solving. In L. Morrow & M. J. Kenney (Eds.), *The teaching and learning of algorithms in school mathematics,* 1998 Yearbook of the National Council of Teachers of Mathematics (pp. 170-182). Reston, VA: NCTM.

Kamii, C. (1985). *Young vhildren reinvent arithmetic.* New York, NY: Teachers College Press.

Kamii, C., & Warrington, M. A. (1995). Division with fractions: A piagetian, constructivist approach. *Hiroshima Journal of Mathematics Education, 3,* 53-62.

Kieren, T. E. (1988). Personal knowledge of rational numbers: Its intuitive and formal development. In J. Hiebert & M. J. Behr (Eds.), *Number concepts and operations in the middle grades* (pp. 162-181). Hillsdale, NJ: Erlbaum.

Mack, N. K. (1990). Learning fractions with understanding: Building on informal knowledge. *Journal for Research in Mathematics Education, 21,* 16-32.

Mack, N. K. (1995). Confounding whole number and fraction concepts when building on informal knowledge. *Journal for Research in Mathematics Education, 26,* 422-441.

Mack, N. K. (2001). Building on informal knowledge through instruction in a complex content domain: Partitioning, units and understanding multiplication of fractions. *Journal for Research in Mathematics Education, 32,* 267-295.

McMeen, G. H. (1962). Division by a fraction–A new method. *The Arithmetic Teacher, 9,* 122-126.

Moss, J., & Case, R. (1999). Developing children's understanding of the rational numbers: A new model and experimental curriculum. *Journal for Research in Mathematics Education, 30,* 122-147.

National Council of Teachers of Mathematics. (2000). *Principles and standards for school mathematics.* Reston, VA: NCTM.

Pothier, Y., & Sawada, D. (1983) Partitioning: The emergence of rational number ideas in young children. *Journal for Research in Mathematics Education, 14,* 307-317.

Sharp, J., & Adams, B. (2002). Children's constructions of knowledge for fraction division after solving realistic problems. *Journal of Educational Research, 95*(6), 333-348.

Sharp, J., Garofalo, J., & Adams, B. (2002). Children's development of meaningful fraction algorithms: A kid's cookies and a puppy's pills. In B. Litwiller & G. Bright (Eds.), *Making sense of fractions, ratios and proportions 2002 NCTM Yearbook* (pp.18-28). Reston VA: NCTM.

Sharp, J., & Hoiberg, K. B. (2005). *Learning and teaching K-8 mathematics.* Boston, MA: Allyn & Bacon publishing.

Streefland L. (1991). *Fractions in realistic mathematics education.* Dordrecht/Boston/London: Kluwer Academic Publishers.

Warrington, M. A. (1997). How children think about division with fractions. *Mathematics Teaching in the Middle School, 2,* 390-394.

Zeichner K. M., & Noffke, S. E. (2001). Practitioner research. In V. Richardson (Ed.), Handbook of Research on Teaching (pp. 298-330). Washington DC: AERA.

CHAPTER 3

REASONING AND SENSE-MAKING

What Can We Expect in Grades Three Through Five?

Tammy Covi
Rochester Elementary School, Rochester, Illinois

Nadene Ratcliffe
Tri-Valley Elementary School, Downs, Illinois

Cheryl A. Lubinski
Illinois State University

Janet Warfield
Illinois State University

A PEDAGOGICAL PROBLEM

Over the past 20 years various mathematics educators have recognized that reasoning, conceptual understanding, and solution processes are important to the learning of mathematics. Russell (1999) noted the importance of

Teachers Engaged in Research
Inquiry Into Mathematics Classrooms, Grades 3–5, pages 33–48
Copyright © 2006 by Information Age Publishing
All rights of reproduction in any form reserved.

reasoning in the process of understanding mathematical abstractions. She said, "If students are to learn to rely on their own mathematical reasoning, they must continually engage in reasoning mathematically" (p.10). In addition, she noted that students need to practice looking for relationships and explaining their reasoning. They must form the habit of reasoning if they are to learn to investigate new problems by themselves. Thompson, Philipp, Thompson, and Boyd (1994) concurred with the importance of helping students become skilled at reasoning and recognized the importance of orienting students' thinking in productive ways. They wrote about conceptual understanding and the need for teachers to help students develop this understanding by adapting a conceptual orientation in their teaching of mathematics, an orientation that requires students to provide an explanation of what quantity is being represented by each expression during the solution process, a form of quantitative reasoning. In this same manner, Frank (1988) recognized the need for teachers to emphasize the entire solution process as well as the correct answer and to encourage students to model how they used various strategies to solve problems.

Even though mathematics educators have been talking about reasoning, conceptual understanding, and explanations as important to mathematics, we have observed that students too often respond to a mathematical problem situation with a strategy that can best be described as a "hit and miss" approach. Many do not use an approach that provides evidence of quantitative reasoning or conceptual understanding. Most do not explain their solution process sufficiently. In our work we address the questions: What evidence do we have to support our belief that many young students often do not use conceptual reasoning to solve mathematical problems? How do we make sense of that evidence? Further, as teachers who are committed to helping our students develop both abilities and tendencies to solve mathematical problems through reasoning, understanding, and explaining, we see the failure of our students to respond in these ways as a pedagogical problem—one that can and should be addressed by teachers. Therefore, we ask: How do we as teachers respond to the evidence that students often do not use conceptual reasoning to solve mathematical problems? How can we implement changes in our classrooms to find solutions to this pedagogical problem?

CREATING A STUDY OF THE PEDAGOGICAL PROBLEM

We are mathematics teacher educators who are working on the pedagogical problem of how to teach elementary students, specifically third through fifth graders, to reason and make sense of the mathematics they are learning. Two of us teach third grade and conduct staff development in mathematics for other teachers. Two of us work with preservice and inservice teachers through our university positions in a department of mathematics. In order to help us think about teaching reasoning to better develop conceptual understanding, we decided to look at the work of several third, fourth, and fifth graders on the following mathematics problem:

> Lizzie collects lizards and beetles. She has 8 creatures in her collection so far. Altogether they have 36 legs. How many of each kind of creature does she have? (Fennema, Carpenter, Levi, Franke, & Empson, 1999, p. 4)

This problem was selected because of its alignment with the algebra standards for grades 3–5, which recommends that all students be able to:

- Understand patterns, relations, and functions
- Use mathematical models to represent and understand quantitative relationships
- Analyze change in various contexts (NCTM, 2000, p. 158)

Through our staff development work with teachers we have come to see that this problem can be modeled by using pictures, tables, equations, or only numbers. Thus, the problem provides students the opportunity to illustrate their reasoning and sense making about change in a variety of ways. Their written work along with their explanations presents us with a window into their mathematical reasoning. When analyzing student work on this problem, we are particularly interested in whether students examine how change in one quantity affects change in a second quantity. That is, do students realize that a change in the number of one or both kinds of creatures leads to a change in the number of legs and additionally, in what direction that change takes place?

Leslie, one of the teachers with whom we work, helped us understand what to look for in analyzing students' strategies. She said students who were making sense of the problem might start with the numbers 4 and 4 to represent the number of beetles and the number of lizards, respectively (a numerical model). She said that when the students calculated the number of legs for this initial guess they would find that they had too many legs: 4 (number of beetles) X 6 (number of legs on one beetle) + 4 (number of lizards) X 4 (number of legs on one lizard) = 24 + 16 = 40 (legs). Leslie said that students who were reasoning about the problem would see that a change in the number of beetles would effect a change in the number of lizards and hence a change in the total number of legs. She predicted students would reason that to reduce the number of legs, it would be necessary to trade in some beetles for some lizards. She hoped that students would see the pattern that one fewer beetle and one more lizard would reduce the total number of legs by two. Since students have to get rid of 4 legs, they would extend the pattern (generalize) and see the need to trade in two beetles for two lizards because 2 lizards have four fewer legs than 2 beetles. This makes sense. We agreed that this is the reasoning that can be expected from third, fourth, and fifth graders if mathematics is taught for conceptual understanding. This reasoning also incorporates knowledge of basic facts that should be well known to students in grades three through five. Surely, we agreed, it is not beyond what is to be expected. We decided to investigate whether students did indeed use this reasoning.

In order to obtain student work on this problem, we e-mailed the Beetle and Lizard Problem primarily to teachers who had taken a summer course at Illinois State University. Teachers were asked to collect solution strategies from their students. We requested that they present the problem without prior instruction. Some of the teachers engaged their colleagues in this task. The result of this effort was that we were able to collect work from students in 14 third-, fourth-, and fifth-grade classrooms of diverse settings. One school has been identified as high needs in an urban area. Most schools were in rural mid-western towns.

EVIDENCE FOR OUR STATEMENT OF CONCERN

Before we looked at the students' work, we predicted what we expected to find. Our predictions included students use of: pictures, tallies or numbers; tables, charts, and organized lists; guess and check strategies carried out with manipulatives; math facts; number sentences; and written explanations. We also expected to find incorrect answers because of the use of the wrong operation. The two of us who teach third grade predicted that from third to fifth grade the percent of students using reasoning would increase from 30% to 60% and those getting the correct answer would range from 40% to 70%. However, we noted that ideally the number of students getting a correct answer using a strategy that reflects reasoning should be between 60% and 90%.

What did we find the students did? Before we began to work in an organized manner, we skimmed through the papers of the students' work. One of us said, "They write what they did but not why." We noticed that often students did not focus on reasoning. They did not make sense of the problem. Some wrote that they added or subtracted. Many didn't get a correct answer. In one class, all students used pictures or tallies, none used only numbers, 6 showed at least some evidence of their thinking, and 9 gave no evidence of what they did – and that was from a fifth-grade class! We were discouraged.

We noted that some students had written 12 lizards and 24 beetles, talking about creatures, not legs as stated in the problem. This reminded us of

Thompson et al.'s (1994) point that students must know what quantities their numbers represent. One of us remarked that several students "did not seem to have a concept of where to start and just drew something." This showed evidence of having a model but being unable to reason quantitatively about the model. Even students who had a correct answer had difficulty explaining their reasoning. Because there was so much erasing on the papers and the most common strategy seemed to involve trial and error, we concluded that the vast majority of the students in grades three, four, and five solved this problem with a "hit and miss" approach. These were not the results we hoped to see.

HOW WE MADE SENSE OF THE STUDENTS' WORK

In order to make better sense of the students' work, we decided to categorize the students' responses. Initially we each looked at students' papers from two or three classrooms and individually developed terms that described the strategies we found. Then, we discussed the strategies and made a master list of categories. We continued to go through several more classroom sets of papers to make sure we had identified all of the strategies represented and agreed on the categories we had developed. When we disagreed, we discussed our findings until we came to a consensus on the categories or we came to an agreement on new categories to create. As a result of this process, we developed categories of correct, incorrect, or unclear answers as well as the categories of strategies presented in Table 3.1.

Table 3.1.   Codes Describing Students' Solution Strategies

Code	Descriptor
ASP	Adding sums or products to get 36
GCM/GCN/CGP/ GCT	Guess and Check: manipulatives, numbers, pictures, tallies
HMM/HMN/ HMP/HMT	Hit and Miss: manipulatives, numbers, pictures, tallies
OA	Only the answer
OAV	Only the answer with verification
OLT	Organized list or table
UN	Using numbers in the problem to $+/-/x/\div$
UC	Uncodeable

We differentiated between *Guess and Check* and *Hit and Miss* based on reasoning and some evidence of a plan (Guess and Check, Figure 3.1) as compared to a wild trial and error approach (Hit and Miss, Figure 3.2).

The difference between the categories *Only the Answer* (OA) and *Only the Answer with Verification* (OAV) was the inclusion of some type of check to determine if all parts of the problem had been considered and calculated correctly (see Figure 3.3). The category *Adding Sums or Products to Get 36* (ASP) included strategies in which students found multiples of 6 (the

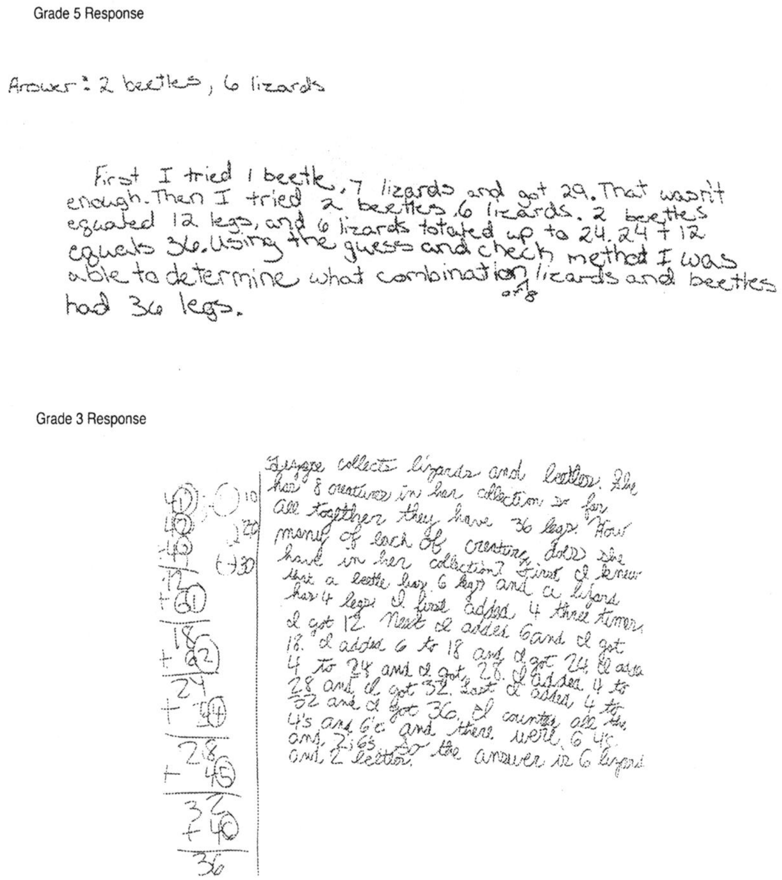

Grade 5 Response

Answer : 2 beetles, 6 lizards

First I tried 1 beetle, 7 lizards and got 29. That wasn't enough. Then I tried 2 beetles, 6 lizards. 2 beetles equaled 12 legs, and 6 lizards totaled up to 24. 24 + 12 equals 36. Using the guess and check method I was able to determine what combination of lizards and beetles had 36 legs.

Grade 3 Response

Figure 3.1.   Guess and check numbers.

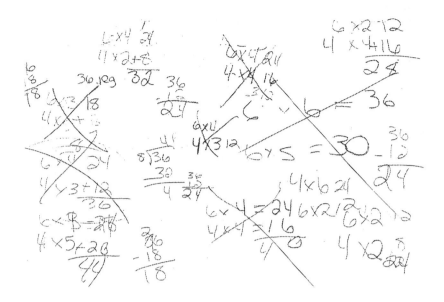

Figure 3.2.   Hit and miss numbers.

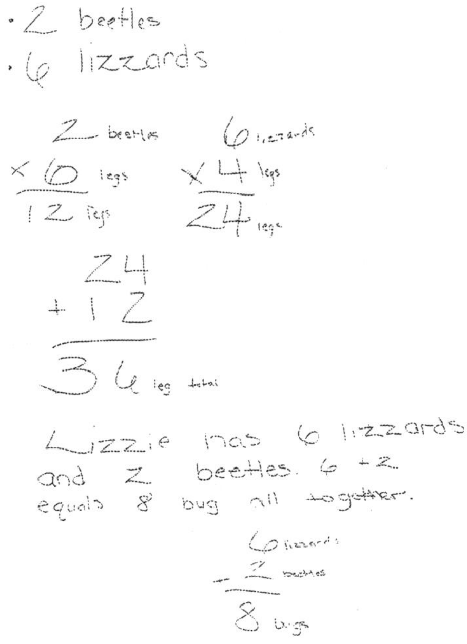

· 2 beetles
· 6 lizzards

2 beetles   6 lizzards
× 6 legs   × 4 legs
12 legs   24 legs

24
+ 1 2
─────
3 6 leg total

Lizzie has 6 lizzards
and 2 beetles. 6 + 2
equals 8 bug all together.

6 lizzards
− 2 beetles
─────
8 bugs

Figure 3.3.   Only the answer with verification.

number of legs per beetle) and 4 (the number of legs per lizard), either by repeated addition or by multiplication, and added them together until they arrived at 36 total legs (see Figure 3.4). The category *Using Numbers in the Problem to +/–/x/÷* (UN) included instances in which students selected numbers from the problem and added, subtracted, multiplied, or divided those numbers. These students completely ignored the context of the problem.

After we had the categories of *strategies*, each of us categorized approximately half of the papers. Then, we worked in pairs for intercoder reliability. That is, in pairs, we looked at how we individually had categorized each paper and if we disagreed as a pair, we discussed our reasons until we reached consensus.

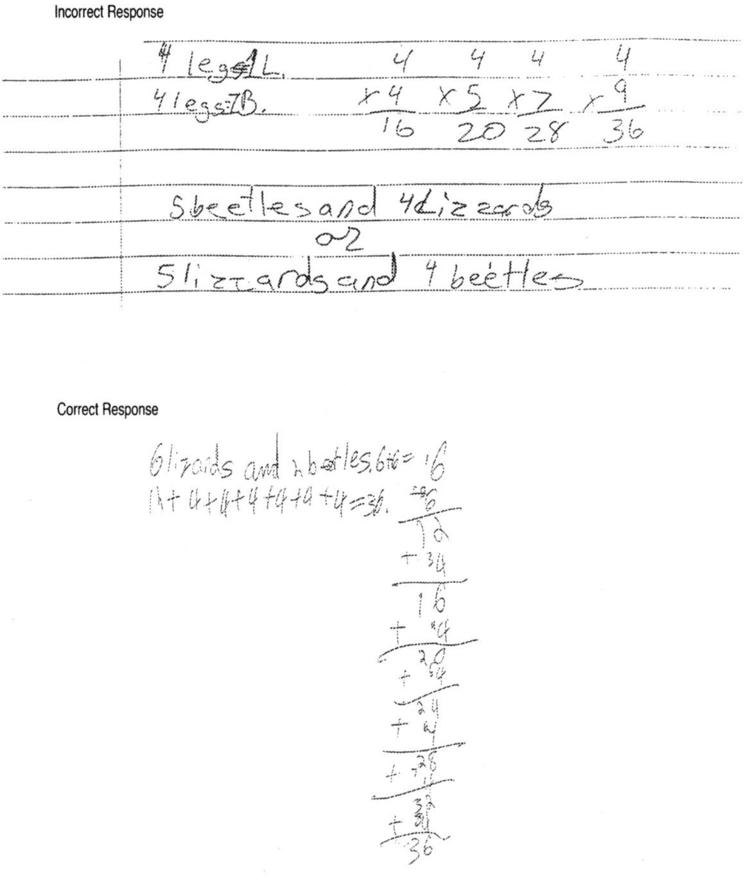

Figure 3.4.   Adding sums or products to get 36.

WHAT THE EVIDENCE SHOWS

The evidence did not support our prediction of an increase across grade levels in the percent of students with correct answers (see Table 3.2). In fact, there was little increase across grade levels, with only 46% of the third graders, 38% of the fourth graders, and 49% of the fifth graders responding correctly to this problem. Of the 317 student responses, 147 of the responses were correct, 143 were incorrect, and 28 were categorized as unclear.

Table 3.3 shows the specific strategies used by students in each grade level. Among the codeable strategies that were used, Guess and Check was most prevalent; 20% of all students used this. The next most frequently used strategy (16% of responses) involved adding sums and products to get 36. This was closely followed by the Hit or Miss approach, used by 15% of the students.

Guess and Check was the most prevalent strategy among third graders; Using Numbers in the Problem to +/-/x/÷ and Hit and Miss among

Table 3.2.   Percent of Correct Responses by Grade Level

Grade	Responses		
	Correct	Incorrect	Not Clear
3rd $(n = 83)$	46%	46%	8%
4th $(n = 50)$	38%	48%	14%
5th $(n = 184)$	49%	43%	8%

Table 3.3.   Percent of Specific Strategies Used by Grade Level

Grade	Strategy							
	ASP	GC	HM	OA	OAV	OLT	UN	UC
3rd ($n = 83$)	23%	31%	22%	0%	1%	1%	4%	18%
4th ($n = 50$)	4%	12%	28%	2%	2%	0%	30%	22%
5th ($n = 184$)	16%	16%	8%	19%	12%	<1%	8%	21%
Total ($n = 317$)	16%	20%	15%	11%	8%	<1%	10%	20%

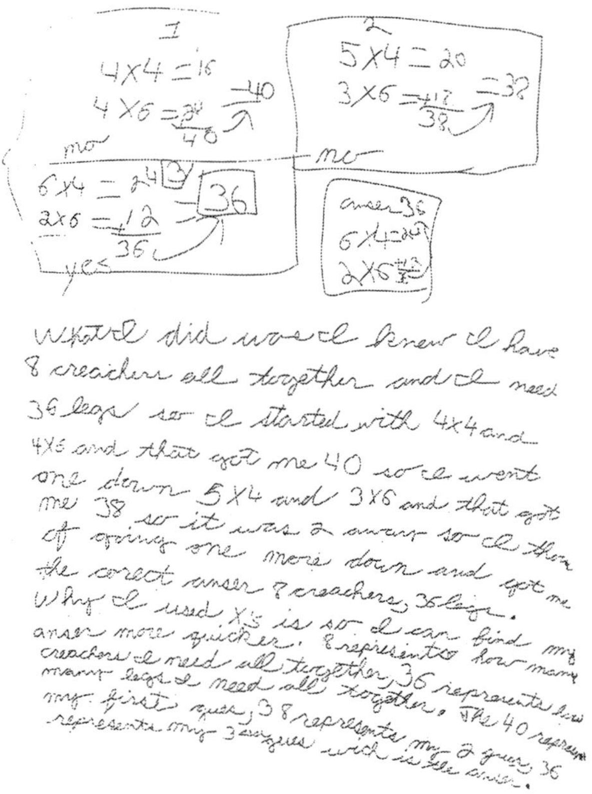

Figure 3.5.   A solution from a third grader.

fourth graders; and fifth graders most often wrote only an answer although Guess and Check and Adding Sums and Products were close behind. We agreed that one of the most complete solutions was reflected in the work of a third grader (see Figure 3.5).

OUR RESPONSE TO THESE FINDINGS

We had read Frank's (1988) article in which she stated that students focus on correct answers rather than on processes. We conjectured that this focus on correct answers is the reason why most adults and young students use a guess and check strategy or make a table (which is tedious and inefficient for this problem). We noted that when the students (and teachers with whom we've worked) use a guess and check strategy, they often adjust the numbers in the wrong direction indicating they do not consider how a change in one quantity affects a change in the other. Using the example of an initial guess of 4 beetles and 4 lizards, many calculate and realize that they have 4 too many legs. Then they try 5 beetles and 3 lizards. This change results in more legs than the initial guess! We surmised that teachers and students do this because their focus is on fast and correct answers, not reasoning.

It appeared that many students in this study were "playing with numbers," not thinking about numbers. Furthermore, few students had explanations of how they arrived at an answer and some had no answer. We noted that too many students did not have a clear understanding of what the problem was asking (i.e. both the 36 legs and 8 creatures need to be considered when finding a solution). We concluded that there was no reasoning behind the process in the majority of strategies we coded.

Thus, we believe that teachers should teach students how to write a good explanation addressing both *how* and *why*. This explanation would provide a check on students' thinking as they write up their reasons. Additionally, we believe that teachers need to ask students to explain why they are doing what they are doing during the problem solving process. Students need help reflecting on what they are doing and identifying what the numbers they are using represent. If students know they are responsible for explaining what they are doing and why, it tends to make them focus more and try harder. Reflection is a necessary part of mathematics and the student must ask, "Does my answer make sense given the elements in the problem?"

We also believe that teachers need to get to know their students' mathematics understanding better. With that in mind, we discussed the importance of encouraging students not to erase mistakes. Too often what is erased tells the story of how and why students came to their final solution.

And finally, we learned that age or grade level did not necessarily reflect mathematical reasoning ability. It was apparent that younger children could solve more difficult problems than older ones if they had number sense and had learned to reason mathematically. What does this mean for our own classrooms?

IMPLEMENTING CHANGES IN OUR CLASSROOMS

Based on the evidence that students too often use a hit-and-miss strategy while problem solving, we have each identified changes we will make in our own classrooms or work with inservice and preservice teachers.

Tammy's Thoughts

Some of these papers indicated that students had no idea what was being asked of them. They did not have a very good understanding of the mathematics. In order to solve these types of problems, students need to be exposed to many different types of mathematics problems. They also need to be encouraged to solve problems their own way. Teachers should do some additional reading on standards-based teaching – maybe even observe some classrooms already using it. And finally, they should use problem solving daily. It promotes learning for understanding and requires more true thinking!

I am always looking for ways to improve my mathematics instruction and my students' learning. This research project has made me feel strongly about the need to use standards-based instruction daily in my own classroom. It confirmed my belief that students learn mathematics better when given opportunities to solve problems on their own. One thing I will be sure to do when writing problems is to use a variety of words. The "key" words that traditional mathematics programs teach can be misleading. For example, the word "altogether" does not necessarily mean addition. Some tests give what many teachers consider "trick questions." A student who is encouraged to solve mathematics problems using his or her own methods is far less apt to be tricked because he or she will not get caught up in the words. I also plan to keep better records indicating just what my students understand. I know that I will continue to use standards-based instruction in my classroom and continue to encourage my students to solve problems in ways they understand.

Nadene's Ideas

I thought about several areas that I want to address next year in my classroom. Reflecting on the number of students who made errors on this problem, I recognized the need to address number sense. I want to have more problem solving that encourages mathematical reasoning and number sense and less bookwork. I realized that bookwork is "how to do" and not "why you do." I think I can help children learn to reason by sitting with individual students, having them take me through the step-by-step process they used as they explain what they did and why. I realize that in the past, I tended to let students work on their own unless they got stuck. However, when I saw all those students' papers from our project, I felt I was not as actively involved in the learning process as I need to be. I think that if my students know I will question them about their work as I walk around the class, they will be more accountable for their own learning.

I also want to improve the written explanations of my third graders. I have required explanations in the past, but I want more details of students' reasoning processes in the future. In conjunction with this idea, I intend to examine more thoroughly the strategies individual students in my class use to solve a problem. I want the sharing and discussion portion of a lesson to take more of the mathematics time than it has in the past. I am more aware of the importance of making mathematical connections among the strategies. For example, when students add a series of same numbers, their work can be connected to a multiplication expression. I plan to take student work and help them organize it into a table so that the information can be more clearly interpreted. I know that in the textbook students are so used to data being given to them and a hint provided to "make a table," that they do not realize how they can use their own strategy to develop a table. I need to help students reason about how to organize their thoughts. Tammy and I both see a need to improve the listening skills of our students. We need to be more attentive and patient when students are describing their solutions. Furthermore, classmates need to focus on the student explaining and show respect for his or her ideas. In order to teach students to listen to each other we think that we, as teachers, will occasionally say, "Tell in your own works what (*student's name*) is trying to explain."

Cheryl and Janet's Reflections

After analyzing the strategies children used to solve the problem used in this project, we have become much more conscious of stressing the importance of encouraging children to reason mathematically as we work with preservice and inservice teachers. We have always used samples of children's work on non-routine problems in our preservice classes and had inservice teachers bring work from their own students when we conduct professional development. However, we have not previously asked our students to analyze the categories of strategies that children use in order to determine what we can learn about their reasoning.

We also emphasize the importance of both spoken and written communication on the part of children and the importance of teachers' helping children learn to communicate their mathematical reasoning clearly. This helps the students, but it also helps teachers understand how children are thinking so that they can make better instructional decisions. From our work on this project we learned that we need to help teachers distinguish between trial-and-error strategies that are used without reasoning and strategies that require reasoning and planning ahead. We are having more discussions about this with both inservice and preservice teachers.

DISCUSSION

As we reflect on our work and the comments of Russell (1999), Thompson et al. (1994), and Frank (1988) that appear in the introduction of our chapter, we realize we have a better understanding of what we need to do both as teachers in our own classes and as teacher educators. We know that reasoning, conceptual understanding, and explanations will not easily evolve in our classrooms unless we provide opportunities for our students to engage in sense-making processes. We can start by finding rich problems for students to solve. Then, we need to create learning environments in which students can share strategies verbally and in writing. We need to help our students make connections among their strategies both with symbols and words. We need problems that promote quantitative reasoning, problems that let our students practice looking for meaningful relationships including change. As Thompson et al. remind us; students need to know what the numbers in their solution processes represent. Our questioning and listening skills are important to this process. Our students need to move beyond a "hit and miss" approach to problem solving and develop reasoning skills.

Our top ten list of suggestions for our colleagues:

10. Ask more, tell less!
9. Be reflective.
8. Be patient.
7. Have students listen to each other's solutions.
6. Monitor students' sense-making processes daily.
5. Help students make connections among their models.
4. Have students share their models with their classmates.
3. Individually listen to students explain their solution processes.
2. Have students solve rich problems encouraging a variety of models.

And, our #1 suggestion: Find rich problems!

ACKNOWLEDGMENT

We'd like to express our thanks to the teachers who helped us collect students' strategies and especially to the teachers from Ritenour School District in Missouri for providing us with the preliminary feedback on the students' strategies. Their comments were helpful to our work. Thanks to Andrea Boeser, Mary Nell Brooke, June Burkhardt, Kristie Kerber, Leslie

O'Neal, and Katherine Richard. And also, thanks to Al Otto for providing helpful suggestions to the algebra sections of this article.

REFERENCES

Fennema, E., Carpenter, T. P., Levi, L., Franke, M., & Empson, S. (1999). *A Guide for Workshop Leaders: Children's Mathematics: Cognitively Guided Instruction*. Portsmouth, NH: Heinemann.

Frank, M. (1988). Problem solving and mathematical beliefs. *Arithmetic Teacher*, *35*(5), 32-34.

National Council of Teachers of Mathematics, (2000). *Principles and Standards for School Mathematics*. Reston, VA: NCTM.

Russell, S. (1999). Mathematical reasoning in the elementary grades. In L.V. Stiff & F. R. Curcio (Eds.). *Developing mathematical reasoning in grades K-12* (pp. 1-12). Reston, VA: NCTM.

Thompson, A. G., Philipp, R. A., Thompson, P. W., & Boyd, B. A. (1994). Calculational and conceptual orientations in teaching mathematics. In *Professional development for teachers of mathematics* (pp. 79-92). Reston, VA: NCTM.

CHAPTER 4

ARITHMETIC TO ALGEBRA

A Teacher's Journey

June Soares
Fowler and Letourneau Elementary Schools,
Fall River, Massachusetts

As part of the *Generalizing to Extend Arithmetic to Algebraic Reasoning* Project[1] [GEAAR], math researchers at the University of Massachusetts Dartmouth were looking for a group of elementary school teachers who would be willing to try mathematics activities that required algebraic reasoning in their classrooms. Their research had shown that students in the elementary grades are capable of thinking algebraically, of making generalizations, and of justifying their thinking. For 30 years, I have been a third-grade teacher in Fall River, Massachusetts, an urban district that is considered typically underachieving. I have been teaching at a Portuguese bilingual school in an economically and culturally diverse community for most of my career. Although I had taken many courses in mathematics instruction, I had not been involved in anything quite like this experience and had no involvement with research-based mathematics instruction. I was not a very good student of mathematics, and felt it was my duty to find a way to make

Teachers Engaged in Research
Inquiry Into Mathematics Classrooms, Grades 3–5, pages 49–58
Copyright © 2006 by Information Age Publishing
All rights of reproduction in any form reserved.

math interesting, fun, and meaningful for my students. Thus, I agreed to participate in the GEAAR project and was involved for four years, as a participant and later as a teacher leader providing professional development for other teachers. Although the project has ended, I have continued to stay in contact with the project team.

PARTICIPATING IN THE GEAAR PROJECT

I joined a small group of Kindergarten to fifth-grade elementary school teachers from my school district as participants in the GEAAR project. The project team (James Kaput and Maria Blanton) explained that they would provide problems that would help students develop algebraic thinking. The teachers would work out the problems under their guidance and then take the problems back to their classrooms where the students would have the opportunities to work on them. Teachers would record student thinking and bring samples of student work to the next session. We were to share our successful and not so successful lessons. We all listened and thought "Algebra!" I started thinking that this was not for me. It wasn't my students that concerned me; it was my fear of a subject (algebra) that intimidated me. After listening to their philosophy, I decided to stay.

Maria and Jim gave us the first problem, the Handshake Problem. The problem asked the following question: How many handshakes would there be if each person in your group shakes the hand of every person once? I'll never forget it. I started to work on my own and found that the problem was not that difficult. I wrote down my answer. I looked around and the other teachers were engaged in conversation. I thought to myself, "What are they talking about?" As I listened, I realized I was so wrong. I had just counted the number of people in my group, which was 5, and subtracted 1 because I couldn't shake my own hand and came up with the answer 4. There was one group of teachers shaking each other's hands and recording the handshakes. Another group had a column of numbers they were adding. A third group attempted a more traditional approach and searched for a formula. One was never found nor did the project team give one.

Again I thought these seminars were not for me. I was totally intimidated. I was embarrassed. I realized how I had misinterpreted the problem. I empathized with my students who were given different problems to solve on their own. I also realized that I was not the only teacher there that thought the same way. We continued to work on the problem in groups and discussed our findings. Our assignment was to go back to the classroom and try this one problem with our students.

I decided to try the Handshake Problem with my students the very next day. I made up my mind that if it didn't go well, I wasn't going back for more. I explained to my students that I had been to a mathematics class the day before and had a problem that I wanted them to try. I read the Handshake Problem and had them work in groups to try to figure out the answer. I told them that they could use any strategies they thought would be helpful. Before they began, I felt that it was important to discuss what a handshake actually meant. If there were only 2 people, how many handshakes would that be? They answered only 1. We did this for 3 people, then 4. I sent them on their way to work out the problem. My goal was for each group to determine the number of handshakes for ten people. At first I wanted to see if they could get an answer. Then I was curious to see how they would organize their information. I later realized that I was looking for so much more. I found that the students were actually finding the relationship between the number of people in a group and the total number of handshakes.

The project team wanted feedback on children's thinking, so I went around with my clipboard trying to write what the children were doing and saying. I was impressed with the way two of my four groups started out. They acted out the actual handshakes and tried to record who they shook hands with. Tommy took charge. He shook hands with one girl in his group, he then wrote her initial down next to his. Tommy did this with the other five children in the group. He had shaken the hands of six children. He then had Katherine do the same while he kept track. She had shaken the hands of five children. He kept the group on task until there were no more hands to shake. Tommy was quite organized.

The other two groups acted very much as I did in the teacher seminar. They jumped right into the problem and came up with an answer. Tim's group had the answer six handshakes for the seven people in their group. At least they remembered not to count their own. When they realized others were very busy doing something else, they went over to other groups and watched. Tommy's group was working with the numbers he had recorded. I watched. His group wrote $1 + 2 + 3 + 4 + 5 + 6$. I asked the group why they didn't have a 7 if there were seven people. Tommy was very exasperated with my question and answered, "You can't shake hands with yourself!" Then they started adding. At first, the group added the numbers in order. Then Jess thought that she could change the order of the numbers to make it easier to add. She grouped the numbers to make sums of 7, $1 + 6$, $2 + 5$, $3 + 4$, and then said. "Add $7 + 7 + 7$." I had her share her strategy with the class. Many had said that they never thought to change the order of the numbers. You could see such a big smile on her face. She was so proud.

I extended the problem with the question: What would happen if one more person joined the group? What surprised me was that Alan said we didn't have to do the problem again, "just add 7 to the answer of the problem." He knew all he had to do was add on. We continued until we reached the goal of ten people in a group. It was interesting, after Jess explained how she changed the order of numbers to make her adding easier, the other students did the same thing. I couldn't believe the amount of mathematics that was being done.

The next day we revisited the Handshake Problem. I joked with the students and asked if anyone in the class would be able to determine the number of handshakes if there were 100 people in the group. I also told them I was interested in *how* they would solve this problem. Well, of course, there were various comments, but two students Alan and Tommy started working together while the rest of the class was still discussing such a difficult problem. After about 10 minutes Alan and Tommy came up and said that they knew how to solve the problem, but they wanted a calculator to get the actual answer. I had them explain to the class just what they needed to do to solve the problem They started writing 99 + 98 + 97 + 96... and explained their reasoning. By the end of the class, the students had an understanding of what Alan and Tommy did.

When I looked at all of the students' work I was convinced – I couldn't quit the seminars. These children could do these types of problems if given the chance. I could not deprive my class the opportunity to work on these rich algebraic problems. By solving the Handshake Problem, my students were thinking in a way quite different than before. They recognized there was a need for organization in their work and they were making generalizations and justifying their thinking.

Two weeks later, our next seminar was held. I was so eager to share what my third graders were able to do. I soon learned that other teachers had many of the same exciting experiences. The kindergarten and first grade teachers had modified the problem by reducing the number of people in the group. The first grade teacher had her students use unifix cubes to keep track of the handshakes. The kindergarten teacher had her students make a graph like that in Figure 1. After the students shook hands with the others in the group, they colored a square above their name on the graph for each handshake they had given.; the last person in the group had no squares to color. Her students then counted all of the colored squares and they knew how many total handshakes had been given. All of these strategies were so fascinating. Here was a problem that is usually given to middle or high school students and we had our K–5 students solving it. Listening to my colleagues describe how their students solved the problem made me realize how important it is for students to share their solutions with one another. It helps them develop a repertoire of strategies that they can apply to other problems.

After our discussion of the various student strategies, some teachers still wanted a formula to solve the Handshake Problem. We worked on it during the seminar and finally one teacher came up with the following: $n(n-1)/2$. I can honestly say that this formula did not mean anything to me; I could substitute numbers, but I did not know why they worked. However, after using this problem with my third graders for three years and becoming much more comfortable with it, I figured it out. One day I looked up at a graph (Table 4.1) we had made to record the number of handshakes in a 6-person group (the strategy used by a kindergarten teacher earlier in the project) and all of a sudden, I finally understood the formula. I was able to "see" the formula geometrically as half the area of a rectangle with dimensions n by n-1, with n representing the number of people in the group.

The Handshake Problem clearly exemplifies the type of problems students need to be exposed to. The National Council of Teachers of Mathematics (NCTM, 2000) *Principles and Standards for School Mathematics* states that students need to understand patterns, relations, and functions. They also need to analyze change in various contexts. The Handshake Problem shows how change in one variable (the number of people) relates to a change in a second variable (the number of handshakes). The students were able to model this problem with objects and use representations such as tables and graphs to draw conclusions, which address other recommendations found in the NCTM Standards.

Although I was amazed at my students' ability to solve the Handshake Problem, I became a true proponent of algebraic thinking with a problem from Tom Carpenter, author and mathematics education researcher from the University of Wisconsin. Tom Carpenter came to one of our seminars because teachers were having difficulty aligning early algebraic problems to the textbook. He started out by giving us the following problem: $4 + 5 = \Box + 6$. He asked us what we thought our students would put in the box. I automatically thought that my third graders would have no problem with this number sentence. Some of the teachers thought the same way and others thought that students might put 9 in the box. Others thought they might put 15. A great discussion developed about the meaning of the equals sign. We were asked to go back and give this problem to our students to solve.

Table 4.1.   Handshake graph

X					
X	X				
X	X	X			
X	X	X	X		
X	X	X	X	X	
Tony	Andrew	John	Katherine	Anna	Sam

Tom Carpenter was right, children misinterpreted the "=" sign! They saw it as a call to action rather than a statement about the relationship between quantities. I was shocked at how many students said that 9 or 15 belonged in the box. They had written the answers that were discussed in our seminar. They DID have a meaning for the equal sign, but it was too narrow. I took out balances and had the students model the problem. They could see that 4 + 5 did not equal 15. Once again clipboard in hand, I asked the students to explain their reasoning. They loved the fact that I was writing down their thoughts. One of the questions I like to ask is, "Does your answer make sense?" Once the students were able to reason that the number in the box (unknown) must preserve the equality between the 2 sides, they were able to solve more problems of this type. I do not think students had been given these kinds of problems before.

To further address the concept of equality, I sent home an addition drill sheet for math homework. However, I did not want the students to write the answers, instead I wanted them to write an equivalent expressions (e.g., 5 + 5 = 6 + 4). I received quite a few notes from parents. Even though there were samples on the page, they felt that their children did not understand the assignment and told them to just write the answer. It was evident that this kind of math required a different way of thinking, a way parents were not used to either.

We discussed these types of problems in our seminar. I think every teacher that tried them was just as amazed as I was with the results. This led us to pose problems such as "Let 8 + a = b + 9. What happens to b as a decreases? What if a increases?" The students could actually see the patterns develop and they started making up problems for others to solve. We realized however, that once the children were exposed to these kinds of problems they were capable of solving others involving an unknown.

Our seminars continued in this fashion for the rest of the school year. Teachers found ways to "algebrafy" arithmetic problems and then shared the problems with the group. I extended a simple multiplication problem such as: " How many legs on one cat? How many legs on two cats? How many on three cats? How many legs on "n" cats?" In the past I would have focused solely on arithmetic problems but now my students were writing equations for the general cases (e.g., $n \times 4$ = legs on cats). As my students continued to solve early algebra problems, I noticed that they were questioning each other's strategies and making their own conjectures. One day, for example, we had been working on identifying prime and composite numbers. We were discussing the number 7 when John expressed the thought that all odd numbers would be prime. When I asked why, he said that he noticed all of the prime numbers we had identified were odd. He told me that was his "conjecture." I loved it! The students all agreed with him. But about a minute later, Tony said that he had to disagree. John very politely disagreed with him and they had quite the discussion going on.

Finally, Tony explained his reasoning that 9 is an odd number, but it is not prime. He came up to the front of the group and drew three groups of three circles on the board. He also took some Unifix cubes and made a one-by-nine array. Tony explained that this was another way to make 9, therefore, it is composite. John was convinced. This type of conversation cannot be planned, but because I now always ask students to share their thinking, these conversations often occur spontaneously during instruction.

The students always looked forward to me coming back from GEAAR seminars with one of my famous problems. Soon I found myself searching out other problems or making up my own. I tried to make math problems resemble real life situations. Students worked on them together as I circulated the classroom trying to record as much student conversation as I could. The children developed a better number sense; they were discovering rules for extending symbolic, arithmetic, and geometric patterns and progressions. I was surprised that they were doing so much mathematics from one meaningful word problem. This didn't happen when they did a page of algorithms. Moreover, because I frequently asked them to slow down so that I could record their thinking, they began to record some of their thoughts so as not to forget what they wanted to share. It was an exciting year.

DEVELOPING CLASSROOM PRACTICE

In the second year of the project, Maria Blanton (one of the GEAAR project leaders) was looking for a third-grade classroom in which to conduct a research study about the project and its impact on teacher practice and student learning. I was very nervous about volunteering my class, but I decided to give it a try. It was one of the best things I did. Maria came in 3 times a week for the whole mathematics class. She took notes throughout the class, and afterwards we talked about the lesson and shared ideas. It was so nice to have someone around to validate all of the hard work being done.

Maria's expertise was invaluable to me. I was becoming more comfortable questioning my children and trying to get them to explain their work. But sometimes when Maria saw an opportunity for the children to think algebraically, she asked questions that extended their thinking and helped them make generalizations. I started taking note of her questioning style because I wanted to use this questioning technique myself. Some of the questions I now ask include the following: Is there another way to solve that? Will it always happen? Why do you think it happened that way? Can you represent that in a more organized way? How can you represent something that is unknown? Why is this equal? There are many more, and I have found that each lesson prompts a different set of questions.

In my classroom, I am not the only one asking questions; students feel quite comfortable to ask questions as well as give answers. All students are encouraged to question another student or me. When a student raises his/her hand and questions another student's thinking, it makes me feel as if I have done my job. They may not have the right answer, but they are thinking. And I have discovered that students' thinking is much more complex than I ever realized. The more I listen, the more I am amazed at the strategies students use to solve problems. Many times students are already thinking algebraically but we haven't listened enough to hear them or looked deeply enough at their solutions.

I have found that when students work with a partner or on their own, without teachers guiding them step-by-step, they start to really understand the mathematics involved. I think the real teaching comes when students are given the opportunity to share their ideas and strategies. I encourage students to explain their thinking using numbers, words, and pictures. Students can then see many different ways to get to a solution. Some of the strategies may not be the way we would solve the problem, but they are often legitimate and make sense to the students. In my classroom, when students share their work, their strategies are validated by their peers. I have found that this validation is important to the students. Although everyone may not be the best reader or writer, everyone has an idea and students in my classroom have become comfortable engaging in conversations about their thinking.

DEVELOPING STUDENTS' ALGEBRAIC REASONING

I have come to learn that early algebra activities are critical to the development of students' understanding of mathematics and that algebraic thinking fits in perfectly with our curriculum. Early algebra concepts do not need to be added to the curriculum; they have always been there. However, we have not always taken the opportunity to emphasize them in our instruction. Through my participation in the GEAAR project, I have come to believe that algebraic thinking should begin with the very young and be built upon through the years. There is evidence that this is possible because Pre-K and kindergarten teachers in the project successfully adapted algebraic problems for their students.

I have come to see that algebra becomes a way of thinking if started early enough. An incident with Tom, a special needs student in one of my classes, highlights this point. We had been solving problems using positive and negative numbers and discussing how some numbers "cancel" each other out. Tom went home and made up a set of problems for the class to solve (see Figure 4.1). He constructed expressions using words instead of numbers and seemed to realize that it is not always necessary to use a numerical representation. I feel that Tom's problems showed that he was reasoning algebraically.

My instruction focuses on concepts of equality. Students recognize and represent equivalent expressions explore properties such as commutativity, and use symbols and other forms of representation to express their ideas. Every year now, I involve my students in activities to recognize, create and extend patterns; give rules; and make generalizations. We begin to explore patterns using the hundreds chart and through skip counting. For example, we will count by 10's beginning with 2, which is often confusing for them until they see the pattern. We also identify patterns in problems involving the relationship between two variables as in the Handshake Problem. I encourage students to describe these patterns verbally and then represent them in an organized fashion. It is important for students to be able to construct their own tables. Typically textbooks only require students to fill in a table that has been provided. I expect students to construct their own tables and charts, and t-charts have become a valuable tool for my students.

I extend our work with patterns by having students graph the data represented in their t-charts. I have discovered that when students become more proficient in algebraic thinking, they learn that change can be predictable. Many students now look at graphs and realize that a straight diagonal line indicates data that has constant differences. This is helpful when they have to make a graph and realize they may have plotted something incorrectly. It also shows their understanding of what they have graphed in terms of the problem situation. Finally, I encourage students to write equations as yet another representation of their solution. This seems to be difficult for them, but the more they do it, the better they get.

I know one thing for sure; all students learn at different rates and even though they may not "get it" right away, they enjoy the challenge of mathematics. I no longer hear "I don't like math!" I believe that the more I enjoy what I do, the more the students enjoy learning. Enthusiasm begets enthusiasm.

$$\text{web} + \text{Garth} - \text{web} = ?$$
$$L2 + L1 - L1 = ?$$
$$\text{blue} + \text{red} - \text{blue} = ?$$
$$\text{car} + \text{red} - \text{red} = ?$$

Figure 4.1.   Garth's problem set.

REFLECTIONS

The highlight of my experience as a participant in the GEAAR project was attending a meeting on teacher development at the University of Wisconsin. I went with the project team and was determined to just sit and listen. I did not want to embarrass myself. The chair of the meeting was Tom Carpenter. Introductions were made around the table and I could not believe what I did — I explained that I was at the seminar he had given in Fall River and described the problem he had us try with our students. I told him how that problem changed the way I teach mathematics. He then started the meeting discussing that very problem.

In closing, I have grown professionally as a teacher of elementary mathematics. I have discovered the power of student thinking and how it impacts my instruction. One of my students, Andrew, commented: "If you want to learn math, you better be in Mrs. Soares class." What a compliment! I owe much of my growth to the Fall River School District for affording me the opportunity to participate in the GEAAR project and to the teachers in the group who shared their early algebra stories with me.

ACKNOWLEDGMENT

I would like to acknowledge all of the support provided to me by James Kaput, Chancellor Professor of Mathematics at the University of Massachusetts, Dartmouth. Jim died in July 2005, unexpectedly. Without his tireless efforts in the Fall River, Massachusetts School District, I would not be the teacher I am today. Words do not express the loss of my mentor and friend.

NOTE

1 . The Generalizing to Extend Arithmetic to Algebraic Reasoning Professional Development Project was supported in part by a grant from the U.S. Department of Education, Office of Educational Research and Improvement, to the National Center for Improving Student Learning and Achievement in Mathematics and Science (R305A60007-98). The opinions expressed herein do not necessarily reflect the position, policy, or endorsement of the supporting agencies.

REFERENCE

National Council of Teachers of Mathematics. (2000). *Principles and standards for school mathematics*. Reston, VA: Author.

CHAPTER 5

EXPLORING MULTIPLICATIVE REASONING[1]

Judy Atcheson

Zippel Elementary School, Presque Isle, Maine

PERSONAL INTRODUCTION

I became involved in this research project in my 24th year as an elementary teacher, having taught in grade 2 and grade 3 classrooms. My goal had always been to strive for excellence, for the benefit of my students. However, over the course of the past few years I had come to realize that following the text and district curriculum and assisting students with assignments was not enough to comprise exemplary mathematics education. My personal journey into research and change was greatly influenced by the opportunity to participate in the New Standards Project and the Maine Assessment Portfolio [MAP] Project over a period of five years. The focus of these projects on state and national standards, aligning curriculum, instruction, and assessment, and the availability of challenging, high quality tasks pushed me to move beyond "arithmetic" to a broader vision of mathematics education. It created within me a greater desire for professional growth and improvement as an elementary teacher of mathematics. I became more involved with reading articles and books related to

Teachers Engaged in Research
Inquiry Into Mathematics Classrooms, Grades 3–5, pages 59–82
Copyright © 2006 by Information Age Publishing

59

mathematics education, including some related to math research (e.g., Burns, 1998, 1999; Herman, Aschbacher, & Winters, 1992). The *Principals and Standards for School Mathematics* (National Council of Teachers of Mathematics [NCTM], 2000) became a guide in reassessing my classroom practice.

During the time I was serving as a participant and teacher leader in the MAP project, I became acquainted with Dr. Zhijun Wu from the University of Maine at Presque Isle. Both of us were interested in providing greater opportunities for pre-service college students to become actively involved in a mathematics classroom where an effort was being made to implement Maine's Learning Results and national standards. We arranged for Dr. Wu to send her pre-service teachers to my classroom to observe grade 3 students working on their MAP tasks. Dr. Wu then invited me to her classroom to share further with the pre-service teachers how the MAP experience was organized in my classroom and how it related to standards based mathematics.

In November of 2000 Dr. Wu approached me about seeking funding for a cooperative research project focusing on multiplicative reasoning through the Edward G. Begle Grant for Classroom Based Research. The idea of doing research on multiplicative reasoning was of keen interest to me. In the *Principles and Standards of School Mathematics* (NCTM, 2000) multiplicative reasoning is considered a central mathematical theme. "In grades 3–5, multiplicative reasoning should become a focus. Multiplicative reasoning is about more than just doing multiplication or division. It is about understanding situations in which multiplication or division is an appropriate operation" (NCTM, p.143). However, my mathematics textbook at the time was not strongly aligned with the Standards. There was too much focus on fact memorization and not much opportunity for concept development or application to challenging real-world problems. So we developed the grant proposal and received notification that our project had been approved in February of 2001. We met several times to plan our research unit over the following summer and fall. We were also selected by NCTM to participate in the Conference on Practitioner Research in Mathematics Education held in Albuquerque, New Mexico in September of 2001. The research project was implemented in my third-grade classroom in January and February of 2002.

THE IMPORTANCE OF IMPLEMENTING STANDARDS

Principles and Standards for School Mathematics (NCTM, 2000) states that "decisions made by teachers, school administrators, and other education professionals about the content and character of school mathematics have important consequences both for students and for society" (p. 11). It also states that "effective mathematics requires understanding what students know and need to learn and then challenging and supporting them to learn it well" (p. 370). The truth of these principles places great responsibility on today's mathematics educators and made our venture into the realm of teacher research in elementary mathematics exciting and challenging.

As mentioned previously, multiplicative reasoning is one of the central mathematics themes for grades 3–5 students. According to NCTM (2000), multiplicative reasoning "involves a way of viewing situations and thinking about them. In grades 3–5 multiplicative reasoning emerges and should be discussed and developed through the study of many different mathematical topics" (p. 144). Some key components related to multiplicative reasoning which are promoted in the standards include the following: use of manipulatives, exploration of various multiplicative reasoning situations (such as combinations, comparison, rates), visual representations (such as arrays), communication, reasoning, and fluency with the easier fact combinations. This knowledge of the standards and the need to delve into *important* mathematical ideas guided the development, structure, and content of our project.

RESEARCH DESIGN

Our research project, *Developing Deep Understanding of Multiplicative Reasoning in 3rd Grade*, was designed to be implemented as a five to six week instructional unit. All lessons, student experiences, and assessments were designed around two questions — *Question One:* How can the learning experience be organized so that students will develop deep understanding of multiplicative reasoning and be able to transfer their knowledge about multiplicative reasoning and representation strategies to a variety of problem situations? *Question Two:* How can teachers evaluate students' representations at different points of the learning process so that necessary assistance and proper instruction can be provided in a productive way?

Participants

A total of 20 elementary students in one third-grade classroom participated in this study. None of the students had received instruction in prior grades in multiplicative reasoning. Our elementary school is located in a rural area of northern Maine. Of the students who participated 47% were boys and 53% were girls. Permission slips were sent to parents, along with a letter explaining our project. Eighty-five percent of the permission slips were returned. Children without permission slips participated in the learning process, but their work will not be displayed in any published form. One difficulty in our project was the attendance rate of a few of the students. Two out of the 20 students missed quite a few classes during the six-week period and did not participate in several activities and assessments. This is a common problem faced by teachers in the classroom on a daily basis, and one that makes instruction, student practice, and accurate assessment data for those particular students difficult to attain.

We considered parents to be important participants in our project. Family involvement was an integral component of the unit, and there were take home activities most weeks. Parents played math games with their children, practiced for beginning fluency, and received information through parent letters which accompanied take home game and practice packets.

As one component of the project, university students from Dr. Wu's *Teaching Mathematics in the Elementary School* class became active participants in our Grade 3 classroom as the research was being conducted. Each of the university students was paired with one of my students. Each university student spent at least one class period a week in our classroom observing instruction and interacting with the children. They also used samples of my students' work, with parent permission, in their university coursework. They assessed children's class work following rubrics that Dr. Wu and I provided for them. They kept grading sheets on the children in the areas of representation, student-generated story problems, and performance tasks. In their class sessions with Dr. Wu they discussed the accuracy and appropriateness of the students' performance they had observed, analyzed the patterns of errors children made, and brainstormed the potential instructional implications. Students kept weekly log entries and submitted a final report after the completion of the project.

Dr. Wu also participated in the project in a valuable way by meeting with me weekly during the implementation of the instructional unit to discuss student progress and make needed modifications to classroom plans. For example, it had been in our research design to explore the concept of rates as a part of multiplicative reasoning. However, during our weekly meetings Dr. Wu and I observed that many of the explorations were taking more time than we had originally thought. More time was also needed for remedial assistance and class discussion and feedback. We made the decision not to include rates, as we were on a timeline and needed the remaining days to conduct post-assessments.

Data Sources

Multiple sources/types of data were collected throughout this project to address the two research questions. I kept daily journal entries based largely on classroom observations, which provided valuable informal data. Most formal data were collected from student practice and assessment pieces that were completed during the instructional unit. These included problem solving sets and performance tasks, progress checks, and a written pretest and posttest. All of these were organized in individual student portfolios. As we developed practice and assessment tasks we focused on a few primary considerations. One was that we wanted to look beyond the student's answer to the reasoning involved in the solution. We were not focusing primarily on "memorization" of multiplication facts, but on concept development. We designed our unit to provide students with ample opportunity for learning and practice. We then wanted to be able to assess progress regularly and systematically, so we could reflect on assessment data and choose directions for future instruction based on the assessments and aligned with our chosen learning goals. Another consideration was our knowledge that students' representations of a problem situation could be used as evidence of their level of understanding. Providing opportunities for students to use representations (e.g., drawings, equations, charts) was a key component in designing assessment tasks for the instructional unit. The information that follows breaks down each data source/type in further detail.

Individual portfolios. As stated above, all student work throughout the instructional unit was collected in individual portfolios. This work was also photocopied for Dr. Wu and her students to use in the university classroom. This provided the opportunity to discuss and analyze the effectiveness of the instructional unit as a whole and to evaluate student progress over time. Many of the pieces of student work collected in portfolios were designed to incorporate three formats or aspects of problem solving. They were (a) writing a story problem of their own for a given number sentence or a given picture, (b) representing and/or solving *mixed* story problems, and (c) explaining their thinking process. We believed that analyzing student-written story problems would indicate differences among students in their degree of understanding of mathematical concepts. Including mixed story problems was important in demonstrating whether students could choose the correct operation (addition, subtraction, or multiplication) for a real life situation. Asking students to explain their thinking would also provide insight into the depth of understanding of individual students and the class as a whole.

Student progress checks. Certain problem-solving sets/tasks were placed strategically throughout the unit to assess progress in one area before moving on to another. In this way feedback could be given to the whole class as needed, and remedial assistance could be given to individual students. For example, the following problem was posed at the conclusion of our exploration of arrays: *To prepare for the evening parent conference, Mrs. Smith arranged her classroom chairs in 4 rows with 5 chairs in each row. How many chairs were in Mrs. Smith's classroom?* Students were asked to draw a picture and also write the equation(s) used to support a solution.

Informal checklists. One form of informal record keeping was designed to assess progress in skip counting, which assists students in developing fluency with the easier combinations (zeros through fives). Students would participate in home and classroom practice in skip counting by twos, threes, fours, and fives. For three weeks of the unit we planned to meet with each student to listen to their counting and record how far they could count fluently in each set.

Teacher journal. In designing the unit, we believed it would be valuable for me to commit 20 to 30 minutes a day to keeping a daily journal of my observations, thoughts, and feelings about each day's lesson. When students played games or worked with partners on problem-solving activities, usually manipulative based, I listened to and joined in their conversations. In my journal time, I documented and reflected on observations of my students. I made and recorded decisions that would inform the next day's instruction. I identified students who I needed to assist, conference with, or observe more closely as they worked. If it was observed that several students had difficulty with the same task or section of a task, I noted the need for a feedback session to share thinking, discuss solutions, identify complete and incomplete responses, revise, and clarify concepts. Listening to students in these sessions gave me valuable information to record about the understanding and thinking of individuals and the class as a whole.

University students' data sheets. As stated earlier, the pre-service teachers in Dr. Wu's class interacted with my students on a weekly basis. They were given photocopies of my students' work for use in their classroom, which they discussed to gain understanding of third graders' mathematical thinking about multiplicative reasoning. They tracked their third-grade partner's performance, graded their work once a week, and kept records on a grading sheet, which finally contributed to the data collection.

Pretest and posttest. A pretest (see Figure 5.1) was designed to determine students' prior knowledge in multiplicative reasoning. A posttest (see Figure 5.1) was designed to allow to us to assess students' growth in their understanding of multiplication concepts over the course of the unit.

Pretest

Mom bought apples for snacks and placed the apples in two bas-kets. In one basket there were 4 apples and in the other one, there were 4 apples. How many apples were there?

Describe what addition is about.

Write down what you know about multiplication.

Posttest

Describe what addition is about.

What is multiplication?

Write a statement about 2 x 5 = 10.

Draw a picture to show 2 x 5 = 10. (please label your picture)
Write a story problem for 2 x 5 = 10.

Figure 5.1.   Example items from pre- and post-test.

Data Analysis

Each of the various types of data was analyzed to respond to the research questions posed at the beginning of the project. For several of the assess-ment tasks we chose to develop rubrics, specific to the type of task. We believed that a rubric would be important for instruction and assessment purposes in the sense that the rubric details the specific aspects of the problem that are most important. Rubrics also allow for clear expectations to be communicated to students. Specific rubrics were developed for com-bination problems, array problems, student representations, and student-generated problems. There was also a holistic rubric that could be used with any type of problem solving, but the task specific rubrics were found to yield more specific data. Rubrics often addressed more than one aspect of problem solving and we used both 3-point (see Table 5.1) and 4-point scales.

Table 5.1.   Rubric used for performance task assessing
             understanding of arrays.

	1	2	3
Computation/ Problem Solving	An inappropriate strategy has been used. The solutions and equations on the array are totally inaccurate.	An appropriate strategy has been used. There are errors in some of the solutions and equations on the array.	An appropriate strategy has been used to solve the problem. The solutions and equations given on the array are accurate.
Reasoning	Explanations are missing OR explanations are not connected to the solution and do not show an understanding of the math used to solve the problem.	Written responses to questions partially explain/ support the arrangement shown on the array OR demonstrate a partial understanding of the math used to solve the problem.	Written responses to questions completely explain/ support the arrangement shown on the array. Written responses demonstrate an understanding of the math used to solve the problem.
Communication	There is little or no visual representation.	The visual representations on the key and the array are slightly unclear or incomplete.	The visual representations on the key and array are clear and complete with appropriate labels.

THE INSTRUCTIONAL UNIT

Developing the Unit

The selection and development of the content of the multiplicative reasoning unit over the summer and fall of 2001 was a challenging learning experience. The information and recommendations contained in the *Principles and Standards for School Mathematics* (NCTM, 2000) informed the development of the unit more than any other source. The Maine Assessment Portfolio Project was chosen as a source or model for some performance tasks and rubrics. I had studied *Math By All Means, Multiplication Grade Three* by Marilyn Burns, which influenced the development of some lessons and games. My desire for change from the traditional math text I had used for many years, which focused primarily on memorization of facts rather than on concept development, also determined the structure of the unit.

After many months of planning, our unit on multiplicative reasoning was ready to implement. We had designed the following primary materials: instructional lessons, practice problem sets and performance tasks for small-group practice, individual assessments to check ongoing progress, and pre/post tests. These, along with games and practice activities from other sources were prepared with the realization that "the goal of school mathematics should be for all students to become increasingly able and willing to engage with and solve problems. Unless students can solve problems, the facts, concepts, and procedures they know are of little use" (NCTM, 2000. p.182). The unit would engage students in exploring different multiplicative problem structures including: equal groups, arrays, Cartesian products (combinations), multiplicative comparisons, and rates (not addressed due to time constraints). There would be many opportunities for students to use representations (e.g., drawings, charts, equations) and manipulatives. Students would also be required to explain their thinking orally and in written form. We were prepared to challenge our students and ourselves! What follows in the remainder of this section, while not a complete writing of all classroom learning, provides a detailed account of many classroom experiences over the course of the unit.

Implementing the Unit

On the first day students were given the pre-test, which demonstrated that most of them had little understanding of the concept of multiplication. The first week was organized to provide opportunities for students to construct their own meaning of what multiplication is and to draw representations of multiplication. In a beginning activity students worked together to create a class chart of things found in groups (Burns, 1991, p. 20). This was done for groups of objects from 2 to 12. For example, when exploring groups of eight, one student suggested that there are eight legs on a spider. The next day we moved on to constructing number sentences, such as 8+8+8 for the number of legs on three spiders. After doing several examples, students observed that in each number sentence there was repeated adding of the same number. This discussion led to the introduction of multiplication as repeated addition. Students also played the game Circles and

Stars (Burns, p.28), a dice game in which one die indicates the number of circles to draw and the other die indicates the number of stars to draw in each circle. Students write related equations (e.g., 2+2+2+2=8 or 4x2=8) for their drawings and the winner is the person with the most stars after seven rounds of play.

Later that week students worked in pairs on an initial problem-solving set (see Figures 5.2 and 5.3 for sample items). The problem set allowed students to explore the following: drawing a picture to show a solution, identifying the meaning of each number in an equation, and attempting to write a story problem for which multiplication would be used to arrive at a solution. Students were also given two take-home activities to reinforce classroom learning. They were given a chart with multiples of 2, 3, 4, and 5 and asked to practice their skip counting with an adult. They also took home a packet containing booklets and rules for Circle and Stars. Students played the game at home through the week and then returned the packet with their game booklets.

The next portion of our unit engaged students in exploring multiplicative reasoning through the use of arrays, often using color tiles and drawings. Using arrays as models proved to be a very effective way for students to visualize multiplication situations and the concept of equal groups. We began with a whole-class lesson, using color tiles. Students were shown a rectangular display of tiles, and asked to think of how the total number of tiles

John, Jeff, and Mary worked in the potato fields. Each picked up 7 baskets of potatoes.   How many baskets of potatoes did they pick?

1. Draw a picture to show the solution

2. Write two different number sentences to show your solution.

$3 \times 7 = 21$ $7+7+7=21$

3. Look back at #2 and describe what each number in the number sentence means. It means 3 people and 7 baskets each. There are 21 baskets.

Figure 5.2.   Jay's solution to an item from the initial problem set.

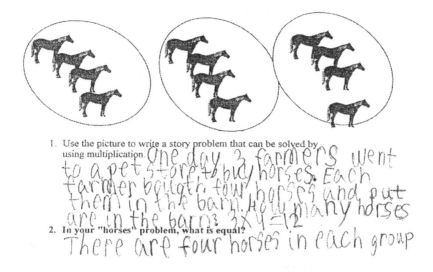

1. Use the picture to write a story problem that can be solved by using multiplication. *One day 3 farmers went to a pet store to buy horses. Each farmer bought four horses and put them in the barn. How many horses are in the barn? 3×4=12*

2. In your "horses" problem, what is equal? *There are four horses in each group*

Figure 5.3.   Mark's solution to an item from the initial problem set.

could be found or proved. Students discussed the strategy that the tiles in each row could be added to find the sum. They were also able to conclude that since the rows were equal the total could be found by multiplying. In the next lesson, students worked with partners to further explore the concept of arrays. They chose a certain number of tiles and were asked to construct all possible arrays for those tiles. They created drawings of the arrays on grid paper and recorded equations reflecting the number of rows and the number of tiles in each row for each array (see Figure 5.4). Students later completed performance tasks in which they explored creating designs in equal rows on grid paper, such as flowers in a garden and shells arranged on a table. Students constructed multiplication equations for their designs and justified the thinking used in their work. The children took part eagerly in these activities, and their excitement about the progress they were beginning to make was visible to all observers.

At home that week students continued to practice skip counting. They also took home packets containing rules, special dice, and game sheets for a multiplication game called "SKUNK"[2]. The game provided an opportunity for students to begin to work on mental computation and fluency. Time had been set aside to teach the game to students during the week. As had been done the first week, students were asked to return their game sheets.

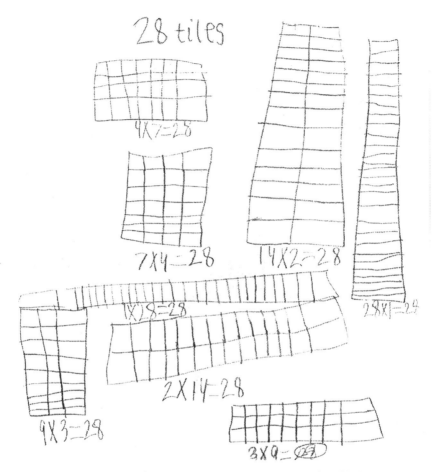

Figure 5.4.   Anna and her partner construct arrays using 28 tiles.

Students next explored combinations as they relate to multiplicative reasoning. Dr. Wu and I believed when we designed the unit that combinations as they relate to multiplicative reasoning might be more complex and more difficult for the children to visualize. We had prepared this component of the unit with that complexity in mind. A memorable and fun introductory lesson centered on the concept of *outfits*. I brought in a shopping bag of my daughter's clothes from home, which created immediate interest in the lesson. I told a story about a student going on vacation, and asked Nancy to come up to demonstrate. She was given two shirts and two pairs of shorts from the bag. I asked students to suggest outfits she could wear. Nancy slipped each outfit on over her clothes, and I recorded the outfits on chart paper. I had set up the headings "pants" and "shirt" on the chart paper so students could see all the combinations that had been made as I wrote them. I then added to the story, saying that her aunt bought her a new sweater while she was visiting. I asked what new outfits could be made and recorded new outfits the children suggested as Nancy tried them on. We discussed what kind of math could be used to find the total number of possible outfits. Students were able to communicate a connection to multiplication, that 2 pairs of shorts each used with 2 shirts would be 2 x 2 = 4 outfits.

Another combinations activity the following day gave students experience with drawing and charting combinations. In this task Clown Bill has three different wigs and 4 different costume noses. Students drew and charted all the different combinations Bill could wear. Students also worked with partners and then individually on performance tasks related to combinations in making ice cream sundaes and pizzas. Students then spent two class periods working with partners to write, exchange, and solve combinations problems they had written. Students constructed and solved combinations problems for such things as: decorating cookies, making sandwiches, choosing house and roof colors (see Figure 5.5), and making candied apples. They gave written comments back to the authors of the problem they solved. This was a very challenging task for some children, but many expressed that this was one of their favorite explorations. It also provided a rich opportunity to informally observe depth of concept understanding in individual students, partners, and the class as a whole.

It was at this time that students were given a set of multiplication flashcards through the fives to take home, to develop fluency. Each student was given a calendar on which parents initialed each weekday for two weeks, showing 10 minutes of daily practice. The calendar was returned to school at the end of the two weeks.

Another real life situation involving multiplicative reasoning is comparison, or "times as many". This was the final concept explored by our students. In the introductory lesson, I brought in a bag of marbles. I asked Jon to come up and take a certain number of marbles from the bag. I then asked Sarah to come up and take two times as many from the bag. Students counted Sarah's marbles along with her, and we created a chart to show what each student had taken. This was repeated with several different students. Each time we wrote on the chart the number the first student had taken, how many "times as many" the next student would be taking, and the number of marbles the second student took. As we described the number of marbles the students were taking, students communicated an understanding that an equal number of marbles was being taken a certain number of times. The following day, students worked with partners to

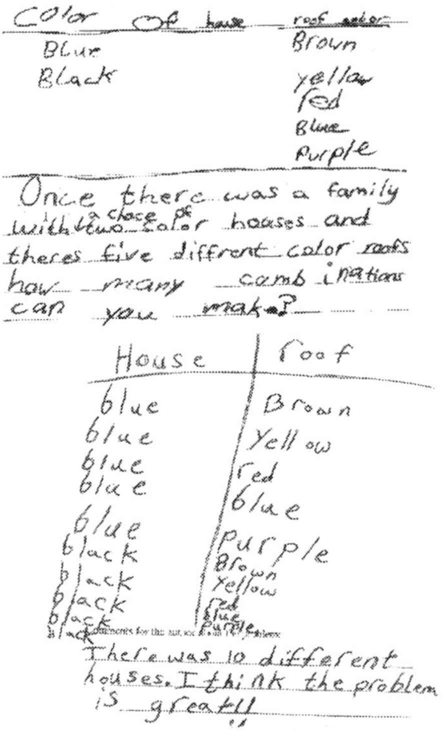

Figure 5.5.   The problem at the top of the page was constructed by two students and given to two other students to solve. Their solution, represented in table form, and comments to the problem's authors are presented below.

explore this concept further. They used "dinosaur" counters, making their own decisions concerning the number of "times as many" and charting their solutions. As we continued to develop this concept students used counters, pictures, charts and equations to represent solutions and worked individually on a set of problems to check their understanding of this concept. Students were asked to demonstrate an understanding of the use of multiplication to solve "comparison" problems, and how they knew that they could use multiplication.

At the conclusion of the unit, two days were set aside for post-testing. These results, along with the student work collected in portfolios, provided us with valuable data from which to draw conclusions about the effectiveness of the instructional unit.

FINDINGS AND CONCLUSIONS

There were important issues to reflect on related to our original research questions as we came to the end of our unit and looked at the informal and formal data that had been collected. How well did students make progress over time? How much information did their drawings, charts, equations, story problems, and explanations give us about the depth of their understanding?

Most of the students made clear progress over time. In looking at their individual portfolios in which all work had been collected, it was evident that students' understanding of multiplicative reasoning had deepened. Specifically, it was clear to us that the third graders as a group performed well in three out of the four areas we had chosen. They did well as a group with "equal-sized groups", "arrays", and "multiplicative comparison" (times as many). Working with "combinations" was the most difficult problem-solving situation of the four areas for students. This was evident as we examined student written work, as well as in our daily observations of students in the classroom. Combinations situations (such as making all possible outfits from 3 shirts and 2 pairs of pants) are complex, and do not as easily suggest the operation of multiplication to young children as the other problem situations do. One data chart related to four unit topics is presented in Figure 5.6, Performance of Representation by Tasks. These data pertain to student success in creating representations (e.g., pictures, charts, or other drawings) to demonstrate understanding and relate to the whole class as a group. The graph shows that on a 3-point scale the group average in tasks related to the concept of equal groups was 2.0. There was an increase in students' scores for tasks related to arrays, with a group average

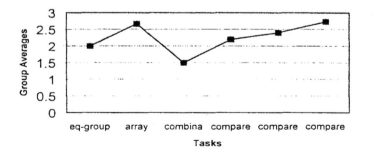

Figure 5.6.   Class average of students' performance for using representations on different problem types.

of 2.5. The group average decreased to 1.5 for combinations tasks. But over the course of work on three comparison tasks, there was an increase in the group average, ending above 2.5.

We agreed as we examined our data that asking students to formulate their own story problems revealed a great range in depth of understanding among the third graders. Figure 5.7, Performance of Generating Story Problems by Types, shows data by group average over the course of the unit as students constructed stories for different types of problems. On a 4-point rubric scale, the group average for student generated story problems over the course of the unit was 2.45. As the graph shows, students did best as a group constructing story problems related to an array situations. They had the most difficulty as a group when the story construction related to the concept of combinations. In the area of constructing story problems we also focused on examining individual work, progress, and difficulties. Data revealed that out of the 18 students who completed this aspect of unit work, two students (11%) received about perfect scores on the story problems they generated over the course of the unit. Four students (22%) scored between 3 and 3.7. Three students (16%) scored between 2.7 and 2.8. Four students (22%) scored between 2 and 2.4 and four students (22%) scored at about 1.3. One student (5%) received less than 1 for his self-generated story problems.

Student success was also documented in classroom observations, informal journal entries, and checklists tracking developing fluency with the easier multiplication combinations. We observed improvements in fluency with multiplication facts as students applied them throughout the unit to

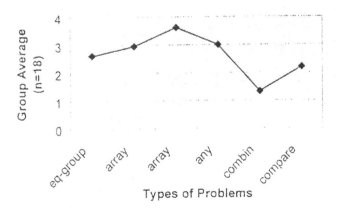

Figure 5.7.   Class average of students' performance for generating story problems for different problem types.

games and real-life problem solving. It was exciting for the students to see their own progress recorded from week to week. For example, skip counting record sheet 1 indicated that Anna could count fluently by twos and fives, but could only count by threes to 6 and by fours to 12. According to skip counting record sheet 3, Anna could count fluently by twos, threes, and fives, and could count by 4s to 32. As shown on skip counting record sheet 1, Danny could count fluently by twos and fives, but could only count by threes to 12 and by fours to 8. On record sheet 3, Danny could count fluently by twos, threes, fours, and fives. These results were typical for most students, and we considered them significant since the NCTM (2000) contends that "through skip counting, using area models, and relating unknown combinations to known ones, students will learn and become fluent with unfamiliar combinations" (p. 153).

Comparing individual student progress from the pretest to the posttest also provided a valuable source of data. I will refer here to Jay, as his progress provides a good example of growth over the course of the unit. On the pretest when told to write down what you know about multiplication Jay wrote: "It is something like math and if the problem was 7x7 it would be 7." On the posttest when asked, "What is multiplication?" Jay wrote the following: "Multiplication is repeated adding". Jay was also able to demonstrate his ability to construct a basic multiplication story problem. On the posttest when asked to write a story problem for 2x5=10 he wrote: "There was once 2 boys. They each got 5 pieces of chocolate. How many pieces did they get?" Jay was also able to successfully explain the meaning of a multiplication equation. When asked to write a statement about 2x5=10 he wrote: "The statement is that you are using 5 repeated twice." Jay's posttest also revealed areas where his understanding still may not be complete. One problem stated "Mom bought apples for snacks and placed the apples in two baskets. In one basket there were 4 apples and in the other one there were 4 apples. How many apples were there?" In his solution Jay correctly drew a picture of 2 baskets with 4 apples in each. However, he wrote the equations 4x4=16 and 4+4=16, which were incorrect. This last data from Jay serves as a good reminder that a research project is not just about seeing "success," but also about further defining areas of incomplete understanding which will inform future decisions about instruction, practice, remediation, and assessment.

The total data from our project (individual student's work and group data) offers support for the following conclusion: children at this grade level can acquire deep understanding of multiplicative reasoning when they have opportunities to examine and explore the multiplicative relationships in the context of real life problem solving situations. Carefully selected problem solving activities and a focus on constructing and using various representations of multiplicative situations encourage meaningful learning among students.

PERSONAL REFLECTIONS

I found myself reflecting on several things as our instructional unit ended and I looked again through all of my students' portfolios. One reality that really struck me was the degree of individual differences among students in the classroom. Teachers must put great effort into finding ways to effectively deal with the range of individual progress and remedial needs, as they focus on how to help those students whose understanding is incomplete.

I also found myself reflecting on the difficulty many students had with constructing their own story problems compared to solving story problems given to them. For a student to generate a story problem of his/her own is clearly more difficult than representing and solving a teacher-written problem. I observed that for students to develop their own problems with all the necessary elements involves a higher level of thinking and understanding. Even though it was a challenge for students, I believe this was an important instructional component of our unit. It allowed students to examine the mathematics involved at a deeper level. These students had little experience in writing their own story problems prior to this project. It was also clear to me in looking at their work that students' basic writing skills are an important consideration in writing story problems in math. In the future as I replicate and improve on this unit I will keep in mind that for some students an "interview" format may be appropriate so they can talk through their story problem idea.

I had very positive feelings about the decision to make family involvement an integral component of our unit design. It was beneficial for parents to play math games with their children and to practice with them using the skip counting charts and flashcards. It helped parents become more aware of the learning that was taking place in the classroom and of their own child's strengths and difficulties. The level of parent involvement and support was high throughout the unit. Nearly all children returned their packets with such things as game record sheets. The packets, when returned to school, often contained positive remarks from parents. Several parents expressed by phone, note, or in person over the course of the unit that their child was enjoying the home activities and that they could see progress being made. One parent told me that she thought the use of drawings and manipulatives was very helpful to her daughter and that her daughter's attitude was very positive. The work we had collected in portfolios was sent home with each student at the end of the project, after we had copied the information we needed. This also provided valuable information for the parents, allowing them to see the whole of their child's work from the beginning to the end of the unit. The feedback received from parents was very encouraging, and reinforced the belief that parents play an important role in a child's education.

Finally, I want to share more about the valuable practice of keeping a teacher journal. Prior to this study, I had never attempted keeping a daily journal for any unit of instruction. As stated earlier in this chapter, Dr. Wu and I felt that a journal would be of great value in reflecting on my teaching and students' learning, and would be a rich source of informal data. Each evening during our study I spent a minimum of twenty minutes, and sometimes more, writing in my journal. Entries included such elements as: my thoughts and feelings about trying some teaching strategies quite different from the traditional text, common problems I had noticed students having with some of the tasks, specific misunderstandings I observed in individual children as they participated in games or written work with notes to myself about how I could provide remediation, lesson components that had been effective, and progress I had observed. Figure 5.8 presents a few brief or partial entries from my journal, the keeping of which was a great professional growth experience.

IMPACT ON MY TEACHING

Participating in this research project was a tremendous professional growth opportunity. My current and future mathematics teaching has been positively impacted by the experience of designing, implementing, and evaluating this multiplicative reasoning unit. I have continued to revise the instruction, practice, and assessment components of the unit as I have used it with new students, and have experienced the joy of seeing greater student success resulting from these revisions. This experience has been a positive force in changing my focus to reflect a more conceptual emphasis. I know that my students need to become fluent in computation, but I have learned that laying a solid conceptual foundation is critical for their future success in mathematics. I have become more convinced of the benefit of providing opportunities for partner activities, exploring a variety of problem solving situations, and using manipulatives more frequently to explore

January 11, 2002
I had felt apprehension all day about how much of a departure it would be from our traditional "text multiplication unit."

January 16, 2002: (relates to playing Circles and Stars)
Terry needed help right away (with the game). He had six sets of three stars and had written 18 times 18 as his equation. I asked why he had written that and he shrugged his shoulders. I asked how many groups of stars do you have? Response-6 How many stars in each group? Response-3 We used the skip counting chart so he could figure what counting 6 times by 3's would equal. Response-18. He then wrote correctly. His partner helped him fix three other equations, then he was able to play and record successfully. I have observed that having a partner is very helpful to the few students who have had difficulty (with the game). The partner stops play and helps the other child fix mistakes, quicker than I would usually notice them. The player who understands more completely is modeling the process for the partner.

January 18, 2002
A teacher who teaches this way has to be willing to accept as positive: less structure, more noise, the presence of others in the classroom.

January 31, 2002: (refers to Clown Bill combinations problem)
As I walked around the room it was interesting to see that some sets of partners used a pattern/strategy. For example, taking one wig at a time and doing drawings with all the noses. Others did not use any strategy as they drew, and had a harder time deciding when they had all the combinations. Students who approached the drawings in an organized way tended to do the same with their charts. I had conversations with these students (the ones having difficulty) as I observed them working asking, "Why is it hard for you to tell if you are done? If you had a problem like this again, how would you do your drawings differently?" After this conversation, some of these students carried that thinking to their charts, and their charts showed more organization, patterning of the combinations than their drawings had.

> **February 8, 2002**
> *I have to remind myself that multiplicative reasoning is a grade 3–5 span and we are laying a foundation, exposing children to many situations and letting them go as far as they can-The range of success is wide.*
>
> **February 13, 2002**
> *The elements in writing a story problem is another area I have worked on with these (a small group of) students. These students also have language/reading difficulties which I believe is somewhat connected to the difficulty they have with such tasks as writing a story problem.*

Figure 5.8.   Sample journal entries.

important mathematics concepts. I have also come to realize the importance of giving my students opportunities to construct their own story problems, not only in multiplication, but for other operations and situations as well. Learning to do so provides students with a greater understanding of mathematical concepts.

> Opportunities to reflect on and refine instructional practice – during class and outside class, alone and with others – are crucial in the vision of school mathematics outlined in *Principles and Standards.* Reflection and analysis are often individual activities, but they can be greatly enhanced by teaming with an experienced and respected colleague, a new teacher, or a community of teachers. Collaborating with colleagues regularly to observe, analyze, and discuss teaching and students' thinking or to do "lesson study" is a powerful, yet neglected, form of professional development in American schools. (NCTM, 2000. P. 19)

I fully agree with this statement encouraging professional development among teachers and have made a commitment to share what I have learned from this research project with others. I recently shared this unit with Grade 3 teachers in another building in our school district. They tried out parts of it in their classrooms, and were positive about the results. One made this statement related to a game activity, "I feel this game provided the children with a visual interpretation of how multiplication is repeated addition. Many who were not sure of the concept of multiplication seemed to have a much better understanding after playing the game. Many were highly motivated to want to learn their multiplication facts after playing the game."

I am a more effective mathematics teacher as a result of my participation in this research project and believe elementary mathematics teachers must continue to seek ways to collaborate with others to improve mathematics education for our students.

ACKNOWLEDGMENT

I would like to acknowledge the efforts of Dr. Zhijun Wu of the University of Maine at Presque Isle in making this such a challenging and rewarding classroom based research experience. Dr. Wu invested countless hours in writing the grant proposal, partnering with me in planning, implementing, and assessing the multiplicative reasoning unit, analyzing data, and writing the final report for the National Council of Teachers of Mathematics. I greatly appreciate her commitment to partnering with classroom teachers, creating greater opportunity for communication and cooperation between the elementary classroom and the college classroom.

NOTES

1. This research project was funded through the Edward G. Begle Grant for Classroom Based Research.
2. SKUNK is a dice game in which a picture of a skunk or the letter "s" replaces the 1 on each of two dice. A scoring sheet consists of 5 columns with the letters S, K, U, N, K printed across the top. Each column (letter) is used to record the score for each of the five rounds of play. This game is played as a whole class with the students standing behind their chairs (at the beginning of play). The teacher tosses the dice and the numbers displayed are multiplied. The product is recorded under the appropriate column (e.g., S for round 1, K for round 2, and so on). A round of play continues until a *skunk* comes up. Thus, after each toss of the dice, players must decide whether they will remain standing and in play, or whether they will sit and take as their score for that round, the total number of points accrued at that time. Students who are standing when a skunk is tossed, receive no points for that round. When a round is complete, all students stand up and the process is repeated. The person with the greatest number of points at the end of the five rounds of play is the winner.

REFERENCES

Burns, M. (1991). *MATH by all means: Multiplication grade 3*. White Plains, NY: Math Solutions Publications.

Burns, M. (1999). *About teaching mathematics: A K-8 resource*. White Plains, NY: Math Solutions Publications.

Burns, M., & Tank, B. (1998). *A collection of math lessons, grades 1-3*. White Plains, NY: Math Solutions Publications.

Herman, J., Aschbacher, P., & Winters, L. (1992). *A practical guide to alternative assessment*. Alexandria, VA: Association for Supervision and Curriculum Development.

Maine assessment portfolio. (n.d.). Retrieved September 13, 2005 from http://www.maptasks.org

National Council of Teachers of Mathematics. (2000). *Principles and standards for school mathematics*. Reston, Virginia: Author.

Maine Department of Education. (1997). *State of Maine Learning Results*. Augusta, ME: Author.

Wu, Z., & Atcheson, J. (2002). Developing a Deep Understanding of Multiplicative Reasoning in Third Grade, A Classroom Based Research. Final Report to NCTM Mathematics Education Trust.

CHAPTER 6

WRITING MATHEMATICAL WRITING

Eileen Phillips
Vancouver School Board, BC, Canada

> Incorporating writing into math class adds an important and valuable dimension to learning by doing. Writing encourages students to examine their ideas and reflect on what they have learned. It helps them deepen and extend their understanding. When students write about mathematics, they are actively involved in thinking and learning about mathematics. (Burns, 1995a, p. 13)

This chapter presents a necessarily brief account of a personal journey into the realm of teacher research: that is, research undertaken by myself as a practicing classroom teacher in my own classroom. Over more than a decade, I have specifically looked at aspects of the mathematical writing of grade three, four and five students who have been in my class. Along the way, there have been four main student-writing vantage points: conventional mathematical journal writing, mathematical pen-pal letter writing, writing about mathematical investigations, and student textbook writing. I have written elsewhere about the pen-pal writing (see Phillips & Crespo, 1996; Phillips, 1996) and my focus in this chapter will predominantly be on writing about mathematical investigations, reflected through an intensive

Teachers Engaged in Research
Inquiry Into Mathematics Classrooms, Grades 3–5, pages 83–112
Copyright © 2006 by Information Age Publishing
All rights of reproduction in any form reserved.

mathematical writing year that my class and I undertook a few years ago. But before getting into more detail, I want to look at some aspects of the recent history of writing and mathematics in school.

THE PROBLEMATIC NATURE OF WRITING IN MATHEMATICS

When I first became aware of the possibility of undertaking writing in a mathematics class, I was excited, seeing a way that I might link some of my other enthusiasms with a love of mathematics. As a teacher, I know that if I can get students to "let me inside their heads," through discussion and/or writing, I am then better able to evaluate their learning and assess their degree of understanding. More importantly, the more knowledgeable I am about my students' understanding, the more informed my teaching decisions can be.

In the early 1990s, I came across some articles (both academic and professional) that introduced me to mathematical writing. These predominantly involved journal writing for mathematics assessment (Kennedy, 1985; Stempien & Borasi, 1985; Waywood, 1992) and pen-pal writing employed as a means of diagnosing mathematics problems (Fennell, 1991).

Much of the research literature concerned with young students' writing suggested that elementary-age students experience too little variation in genre, claiming that they neither read enough nor write sufficiently using different available styles and forms. This claim matched my personal experience. In terms of written genres, students usually enter my class knowing loosely how to weave a creative short story, how to retell an event (often using "and" and "then" as the major organizing connectives) and how to produce a short "research" project (e.g., on an animal), often in point form under pre-determined headings. In the field of mathematics, they know how to record computations, draw some diagrams and write a word problem to support a simple equation such as $12 - 9 = 3$. They do not arrive knowing how to *write* mathematically nor, for the most part, how to *speak* mathematically (Pimm, 1987) nor read mathematically. Many of my questions about mathematical process and thinking in the early part of the new school year are met with "I don't know" or "I can't explain it" or "I just did it."

As a result of becoming familiar with the research literature mentioned above, I identified a missed opportunity both for my students and myself – I had not been asking for extended nor extensive writing in my mathematics classes. Initially, the opportunity I saw was for my students to experience linking their mathematical work to personal narrative, and in this way offering me a route into gaining additional access to their mathematical attitudes and thinking. I started by asking them to write about their successes and difficulties related to the mathematics we were doing. I requested they write to me about their solutions and justify them. Initially, I was pleased with anything and everything that was handed in: to my uncritical eye, it all looked good and it was certainly better than nothing being reported.

Gradually, however, I began to mistrust aspects of the writing I received. Often, it seemed as if students had discovered a formula and were feeding it back to me. For example, if I were provided with the words, "This made me wonder about ..." or "I am still struggling with ...," I was easily deluded (for a while) into believing that these were meaningful reflections from my students. But when the writing about mathematics of these students did not seem to be developing depth in the way that I knew that it was in their language arts, science or social studies work, I began to suspect that they were simply *reacting* to my prompts, when I had hoped they would *respond* to them.

I asked these students about my suspicion of their using a "formula" for writing in mathematics classes, and they agreed, opening the door for a torrent of complaints. They told me that they hated writing in mathematics and could see no purpose for it. Some even said that writing was making them dislike mathematics, because one of the things that mathematics traditionally offered was "not having to do all that written stuff."

They additionally responded that they did not worry about forgetting and that they never used the writing again—two of the purposes I had offered them by way of public justification for my request for writing. They also complained that it took too long and they sometimes lost track of a problem's solution when they were also aware of the need to write about it. What they really wanted was "just to do the work," suggesting they saw such writing as peripheral to the mathematics. And admittedly, for me, it was very time-consuming to have them use class time to write and, moreover, it resulted in one more thing for me to read and respond to. I began to question the value of writing in mathematics, at least for this age level.

Mostly because of the time this writing took for the relatively minor "reward" it gave, I found my enthusiasm waning. But my interest and belief that there was value in writing as a *learning* tool for mathematics, and not just as an *assessment* tool, remained. I started reading about *writing to learn mathematics* (Countryman, 1992) and wanted to find ways, within my classroom, that would support this possibility. I also started thinking about the interconnections between form, audience and purpose that I would later focus on in more depth. Burns (1995b) broadly discussed purposes of writing in mathematics, claiming it is necessary for students to understand that the two basic reasons for writing are to "enhance and support their learning and to help you [teacher] assess their progress" (p. 41).

She also advised teachers to establish themselves as the audience and to have students discuss their ideas before writing them, suggesting that prompts are important to help students start to write and that lists of mathematics words might be posted in the room.

I kept seeing examples in print of writing from students that far exceeded the products that I was receiving, both in length and in significant detail. Educators whom I respected (e.g., Burns, 1987; Pimm, 1987; Borasi & Rose, 1989; more recently, Morgan, 1998; Borasi and Siegel, 2000), as well as the more anonymous voices of the National Council of Teachers of Mathematics Standards documents (NCTM, 1989, 1991, 2000), were indicating through books and journal articles how successful writing in mathematics (as part of a growing emphasis on communication in mathematics classrooms) on occasion *could* be.

If writing in mathematics classes could be more successful than that within my experience, then I began wondering what my teaching lacked. Once identified, this deficiency would then presumably explain why the results of my students (many of whom seemed set to succeed both academically and socially, coming from predominantly middle-class homes with high educational expectations) did not appear as noteworthy as the ones I was reading about. Equally obvious to me, I needed to work on my writing-in-mathematics tasks, while still seriously considering some of the claims being made elsewhere.

THE NATURE OF WRITING PROMPTS IN TEXTBOOKS

Over the past decade, I have noticed an increasing number of claims for the merits of using writing in mathematics, culminating in the ultimate accolade of acceptance – sections of school textbooks dedicated to pointing students and their teachers toward opportunities for writing in mathematics classes. These sections often remind me of those picture-taking spots found at various tourist locations. They have been pre-determined; they are set for anyone who comes along; the answer to the question 'Why take this photo?' ('Why write about this?') is believed to be so obvious that no justification is offered and no samples of a potential finished product are given.

Many of the writing directives in texts, taken at face value, make much more sense as suggestions for oral discussion. They are usually too general to prompt specific, in-depth writing. To me, many textbook writing prompts ask for story writing more than focused mathematical writing, at best pointing to instances of writing *about* mathematics. It is the writing that is apparently the goal in itself here, rather than writing as an additional way to represent or help to learn mathematics: that is, writing as a way to clarify one's own thinking or as a means to show personal understanding.

Here are some instances of self-styled writing prompts, taken from a Canadian grade four textbook *Quest 2000: Exploring Mathematics* (Wortzman *et al.*, 1996). The proposed journal entries I have selected are taken from throughout the book. These are typical of the whole in that they have an open quality and promote a narrative, summative response.

- What do you know about figures? [in response to an activity on constellations] (pp. 58–59)
- What did you find interesting about finding squares and parallelograms? [in reaction to a quilt picture] (p. 71)
- Design your own flag. Use fractions to describe its coloured sections. Tell what is important to you about your flag. [following an exercise on fractions and flags] (p. 141)
- What have you learned about multiplying? [following an exercise on the distributive principle in relation to multiplication] (p. 175)
- Do you enjoy making and recording patterns? Explain. [following the use of T-table columns to show patterns] (p. 229)

Why would I ask students to write about these things and, in turn, why might they conceivably want to *write* about them?

A more recent example, taken from a US middle-school textbook unit *Connected Mathematics: Thinking with Mathematical Models* (Lappan, Fey, Fitzgerald, & Friel, 1998), falls at the end of pages entitled *Mathematical Reflections* that consist of five investigative questions, many of them having more than one part. The student is directed to: "Think about your answers to these questions, discuss your ideas with other students and your teacher, and then write a summary of your findings in your journal" (p. 25). This generic writing instruction is presented again on pages 36, 46 and 59 of the student text.

I cannot imagine students writing, having already explored, concluded, and discussed all this work orally. Why would they want to? What could they see as a purpose that would be plausible to them? Looking through the tests in this CMP unit, I found no written summaries required as part of any assessment. So, a student could not even see a *pragmatic* reason for undertaking such comprehensive writing tasks (e.g., 'I might do better on this type of test question if I practiced my mathematical writing').

What other potential purposes can be offered to students? Reflection has already been started by the doing and discussing, signaled by the imperatives "describe," "explain," and "give reasons" found in the text exercises. What middle-grade student would really be lured into willingly writing a summary as well? As an adult and a teacher, I value the writing process and I know that it will frequently stimulate new connections for me, but would many uninstructed and inexperienced students of this age know and feel the same way?

So far, I have detailed some outside reading in interaction with my initial experiences in writing and mathematics within my own classroom, and indicated both my interest and hope, as well as some of my reservations at the outset. In addition, I have outlined my sense that much of the justification for writing in mathematics is problematic or insufficiently clear, at least as offered to practicing teachers through both the professional and research literatures, as well as being increasingly promoted through textbook and curriculum/assessment requirements. This is the broad context in which my own work developed.

THINKING FURTHER ABOUT CLASSROOM MATHEMATICAL WRITING

My over-riding question for exploratory research became: What types of writing and settings could I find or develop that would enable my students to write genuinely and mathematically? Because my initial attempts at straightforward journal writing did not yield the products I was expecting, I needed to change how I presented the writing tasks to students and/or I needed to change my expectations about the result. Increasingly, I came to believe that I needed to develop new strategies for including writing in mathematics class.

Prior to the beginning of the school year that gave rise to the writing samples that will be offered in this chapter, I had done a considerable amount of thinking about how to structure the time and format of my *Mathematics Writing* program. The writing of pieces could not be left to chance, yet I would not overload the students with writing at every opportunity either. This was because I was wary of triggering an "Oh, no, do we haaaaaave to?" response in my students and also of trying to keep mathematical writing within the usual curricular time frame (namely, six forty-minute periods per week) that my regular mathematics curriculum allowed.

I did not want to be viewed as spending too much time on my personal project and not enough on the required mathematics curriculum which, although containing communication goals, did not specify how much time was to be spent on them. I was also aware that my colleagues generally paid less attention to these particular goals (at least as far as writing was concerned), spending more time on arithmetic practice and teacher-to-student communication than on writing strategies and student-to-student and/or student-to-teacher communication.

According to the British Columbia provincial guidelines, elementary students should have the equivalent of at least five (forty-minute) periods of mathematics each week. I set aside one class period every Wednesday afternoon for mathematics writing, in addition to the morning period we had daily for 'regular' mathematics. The mathematics writing period was thus in addition to the required mathematics time: in reality, this additional time co-existed within the language arts program and the discretionary time allotment available for locally developed programs.[1] The students themselves gave no indication of distinguishing mathematics writing time from any other mathematical work: this was one of the advantages of working across the whole year, where students have no real sense that what they were doing might be seen as unusual.

I decided to provide mathematical problems and projects that would necessitate writing and take more than a period to complete. Some were to be started at school and finished at home. Others would run across several mathematics writing periods (hence across consecutive weeks), requiring students to write about their extended assignments as they went along and not to leave all their writing till the end. This would give some force to my comments that one purpose for writing was to assist them in recalling where they were, both in their thinking and in their solution process.

Students would have opportunities to write in varied genres, that is, recognizably different forms of writing to achieve different ends. (Examples of mathematical genres might include 'report', 'recount' or 'summary' – see Marks and Mousley, 1990; for more on genre in mathematics education in general, see Pimm and Wagner, 2003.) Thus, I planned to explore informally more explicit teaching of forms and making overt genre suggestions with my class concerning how to focus on stylistic features that would improve the written form. I also knew that I would be relying heavily on purposeful writing, that is, writing where students could readily appreciate and acknowledge a genuine purpose for it, since part of my initial challenge to students was to write for an audience who was to be found within the classroom.

Additionally, and unlike in previous years, I introduced the notions of caring, safety, trust, and kindness (our four overall classroom themes) immediately into this year's discussion of writing. I wanted the students to know that most of their work, throughout the year, would be discussed in an individual writer's conference initiated at their request. However, out of necessity, I would sometimes take work home to read and make comments on, but I was not keen on 'red-marking' work without the author present. I also wanted them to know that if a piece of writing were going to be used for assessment, I would tell them ahead of time.

They were also informed I would not tolerate anyone laughing at someone else's efforts – unless humor was the intent – and that they would need to request permission before using someone else's name or another's ideas in their writing. I introduced the idea of writing to learn and told them that sometimes I would be asking them to write as they were thinking about something or as they were struggling to understand it. Finally, I told them that I was interested in this as my research for the year and that I would be using samples of their work to help further my understanding of "how writing works." This went for all of their writing – mathematics writing included.

As their teacher, I was also responsible for, and in control of, the writing that was being done concurrently in other subjects. Sometimes writing in language arts or science would influence a mathematics writing assignment. As a class teacher, I am aware of much more of the general running of the classroom than I would be as a visiting researcher. My timetable was also more flexible than that of an outside researcher (who, in my experience, would usually schedule the visit to the classroom in advance and, thus, we would need to stop what we were doing in order to give our time and energy to his or her research focus). There were times when my scheduling flexibility encroached upon my research time, as well as situations where I was able to extend research time into other subject time allocations.

THE WRITING TASKS THEMSELVES

Throughout the course of the school year, students engaged in a broad range of tasks involving writing within the context of what I called the mathematics writing period. These varied considerably in nature and scope. Instances included: open-ended writing in response to prompts like 'mathematics is …'; a wish poem; elements of their own mathematical autobiography; and, procedural writing (e.g., how to make a 3-D snowflake cut-out or explaining the moves of the different pieces in chess or the process of long division). I also elicited responses to some challenging mathematical problems and investigations, culminating in an extended project to produce chapters for inclusion in the mathematics textbook the class was jointly writing. (See the Appendix for a full list of these tasks. For more on the general research frame of my work on student mathematical writing, see Phillips, 2002.)

The mathematical topics were selected because they were larger in scope than the ones generally presented in mathematics textbooks and they were (to my mind) ones where keeping a written record or writing a description, solution, or explanation would be plausible and even necessary for successful completion of the task. My planning of the order in which they would be offered was intended to lead the students sequentially from one type of genre writing to the next, with the proviso of some overlap between each. One of the stated purposes for writing that I gave my students was that it would allow them an opportunity to make me (in September, their new and known-only-by-reputation teacher) aware of how much they knew about mathematics. Later, they were encouraged to let me in on their current thinking in and about mathematics. Through writing, each of them could have my undivided attention: something that was explicitly declared to the class when discussing "Why write?" The open and social context of writing did not change. Although in some cases students worked by themselves and sometimes in a writing team, they were permitted to talk to others throughout in order to gain and clarify ideas. Writing here was not proclaimed a necessarily private or solitary act and collaboration was generally encouraged.

The tasks I employed have some similarity to writing assignments offered by others (see, for example, Burns, 1995a, and Countryman, 1992). However, I think the range of genres, the richness of many of the writing tasks that required writing over a period of weeks and the regularity of the writing program over the year meant this class of students wrote more mathematics that any other group I have taught or read about in the research literature. To help the students with their writing, lists of words that might be useful were posted in the room. As well as this, some ideas about what to include in a specific writing form/genre were also pinned up. I felt it important that students have writing aids (e.g., prompts, lists, definitions) available to them. Naturally, some of the students used these aids, while others ignored them. The main point was that they were there, available for the students and myself to refer to.

WHAT EVIDENCE DID I GATHER TO ANALYZE AND WHY?

I believe that research in classrooms needs to be caring and respectful of the culture, atmosphere, and relationships that exist (and are constantly emerging and developing) in a classroom. For myself, classroom research should not be carried out as a completely separate activity, for its sake alone. My classroom research has needed to align itself with my teacher sense of both curricular constraints and the central importance of providing *educational* opportunities for my students. I have a similar tenet in mind to a doctor's Hippocratic oath: do no harm. Research should not, intentionally or unintentionally, be harmful to any of the students and hence must be conducted with both considerable care and deliberate attention to this possibility.

Because of this belief, I am unwilling, for instance, to undertake research in my classroom that relies on or results in identifiable comparisons of one method over another by overt means of comparing group achievement standards. There is perhaps room for such comparative educational research to be done on a broad scale over districts, but I strongly believe that each method of instruction used with my students has to be the best I can knowingly offer at the time. Thus, rather than generating comparative data in the moment, I find that *my* work generates data that is cumulative – each element adding to or constraining something that was known or believed before.

The research that I have done in my classroom over the years has mainly arisen from the teaching that I would normally have done. But it is a particular part of that teaching: it is both teaching and more than teaching at the same time (involving instructing, discussing, assessing, questioning, searching and re-searching) in an area that I am specifically and passionately interested in. It is thus acutely personal classroom work.

One core difference between my usual teaching practice and my researched teaching practice is in the degree of reflection I undertake about the teaching/learning relationship I have with my students, as well as some of the tasks I have them carry out. When my intent is to research an area, I collect more student work than I usually do—often because I am unsure what might prove to be significant, and do not want to limit my search. (A research partner, Rena Upitis, once remarked to me that *everything* is potentially data.) I write notes to myself before, during, and after the teaching events that are intended to be part of my research records. I try to ensure complete participation by all of my studentss—finding ways for them to make up any missed work. I also deploy varying means to collect/create data seen as records of particular events located in space and time. For this study, for instance, I used students' written work done in notebooks, on separate assignment sheets, and in folders containing the pupils' attempts at textbook writing. Additionally, I have drawn on class-meeting notes and my own personal research journal and day plans.

Partly because of my combined interest in both mathematics and language, the analytic frame I brought was primarily a linguistic one, looking closely and systematically at aspects of the written language the students produced in relation to the specifics of the communication situation. By attending to the way the form of and voice inherent in the writing interacted with the audience and purpose of the writing in giving expression to the content, I aimed to be able to determine features of significant school mathematical writing tasks.

SAMPLES ARISING FROM A
MATHEMATICAL WRITING TASK

I now present a set of examples of grade-four student mathematical writing in response to a task (pattern block writing – task ten, see Appendix). The purpose of this task was to develop skill at writing *explanatory* language, language that fulfilled a function independent of the presence of the author. The context required making a shape from more than one pattern block and then writing instructions for others in our class (or possibly in next year's class) that would enable them to duplicate the shape – sight unseen. This is similar to the task where two people sit back-to-back with one describing what he or she is doing so that the other partner can replicate the design. In fact, the rehearsal for this writing task was the oral version just described. Later, the students acted as critical readers of each other's work. The presence of the author's coloured image (on the reverse side of the paper) provided an immediate source of comparison by which the measure of success (or otherwise) of the instructions could be evaluated by the reader. In some sense, the illustration itself provided both the meaning and the goal of the written text.

As the teacher, part of my pedagogic purpose for having the students undertake this task was to impress upon them the power of written text to conjure images (by means of correct vocabulary and sequencing of instructions). Furthermore, I wanted them to become more aware of the precise amount of information to give, in order to rule out viable alternatives at any point. In addition, I increased the mathematical challenge of the task by prohibiting the use of colour names in written descriptions that would otherwise have allowed simple shape identification (e.g., the blue one). I also wanted the students to appreciate the value of an illustration in providing clarity and confirmation of a written text, as well as providing a sense of *successful* text.

This was important work because I knew that I would be asking these students to write textbook chapters later on in the school year, so it would provide a specific instance of the clarity of writing that I would want to draw on for the textbook writing challenge. The student readers were requested to make focused, critical comments about the effectiveness of the communication and to provide written feedback augmenting and altering the text that was there. This task involved comparing the present form of a text with the desired purpose it was intended to achieve, as well as confirming that texts were not inviolable, but improvable. Many of the students provided useful critiques, modifying what had been written, indicating places of potential confusion, misuse of vocabulary (e.g., *This worked out perfectly once I realised you were calling parallelograms "triangles"*), and commenting on places of particular clarity.

A further look at the comments also alerted me to a striking feature of these amended texts: student perceptions of politeness and decorum in the "teacher" role (one who is allowed to make suggestions and critical comments on another's work). These students seemed to feel that generally it was necessary to include a "Well done!" sort of comment, even to the extent that one writer who could not follow any of the written text wrote: "Even though mine didn't turn out anything like yours, I thought you did a great job."

When the students started this task, there were two main strategies they used: some wrote as they placed the blocks down and some made a complete design and then described how to make it. The written sequence of making the shapes might vary from the actual sequence employed, depending on the focus of the writer. Usually, when construction was described while the shape was being made, the writing more closely followed the actual sequence. When the design was completed before the construction was explained, the focus seemed to be the final shape and the written construction sequence might vary from that used in the actual construction.

Part of the assignment was to include a picture of the shape being explained. The drawing had to be separate from the words, so it could be used by the reader only as a final check, but not as a construction guide or model. There were several different strategies used to complete this part of the task:

- some students made the design, drew it, then wrote about it;
- some made the design, wrote about it, then drew it;
- some partially made it, wrote about what they had made, then added more, and finally drew it all at the end;
- some partially made it and drew it as they went along, while also writing as they went.

Most made the shape and described it before drawing it. This proved advantageous at times: a few, upon finding their design too complex to write construction notes for, changed the part that was proving too hard to explain. Then they finished the explanation and drew the altered shape.

I, as teacher and researcher, was interested in the different strategies used. But managing the project (as teacher), while also attempting to do at least one task myself (something I often try to do), took effort and time. As a result, more detailed recording (as researcher) about who was using which method did not happen. This was an instance when a serendipitous interest arising unexpectedly from a project could not be followed up. If I had been solely the researcher, rather than a teacher–researcher, I could have made the observations or if I had had a video camera set up I could have recorded the students working in one area of the room.

As the writing/drawing was completed, the students put their finished work into a collection box. They had the option of doing another or completing work on a different assignment. Another research road not taken was a comparison of first product to subsequent products. Classroom research is often contingent on trade-offs, mostly of time. When some students had made three artifacts and others two, and all (including me) had made one, we each selected a folded page from the finished box and tried to create the shape we were reading about. The constraint was that only the writing on the paper could be used as a resource – no peeking at the drawing, no asking what someone else thought, no seeking out the actual author for clarification.

As students attempted to make the design, any parts that were found difficult were described in written notes. If the reader could not decide what was meant, she was to continue with her best guess at each stage until done. When the reader had completed the design, the paper was to be flipped to the drawing. Readers then compared the model they had just constructed with the pictured design and wrote more about where the explanation/instructions had succeeded and tried to identify where the problem areas were as well as, at times, attempt a diagnosis of the nature of the difficulty. In order to be more helpful to the writer, the reader also drew a picture of the shape she had just constructed.

During subsequent class discussion, student comments indicated they realized that their written language had to become more precise. Two particular areas quickly arose as generally problematic – the use of prepositions (e.g., above) and the use of rhombus to describe two different pieces (one beige and one blue: but with colour adjectives not being permitted). Some students had used *above* to mean "stacked on top of" and others had used it to mean "placed to the north of" ("north" being "up the page"). The various solutions taken for rhombus were imaginative: "large rhombus" and "small rhombus"; "rhombus senior" and "rhombus junior"; "rhombus major" and "rhombus minor"; rhombus 1 and rhombus 2. Many students constructed a legend to help the reader identify the pieces.

The samples below were selected because they depict different writing forms that were used: the first (Figure 6.1) is written in steps and includes a list of shapes required to do the task; the second (Figure 6.3) is written in paragraph form, as is the third (Figure 6.5). The third also received contrasting critiques from the reviewers (Figures 6.6 and 6.7).

Sample One: Lillian's Dragon

Lillian's explanation is formatted in discrete, numbered steps and uses the strong, imperative form of verbs: take, put, have. In consequence, in

1. Take 2 hexagons and lay them flat on the floor. Have
an edge on both of the hexagons touch each other
horizontally
*2. Then take 2 triangles and put them in the sides
of the hexagon where there's a gap.
*3. Then take 2 more triangles and put them on the
bottom sides of the hexagon
#4 Then take 2 trapezoids and put the shorter side of
i on the top of the top hexagon. Then put the other trapezo,
(the long side) on the other trapezoid
*5. Next on one side, take rombus senior and put it on the side
of the trapezoid so it on the side of the trapezoid
and the other one on on the top right side of the top rombus
senior

- 2 hexag
- 2 rombus
- 4 triangles senior
- 2 trapezoid

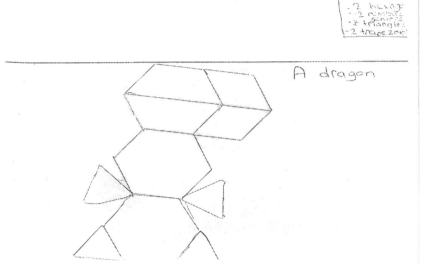

A dragon

Figure 6.1.   Lillian's pattern block explanation and design.

terms of voice, there are no pronouns deployed and the tense is the running present throughout. The sequence is well marked with numbers and
uses some words (*then, next*) that designate sequential (temporal) order.
There is a 'pieces needed' recipe list, placed like a map legend in the lower
right corner.

Mathematical nouns (*hexagons, triangles, trapezoid, r[h]ombus*) and positional terms and expressions (*horizontally, in the sides, edge*) are used.
Descriptive words and phrases from the everyday lexicon are also
employed: *lay them flat, touch each other, where there's a gap, on the right side, on
the top, of the top, on the bottom*. Words that compare are also used: *long,
shorter, senior*.

The audience is addressed generally, in the manner of one being impe-
riously commanded. There is an authoritative "I know this" quality to the

author voice that is reflected in the format. When the paper is flipped over in order to see the shape, the reader also sees that it has been named: a dragon. I often encouraged the naming of a finished piece, whether in art, social studies or science. Although I had not requested labels for this product, many of the students who could see an object in their finished illustration tended to use the name to label their image.

Figure 6.2 presents comments from Jane and the diagram that shows her final product where the pattern blocks have been individually outlined.

The criticism is done gently – Jane tells Lillian where her problem occurred, though she does not specifically refer to what it was in the ending that she *didn't quite get*. Also, the problem is only indirectly attributed to the text. Lillian is addressed by name (although not visible in the figure)

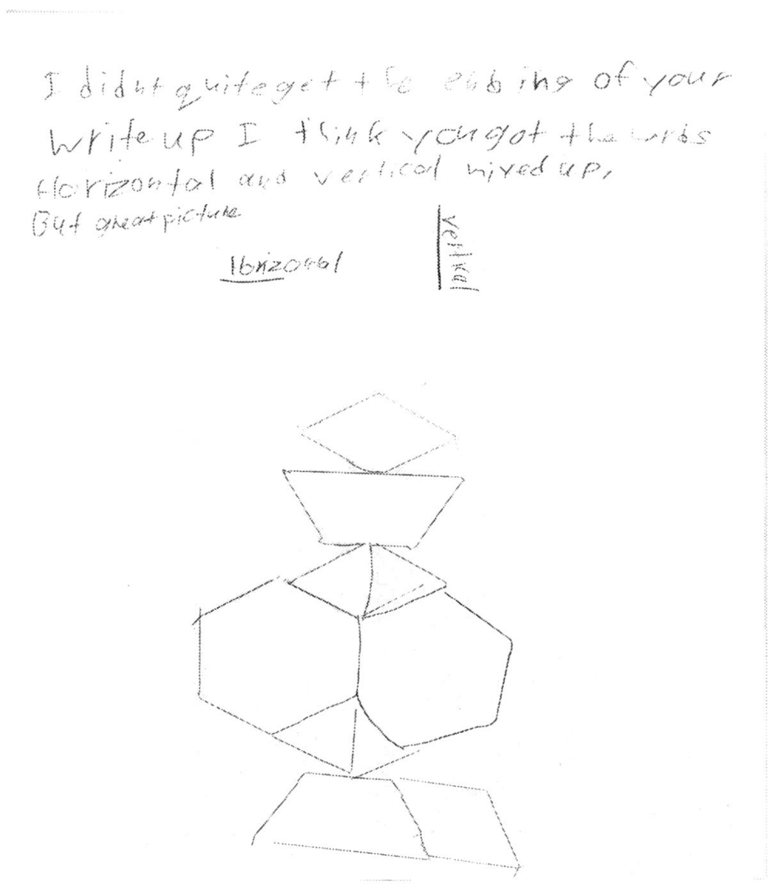

Figure 6.2.   Jane' response to Lillian.

and as *you* and the product is *your write-up*. A reassuring compliment is paid, as is common with many teachers (say something encouraging) and the compliment is specific: *great picture*. Then there is a teaching moment, one where Jane explains the difference between *vertical* and *horizontal*, even though the only place where this term is used is in the first instruction.

Looking at the drawings of both writers, it seems that Lillian placed the hexagons adjacent to each other, one immediately above the other, in a north/south relationship, whereas Jane also placed the hexagons adjacent to one another but in an east/west orientation. Lillian correctly stated that the touching edges would be horizontal and Jane interpreted what she read to mean that the hexagons were to be placed touching, but horizontally. Careful reading is therefore needed, as well as specific and detailed writing. Where would readers learn to read and follow mathematical instructions such as this? Certainly not in the textbooks they have been using.

Sample Two: Brian

To the right of Brian's explanation (Figure 6.3), there is a legend that includes illustrations of all the pattern-block shapes. This is necessary, because it offers the only way toidentify what is meant by "rhombus 1." In elementary school textbooks, much information contained in drawings or illustrations merely repeats information in the text. However, in some instances, like this one, the diagram or legend is essential in glueing the words to the world beyond the text.

The format is like a paragraph, though the use of *then* as a sequencing word signals a stepped task for the reader who is referred to as *you*. The use of *you* is also important because the reader her- or himself is used by Brian as a positional referent – *is facing you*. The verbs used are again in imperative form (*put, make, do*) and the voice is commanding.

There is one attempt to predict and remove ambiguity over a problem area, indicating an orientation toward the reader's task, which in some sense makes this partially a teaching text – *make sure the rhombus 1 is not sticking up,* This can be seen as help or a hint: a caring offer made by Brian to the reader. The mathematical nouns used include the names for all the shapes, even ones not used in the finished shape, as well as *edge* and *sides*. Positional terms are in abundance – *is facing you, on the flat edge, the closest edge, on the opposite edge, on the diag[o]nal edge, beside the square, on the other side, on the bottom sides*. Many of these stress the use of prepositions and demonstrate the importance of prepositions in descriptive/explanatory constructive language.

Figure 6.4 presents comments from Carl. Carl addresses Brian as *you* and gives him personal ownership of the instructions – *your instructions*.

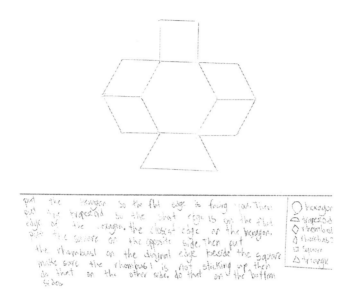

Figure 6.3.   Brian's pattern block diagram and explanation.

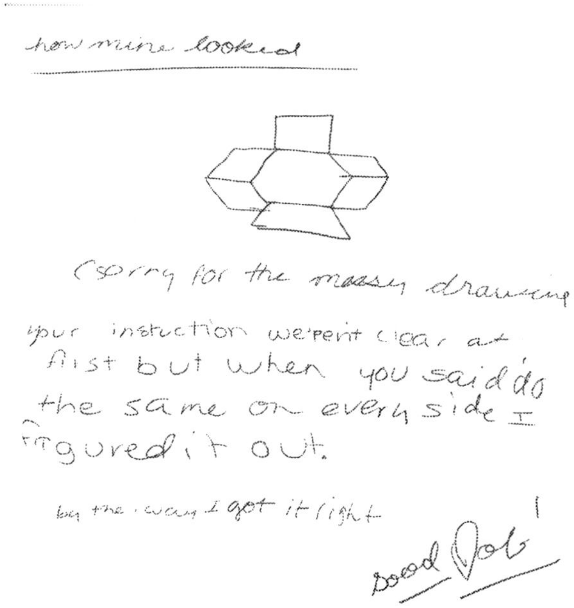

Figure 6.4.   Carl's response to Brian.

Also, the point of clarification is identified—*when you said ...*—but Carl also takes credit for getting it right, by asserting *I figured it out.* For the most part, except when directly addressing Brian, Carl is writing in the past tense and reporting back very generally on what he did. *By the way* is an interesting parenthetic marker that allows success to be both claimed and reported, but this marker suggests it is less than centrally important.

The writing of *Good Job!* (at the teacher's angle on the page, even) is very much in the mode that used to be drilled into teachers ("Say/write something nice or show encouragement") and in this case is non-specific. Over almost five years of schooling, these students will have been the recipients of many such comments.

Sample Three: Eric

To the right of Eric's explanation (Figure 6.5), there is a *legend* that includes drawings and labels for *hexagon, trapezoid, rhombus Jr, rhombus,* and

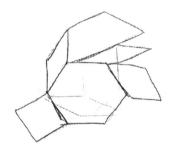

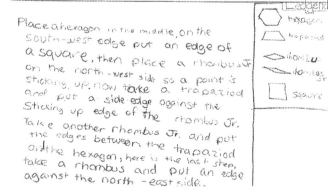

Figure 6.5.   Eric's pattern block design and explanation.

square. Eric had noticed that signifying a change in labeling of one of the two rhombuses is all that is needed to differentiate between the two.

The explanation is once again written as an imperative, instructional paragraph. The only break in the flow is an aside alerting the reader that *here is the last step.* Eric sees this as a sequence, as signaled by the word *step,* though there are few of the usual sequence signifiers used to begin sentences: *then* is included within a sentence and *now* begins a sentence, but is not marked with an uppercase letter. Eric uses action-filled placement verbs: *place, take, put.* Some positional indicators are direction-related: *south-west, north-west, north-east;* some are mathematical: on the *edge,* so a *point* is sticking up, a side *edge,* against the sticking-up *edge,* put an *edge,* and some use everyday language: *in the middle, sticking up, between, on the side.* When Eric writes, *here is the last step,* he is directly addressing the audience with what can be seen as a caring comment. Often telling students that the end is near ("this is the last question," "you're almost done") is a way to encourage the student to keep striving and not to give up.

Figure 6.6 presents comments from Susie. Susie is an ESL (English as a second language) learner and possibly found the density of instructions

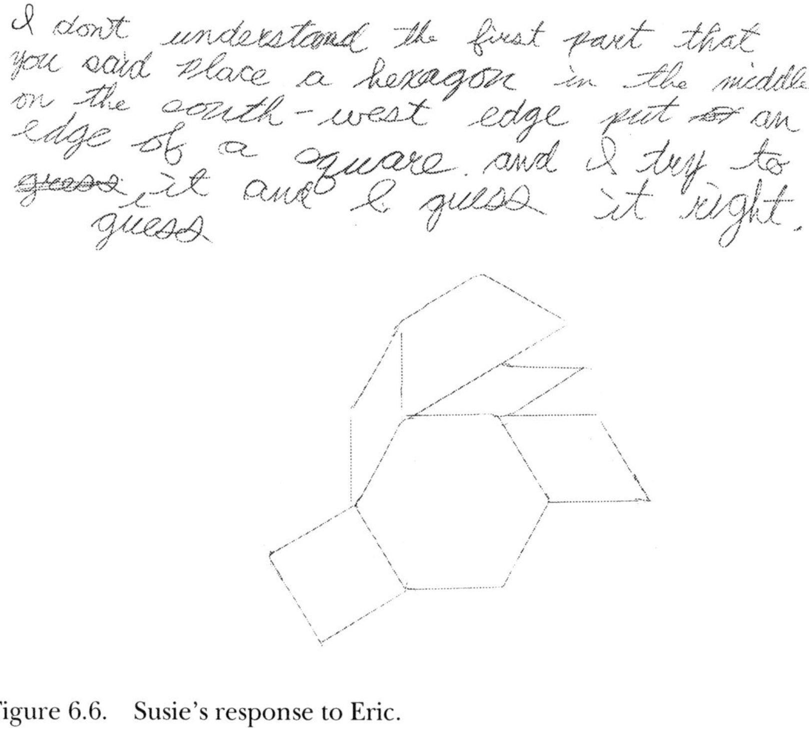

Figure 6.6.   Susie's response to Eric.

overwhelming. She tried to be specific and was able to identify the difficult spot, though she did not identify what it was about this that was unclear. She said she guessed, but did not tell what the possible guesses were that she might have tried. She seems to have followed one guess through and it proved correct, so there was no need to keep on trying. There is a tracing of the shapes to validate this. There is no comment of praise or encouragement like many of the other students made. I suspect that this is because her early educational experiences were not filled with the modeling of such comments.

Jane also worked on this set of instructions, as shown in Figure 6.7. There is no proof offered – no drawing. The friendly letter form is unusual for feedback of this sort: it makes it easy to address Eric directly and perhaps this is the most common way that Jean has written to another student. Praise is there, somewhat specific, since it refers to the writing but does not particularize any part of it. The past tense is used to indicate this was written after the shape was made. *Very well written!* is timeless.

The students demonstrated in the above examples that they had their own clear ideas of what a response to work entailed. Their inclusion of positive, teacher-like comments, even when unwarranted, was surprising to me. My plan had been to have the students use the feedback they received to re-write their original versions, but I decided not to do this, believing they had benefited enough from reading the critiques. In the end, it seemed that more experience writing and commenting on the second and third tasks was better than re-working a piece. Each new task was carried out more successfully than the one before, possibly because they became better at both writing and choosing the type of finished shape that would write up well.

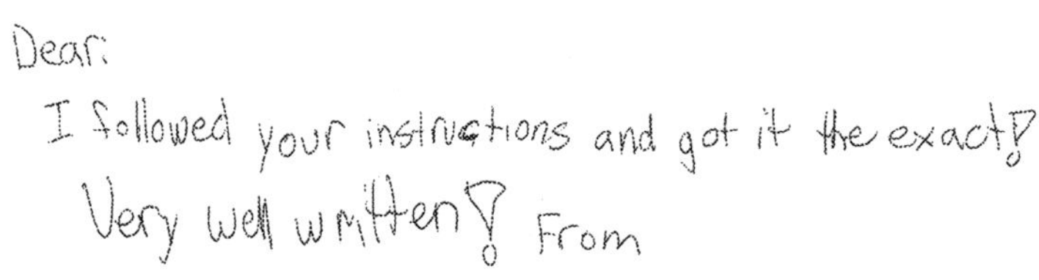

Dear:

I followed your instructions and got it the exact?

Very well written? From

Figure 6.7.   Jane's response to Eric.

IN CONCLUSION

I have discussed one task in detail in this chapter and included a linguistic analysis of my students' writing on it, particularly in relation to the means they developed to engage and hold the reader's attention. Some of the specific features that they learned to attend to in this task include: the value of clarity and precision in language use; the ability of language to help conjure an image; the importance of prepositions; the significance of sequence; and, the editing role of determining what elements are necessary or require modification. Additionally, the students began to appreciate and value the use of specific vocabulary and to pay greater attention to detail in relation to purpose. I increased my understanding of the importance that form plays in relation to the content expressed and also solidified my belief that learning to write in mathematics takes a long time, over many varied opportunities.

When my students write in mathematics class, I ask them to consider their answers to five questions as they start to write. *Who* am I writing for? (audience) *Why* am I writing this? (purpose) *How* do I expect the finished product to look? (form/genre) *What* do I know and/or what am I thinking about this topic? (content) *Where* am I in relation to the writing? (aspects of voice). Although the audience was known (or somewhat known) for all of the writing tasks I provided, student awareness of writing for another was most heightened in the pattern-block writing. This task contained the greatest opportunity for the students to become more aware of writing to/ for an audience, because they were also reading others' responses and acting on the language in such a way that comprehension and successful communication (or not) were evident. The task framed them as both readers and writers of such texts.

This task, although not contextualized as a 'read-and-respond' journal, had some of the same characteristics reported in the literature of teacher–student writing by Gordon and MacInnis (1993) and Kennedy (1985) – for instance, a reader who could provide prompts. Pattern block writing differed from such journals in that it required a procedural report rather than the less-structured narrative of dialogue. There was an additional awareness developed in the receiving student (who was acting somewhat 'in the role of a teacher') about areas that the writing student did not express clearly; and, reading the explanations allowed the "reader–teacher" more insight into the difficulty of writing a report about a construction. To press this point further, since the action of responding was taken immediately (either while reading or just after), the response writing served to inform the original writer in an obviously helpful way about areas that needed clarifying. It also served to identify areas of difficulty to the reader that he or she could be aware of when acting in the role of writer. This type of mathematical writing was unique among all the tasks because the language was, in this sense, *enacted*. I also claim my students felt the exigencies of some of the role of teacher when placed in the position of commenter on the text of others, indicated by their teacherly comments of praise (sometimes somewhat independent of the reality).

I had offered these students many more opportunities to write than I had any other class. However, at the time I wondered (and do so, still, now) whether I had touched the surface of too many genres, but failed to move deeply into any particular one. What would the results of fewer genres and more experience with each have been? Would the writing have been more intensely mathematical? This is an example of research generating its own questions, unanswerable without further explorations, thereby creating a cycle of research. It is also a defining difference between being a classroom teacher who is also a researcher and an outside researcher. Because of the nature of teaching an elementary class, the teacher–researcher must attend to all students and all subjects, whereas an outside researcher can focus on a specific topic, and even on only a few students, perhaps with greater intensity over a shorter period of time. As a teacher–researcher, any further actions taken from my reflections are left to next year and a new group of students. An outside researcher may be able to move immediately to a similar classroom and explore a new question or may be conducting several pieces of research concurrently, each with a different focus. However, as a teacher–researcher, I have the advantage of knowing both my students and the teaching/learning context intimately and intensely. I also have the benefit of being known and trusted by my students and their parents. Next year is soon enough to further my explorations.

ACKNOWLEDGMENT

I would like to acknowledge the comments and support of David Pimm in preparing this chapter.

NOTE

1. In British Columbia, about 10% of curriculum programming can be used by individual teachers to pursue class-based areas of interest. I made use of this time, together with some allocated inside language arts for *writing in the content areas,* to provide the periods needed to pursue this project. Thus, I

could allay any parental or administrative concerns that students might be missing required curriculum due to my research interests.

REFERENCES

Borasi, R., & Rose, B. (1989). Journal writing and mathematics instruction. *Educational Studies in Mathematics, 20*, 347-365.

Borasi, R., & Siegel, M. (2000). *Reading counts: Expanding the role of reading in mathematics classrooms.* New York: Teachers College Press.

Burns, M. (1987). *A collection of math lessons: From Grades 3 through 6.* Sausalito, CA: Math Solutions Publications.

Burns, M. (1995a). *Writing in Math Class.* Sausalito, CA: Math Solutions Publications.

Burns, M. (1995b). Writing in math class? Absolutely! *Instructor, 104*(7), 40-47.

Countryman, J. (1992). *Writing to learn mathematics: Strategies that work.* Portsmouth, NH: Heinemann.

Fennell, F. (1991). Diagnostic teaching, writing and mathematics. *Focus on Learning Problems in Mathematics, 13*(3), 39-50.

Gordon, C., & MacInnis, D. (1993). Using journals as a window on students' thinking in mathematics. *Language Arts, 70*(1), 37-43.

Kennedy, B. (1985). Writing letters to learn math. *Learning, 13*(6), 59-61.

Lappan, G., Fey, J., Fitzgerald, W., & Friel, S. (1998). *Connected mathematics: Thinking with mathematical models.* Menlo Park, CA: Dale Seymour.

Marks, G., & Mousley, J. (1990). Mathematics education and genre: Dare we make the process writing mistake again? *Language and Education, 4*(2), 117-135.

Morgan, C. (1998). *Writing mathematically: The discourse of investigation.* London: Falmer Press.

National Council of Teachers of Mathematics. (1989). Curriculum and evaluation standards for school mathematics. Reston, VA: Author.

National Council of Teachers of Mathematics. (1991). *Professional standards for teaching mathematics.* Reston, VA: Author.

National Council of Teachers of Mathematics. (2000). *Principles and standards for school mathematics.* Reston, VA: Author.

Phillips, E. (1996). Mathematics pen-pal letter writing. In P. Elliott, & M. Kenney (Eds.), *Communication in Mathematics: K–12 and Beyond,* 1996 Yearbook (pp. 197-203). Reston, VA: National Council of Teachers of Mathematics.

Phillips, E. (2002). Classroom explorations of mathematical writing with nine- and ten-year-olds. Unpublished doctoral thesis, The Open University, Milton Keynes, Bucks, UK.

Phillips, E., & Crespo, S. (1996). Developing written communication in mathematics through math penpal letters. *For the Learning of Mathematics, 16*(1), 15-22.

Pimm, D. (1987). *Speaking mathematically: Communication in mathematics classrooms.* London: Routledge and Kegan Paul.

Pimm, D., & Wagner, D. (2003). Investigation, mathematics education and genre: An essay review of Candia Morgan's *Writing Mathematically: The Discourse of Investigation. Educational Studies in Mathematics, 50*, 159-178.

Stempien, M., & Borasi, R. (1985). Students' writing in mathematics: Some ideas and experiences. *For the Learning of Mathematics, 5*(3), 14-17.

Waywood, A. (1992). Journal writing and learning mathematics. *For the Learning of Mathematics, 12*(2), 34-43.

Wortzmann, R., Harcourt, L., Kelly, B., Morrow, P., Charles, R., Brummett, D., *et al.* (1996). *Quest 2000: Exploring mathematics* (Grade 4, revised edition). Don Mills, ON: Addison-Wesley.

APPENDIX: CLASS MATHEMATICAL TASKS

Task One: Mathematics Is ...

Features: self-brainstormed ideas; expressive writing; points made, no particular order; formative – one period, then added to as the year progresses.

Form: list.

Content: beliefs about what mathematics involves, probably based on arithmetic operations, geometric figures, and story problems.

Audience: the self, the teacher.

Purpose: to see how self and others view mathematics and to see if (and how) ideas about 'what mathematics is' change or develop as the year progresses.

Task Two: Other Names for 25

Features: self-generated ideas; symbols, diagrams and words used; mathematical elaboration; done in a period; random order of ideas and equations.

Form: web.

Content: ways to indicate 25 (e.g., $100 - 80 + 5$), decomposition of whole numbers based on choice of operation (e.g., division) and type of numbers involved (e.g., fractions).

Audience: the self, the teacher, others who look at the display.

Purpose: to encourage flexible thinking and to represent a number in multiple ways; to see others' results and gain ideas from them.

Task Three: King's Poisoner

Description: This is a problem presented in oral story tradition. Briefly, a king finds out about a plot to poison him and he creates a plan to poison the poisoner instead. He arranges the seating and determines the order of serving of glasses of wine, so that the last person served gets the glass that has the poison. The problem is to get the plan right given settings like: if there are 21 people and the server gives wine to every fourth person, starting at person 1, and no person gets more than one glass of wine, where—on a round table—would the last person to receive wine need to be seated?

Features: explanatory writing; formative and summative; diagrams used to clarify and to show strategies; tables used to represent results; continued over several sessions; report on progress; prediction, messy drafts with an organised, tidier final presentation.

Form: paragraphs with illustrations, perhaps multiple illustrative strategies.

Content: solution strategies leading to the problem solution, involving systematic elimination of multiples of a fixed number, iterated on the partially eliminated list.

Audience: self, teacher, other members of the problem-solving team.

Purpose: to write, over time, about developing strategies and solution formation. Also, to write new organizational features, within the same context (e.g., there are 26 people, start at person 3, serve every third person, who is last?).

Task Four: The Recess Problem

Description: Which would you prefer if we could change recess from 15 minutes each day to either (a) 30 minutes of recess every day, for 2 school weeks (ten days) or (b) one minute on the first day, two on the second, four on the third, and this pattern keeps up for the ten school days? Explain your choice.

Features: explanatory writing; argument – opinion needed with supporting detail (optimum solution may vary depending on the point of view of the student); formative and summative; continued over several sessions; tables used to represent results.

Form: paragraphs of the explanation and argument to defend choice, table showing mathematical growth.

Content: supporting one's answer, based on comparing results of multiplication or repeated doubling (powers of 2).

Audience: self, teacher.

Purpose: to write, over time, about developing strategies and solution formation; to be able to explain and justify reason(s) for the solution preference chosen; to use written language to argue in support of a mathematical solution.

Task Five: King to Castle Grid

Description: a problem of finding a general rule to determine the least number of moves it takes to move a piece from one corner of a square grid to the diagonally opposite corner. All moves need to be made into the open space and diagonal moves are not allowed. There is only one open space at a time and it starts as the destination position. I begin the problem with a 3 by 3 grid and with the students acting the initial problem out before going to models and paper and pencil strategies. It extends up to grids of 20 by 20, depending on the challenges the pupils choose and how long it takes them to find a pattern.

Features: explanatory writing; formative and summative; continued over several sessions; diagrams used to clarify and to show strategies; tables used to represent results; prediction.

Form: paragraphs, chart of movement.

Content: solution to the problem, including mathematical (e.g., counting by 8s and expressing a linear generalization in words) and illustrative thinking (drawing diagrams and using them to support the written explanation).

Audience: self, teacher, other members of the solving team.

Purpose: to write, over time, about developing strategies; to explain solution formation; and to try to generate a proof for the solution.

Task Six: Handshake Problem

Features: diagrams; notes; reporting on testing trials; conclusion.

Form: paragraph and table or diagrams.

Content: solution to the problem or attempts at solving (the relationship is quadratic in the number of people, expressible in a number of different ways).

Audience: self, teacher, partner.

Purpose: to develop a plan, enact the procedure and report back; to try to develop a proof for other numbers of handshakes.

Task Seven: Snowflake

Description: steps to make a 3-D snowflake cut-out.

Features: procedural writing that shows sequence; some illustrations; recall and formative writing.

Form: steps, in sequential order; like a recipe.

Content: explain how to make a 3-D paper snowflake, iterating procedures involving fractional language, notions of symmetry, and measurement.

Audience: the teacher, students in next year's class.

Purpose: to explain, using mathematical descriptors, a sequence that leads to a project sometimes seen as a craft activity; to mathematize a craft project.

Task Eight: Chess

Description: explain how the pieces move in chess.

Features: explanation, diagrams, predicting and reporting.

Form: paragraph, illustrative moves.

Content: make a chess piece movement guide for someone who is learning to play chess, describing the effects of certain transformations of the plane, drawing on notions of vertical, horizontal and diagonal in relation to an underlying grid.

Audience: self, others in the class, grade two chess buddies.

Purpose: to use words and diagrams to explain movement to a younger student (who is known to the writer) about a game that many are learning to play.

Task Nine: Long Division

Description: explain the process of long division (using 69 divided by 3) and write a suitable context problem for the worked example.

Features: explanation; directions; illustrated steps; short vignette; a question.

Form: steps supported by long division algorithm; an arithmetic word problem.

Content: use of a one-digit divisor and a two-digit dividend as an example: also, students are to make up a word problem that goes with this example.

Audience: a classmate, the teacher.

Purpose: to clarify the long division process and to create a problem context requiring dividing.

Task Ten: Pattern Blocks

Description: make a design using pattern blocks and separately, in writing, explain how to create it to someone who cannot see it and is either not present or is present but involved in their own work. (No colours to be named in the writing.)

Features: descriptive mathematical vocabulary, careful use of prepositions, explanation, generative language, definitions. Also, response writing and editing in the next stage; illustration of the finished work.

Form: paragraph or steps.

Content: description of how to make a design, using unambiguous instructions, naming geometric shapes (trapezoid, hexagon, rhombus, square and triangle) and using their properties and orientation to create a figure.

Audience: the student editors, next year's grade fours.

Purpose: to stress the importance of precise language.

Task Eleven: I Wish

Description: a mathematics poem

Features: pattern poem; mathematical topics and vocabulary; attitudes and feelings; exaggeration; make-believe.

Form: pattern poem, in the style of:

I wish ...

I also wish ...

I sometimes wish ...

I mostly wish ...

Finally, I wish ...

Content: feelings, mathematical topics such as multiplication, sub-traction, and fractions.

Audience: teacher, others in the class.

Purpose: to use personal language to express some attitudes about mathematics; to blend human features with mathematics.

Task Twelve: Mathematics Autobiography

Features: personal writing, narrative report, emotions, prediction, mathematical benchmarks.

Form: paragraphs.

Content: memories, present highlights, feelings, predictions of mathematical experiences.

Audience: self, teacher.

Purpose: to identify benchmarks in mathematical experiences and to indicate the continuum of past, present and future mathematics; to blend human features with mathematical events.

Task Thirteen: Mathematics Textbook Chapters

Description: writing chapters for a grade four mathematics textbook.

Features: explanations; definitions; headings; examples; procedures; word problems; exercises; answer keys; diagrams with labels; games; puzzles.

Form: textbook chapter.

Content: mathematical topic selected, such as problem solving, Roman numerals, multiplication, measurement, subtrac-tion, and geometry.

Audience: next year's grade fours; self and/or writing group; teacher.

Purpose: to promote the synthesis of some of the writing genres used during the year into a creative product.

CHAPTER 7

APPLYING RESEARCH IN THE CLASSROOM

Investigating Problem-Solving Instruction

Christina Nugent

Dubuque Community School District, Dubuque, Iowa

Researchers do research and teachers teach, often times operating totally independent of each other. In the best of circumstances it is hard for teachers to keep up with current research, let alone do original research in the classroom. In the day and age of No Child Left Behind, education is driven by the use of data in the classroom. However, many teachers are unsure of how to use data to make decisions about teaching and student learning. To facilitate this process, the FINE Foundation[1] designed a project, ARC: Applying Research in the Classroom, to create a bridge between theory and practice and to help elementary school teachers conduct action research in the classroom. I was fortunate enough to be in on the ground floor of this project. The process of looking at research in education, applying it to my classroom, and collecting data to study the results was an awesome opportunity that had long-term effects on my teaching of mathematics.

Teachers Engaged in Research
Inquiry Into Mathematics Classrooms, Grades 3–5, pages 113–128
Copyright © 2006 by Information Age Publishing
All rights of reproduction in any form reserved.

The first thing the FINE Foundation needed was teachers willing to participate in the project. In order to do this they enlisted the help of Iowa's Area Education Associations (AEAs). AEAs in Iowa provide professional development opportunities, educational support materials, and other services to schools across Iowa. FINE staff contacted the math support person in each AEA to recruit teachers to participate in the pilot year of the project. Six teachers were chosen to participate. When the AEA staff contacted me, I was very excited about the opportunity to participate. I love mathematics and take advantage of every opportunity I can to improve my teaching of the subject. I was especially intrigued by the opportunity to study research and apply it to my classroom. Each month, faithfully, I had attempted to keep up with the professional literature in the field. I enjoyed trying the suggestions given for best practice in mathematics in journals like *Teaching Children Mathematics.* However, I had never taken data to evaluate my use of these suggestions. I was anxious to give it a try.

SUMMER WORKSHOP

The project started with a two-day summer workshop. During the workshop, participants met with experts in the field of mathematics educational research. We read and discussed current research from the *Handbook of Research on Improving Student Achievement Second Edition* (Cawelti, 1999). The research had several important implications for improving student achievement in mathematics. First of all, a student's opportunity to learn mathematics is directly related to student achievement. This point is obvious. If a student is not given the opportunity to learn challenging mathematical content, his or her mathematical achievement will be negatively affected. Secondly, mathematics instruction should focus on meaning, rather than the memorization of algorithms. Students can learn both concepts and skills by solving problems. Allowing students to discover mathematical concepts and ideas through problem solving improves mathematical achievement. Invention and practice should be a part of the mathematical classroom. Students should have an opportunity to discover and invent new knowledge as well as an opportunity to practice what they have learned. There needs to be a balance between discovery and practice. Along with problem solving skills, students need to have number sense. Teaching mathematics with a focus on number sense encourages students to become problem solvers in a wide variety of situations and to view mathematics as an area where critical thinking is valued. The mathematics classroom needs to have an openness to student solution methods and student interaction. Using small groups of students to work on activities, problems and assignments can increase student mathematics achievement. However, this small group time should be followed by whole class discussion. Teachers need to ensure that there is closure to the group work, where key ideas and methods are lifted out of the activity. It isn't a time for teachers to lecture, but as a follow-up to individual and small group work. Long-term use of concrete materials as well as the use of calculators and other forms of technology is also positively related to student achievement in mathematics.

Another focus of the workshop was to read and discuss the National Council of Teachers of Mathematics (NCTM, 2000) *Principles and Standards for School Mathematics* (*PSSM*). Although many participants were familiar with the original standards document (NCTM, 1989), there was enough difference between the two that a study of the new document was imperative. Essentially, *PSSM* addressed the same standards, relaying the message that students still need to learn numbers and operations, algebra, geometry, measurement and data analysis and probability through problem solving, reasoning and proof, a variety of representations, communications, and connections. However, to me *PSSM* seemed to emphasize mathematical fluency, the ability to reason mathematically quickly, accurately, and efficiently. It also emphasized the equity principle and providing equal access to all. These were two very important points I wanted to address in my instructional practice.

The second day of the summer workshop kicked off with background on writing an action plan as part of the action research we would be conducting. Action plans include a goal, a plan to meet the goal, a way to collect data on the effectiveness of the plan, and time built in to look at the data and tweak the plan. The researchers provided us with an example plan and a form to help us organize our plans. Then we were given time to reflect on our teaching and students' learning to determine a goal.

I examined achievement data on the students who would be in my fifth-grade class in the upcoming school year. The results of the 4th-grade Iowa Test of Basic Skills (ITBS) showed that they were weak in problem solving. Most students scored below 50% on the Problem Solving and Data Interpretation subtest of ITBS. As I looked at the test I noticed a difference between the test and the problems I traditionally gave in my classroom. First of all, every problem was different. Traditionally, the problems I used centered around a theme or strategy. Students did several of the same problems or problems that used the same strategy consecutively. On the ITBS Problem Solving subtest students needed to draw from a variety of strategies. They also needed to know when to apply each strategy. Students couldn't just regurgitate knowledge that they had memorized or I had spoon fed them. Secondly, problems on the ITBS required more than one step to solve, whereas the problems I used in class were simplistic. I also recalled that when former students took the ITBS in my classroom, many finished before the time was up and when answers to problems weren't obvious many students just guessed rather than continuing to work hard and try a variety of strategies. I surmised that my current students might do the same.

In determining a goal for my action plan, I was also influenced by the huge emphasis on problem solving in the research we studied and in the NCTM Standards. The research said that students could both learn new concepts and practice skills through problem solving. Data from the Third International Mathematics and Science Video Study (Hiebert, 2003) indicated that students in Asia spent more time solving problems than drilling skills. So, I decided that my focus needed to be problem solving.

INSTRUCTIONAL PLAN

As I designed my plan, I wanted to make sure that the plan was attainable. It was easy to sit in a workshop in the middle of the summer and concoct lofty ideals that when put in to practice in the fall would be impossible to do. I decided on a plan that was based on a three step process but required just a few small changes in my weekly routine. The three steps had students working on problems individually first, then in small groups, and finally explaining their solution to the whole group. I chose these steps based on the research we read at the workshop that said using small groups of students to work on activities, problems and assignments followed by a whole class discussion increases student mathematics achievement (Calwelti, 1999). I was hesitant to give up an entire class once a week for problem solving. How would I cover the curriculum I needed to if once a week I gave up a class period for problem solving? So I decided that every day, students would spend 15 minutes solving a unique problem. The problems I chose for this activity were problems where the solution was not immediately obvious and which required the use of strategies in order to solve them successfully. They also included problems with one solution as well as problems with more than one solution.

My plan was as follows: On Monday, students would be given a problem like those described above to solve. They would work on the problem individually. On Tuesday, Wednesday, and Thursday they would work together in small groups to solve the problem. I would facilitate this process. During this time, I would be careful to focus on the process rather than the answer and to ask guiding questions instead of giving suggestions. For example: How did you get this answer? What do you think would happen ...? What if ...? Did you think about...? Once again the focus would be on explaining thinking and solution methods rather than giving the answer. Finally, on Friday they would explain their solutions to each other. At this time, I would lead the students in a discussion highlighting efficient solution methods as well as unique solutions. To solve these problems, students would need to apply a variety of skills. They could draw pictures, make charts, or guess and check just to name a few. However, the skills would not be directly taught, but discovered by the students instead.

The next question that came to mind was how to measure the success of my plan. Since my goal was improved problem solving, I needed to measure growth in problem solving. The research question I wanted to answer was: Would my problem-solving plan raise students' scores on the Problem Solving subtest of the ITBS? However, ITBS is a summative form of assessment given only in the fall of the year. I couldn't go the whole year without some type of formative data to guide my instruction. I hypothesized that students needed to persist when solving problems and to have a more positive attitude toward mathematics and confidence in their mathematics abilities in order to succeed in problem solving. Therefore, I decided to measure students' persistence and attitude in solving problems several times throughout the year. How long did students persist when solving problems before giving up? In order to measure this easily and efficiently, I decided to use an anecdotal checklist. As students worked on problems individually, I devised a code to record how long they persisted before giving up. Students who worked less than a minute received a minus. If they worked for five minutes, they received an okay, and if they worked for 10 minutes they received a plus. Students received a star if they worked the whole time. During the summer workshop I constructed a student attitude survey (Figure 1) to be given at the beginning of the school year and again at the end. My hypothesis was that if students had a positive attitude towards mathematics they would be more successful and vice versa, if students were successful in mathematics, then they would have a better attitude.

Table 7.1.   Student attitude survey.

	Strongly Agree	Agree	Disagree	Strongly Disagree
Mathematics is as important as any school subject.	1	2	3	4
I like math because I can f igure things out.	1	2	3	4
There is more to math than just getting the right answer.	1	2	3	4
I enjoy doing word problems.	1	2	3	4

Table 7.1.   Student attitude survey.

I can estimate answers very well.	1	2	3	4
Math is one of my favorite subjects.	1	2	3	4
I like the challenge of a problem.	1	2	3	4
I can explain to others my thinking in solving a math problem.	1	2	3	4
I like doing math problem solving.	1	2	3	4

IMPLEMENTING THE PLAN

The school in which I taught that year was an excellent place to apply research. I had a very diverse group of fifth-grade students with approximately 80% of the students receiving free/reduced lunch. Though there was a fairly even distribution of boys and girls, approximately 25% of the students were minority and 33% were identified as students with special needs. One thing that really made data collection difficult was the high mobility rate of my student population. It was hard to keep track of pre and post data when only 15 of the 25 students who started in my classroom at the beginning of the year were in my classroom at the end of the year.

August arrived and the school year started. I was anxious to put my plan in to place. I selected problems that I thought the students would find challenging. My main resource for problems was the book *The Problem Solver 5* (Creative Publications, 1987). An example of a problem I used was,

> With loud beeps, the spaceships from the planets Morunda and Boranda touched down. The Morunda spaceships each landed on 9 robot "feet," and the Boranda spaceships each landed on 12 robot "feet." When the spaceships left, someone counted 208 "feet" marks in the dust. How many spaceships had been there from each planet?

With my clipboard and anecdotal checklist handy, I presented the problem and instructed the students to get started. Before a minute was up, everyone in the class had given up. According to my plan, I had to stop for the day and go on with the rest of my regular math class. Tuesday arrived and the students worked in mixed-ability groups of three to four. The groups were fairly productive. Students bounced ideas off of each other, argued over how to solve the problem, and tried different strategies. I was kept busy going from group to group, asking clarifying questions and guiding groups in the right direction. Things were moving along brilliantly, when I looked at the clock and noticed that the fifteen minutes allotted for problem solving had expired. I hated to stop the students because some groups were close to successfully solving the problem. On Wednesday, we continued with our problem. It was difficult for the students to start where they had left off on the problem. It took them a while to build up the momentum. Once again, just as they were sinking their teeth in to the problem, it was time to stop.

This same scenario happened again in the next several weeks. It never failed, students would just get started solving a problem and it would be time to stop. Something had to be done; I needed to make some changes to the plan. I decided to bite the bullet and devote one whole day to problem solving. The research said that students could learn and practice concepts through problems. Therefore, I tried to choose problems that centered around tropics we were discussing in class. If we were on the fractions chapter, I tried to find problems that involved fractions. For example:

Each year down at the bottom of the sea, the codfish hold their annual ball. This year 1/3 of the invited guests are codfish, since they are giving the party; 2/6 of the guests are in the tuna family; 1/6 are flounders, who get in everyone's way; 1/12 are salmon, who always want to dance upstream; and the last 32 are electric eels, who provide the lighting. How many fish are coming to the party, and how many are in each group?

According to the revised plan, students worked individually on the problem, then in groups, and then shared with the whole class all in the same day.

As we continued to work on problem solving, I discovered that I needed more data. There were lots of "ah ha" moments that happened during our problem solving sessions. It was exciting when Fred, an identified special needs student, was the one in the group that came up with the key to solving the problem. Still another time, Keesha was so proud when she explained her solution strategy to the class for the first time. I was sure I would remember those moments. After all, that is why we teach, to see the excitement and share in the moments of triumph as the students learn new knowledge and skills. However, I didn't want to trust myself. Along with my anecdotal checklist, I decided to keep notes as well. They were not necessarily systematic, they were just comments, reflections, and impressions from the problem solving sessions. Examples of my notes are illustrated in Table 7.2.

Table 7.2.   Examples of anecdotal notes.

October 23	I brought in a quilt since we were studying freedom quilts in reading and social studies. The problem of the day was to determine how many stitches were in the quilt. There were kids all over the floor counting stitches. "There's 36 in this triangle." "This one is the same size and there are 38 stitches." "Maybe we should average them!" Everyone worked together both at their seats and at the quilt. The whole lesson went well, however, I need to work more on the whole class discussion piece. I tend to be the only one listening as the other students present.
November 20	What will the 10th shape look like?

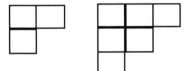

There was a crush around the overhead to see the clues. Other students had heads bent over their desks glancing up at the overhead. One person wrote clues in their notebook. At least one person in each group drew a picture of the building. Everyone worked together. There was lots of discussion and arguing about what the clues meant in their small groups. It is odd that some kids still insist upon adding / subtracting/ multiplying / dividing to find the answer instead of seeking to understand what the problem is asking them.

March 13   My problem-solving lesson involved a mixed group including my students and others in fourth and fifth grade. My class definitely worked harder on problems and persevered longer. They might not have all gotten the correct answer, but at least they had a plan to go about it.

These anecdotal notes also helped me to decide whom to call on to explain their thinking to the class at the end of each problem-solving day. After all, the summarizing of solution methods was the most important part. As the students worked I recorded who used what solution method. Then when students got ready to explain their answers, I had a plan in mind as to who was going to explain first, second, etc. I did not have everyone explain every class period. I usually started with someone explaining the most common solution method. Then I had students explain unique methods. At the end, I summarized the most efficient way of solving the problem. The anecdotal notes helped me to keep this information organized.

In addition to the anecdotal notes, I felt I needed more hard data than I was gathering. I had data that students were persisting and data on improved student attitude, but I needed more formative assessment data to guide my teaching. ITBS data would not be available until the following fall, so it did not give me what I needed. What I needed was data on weekly individual student performance in problem solving. The FINE Foundation came to the rescue. As part of their support for teachers participating in the ARC project, they planned a full group meeting in November. ARC participants met in Des Moines to discuss the progress of their action research plans and to refocus and refine their plans. Matter of fact, the November whole group meeting was such a success that the Fine Foundation scheduled a second full-group meeting in February. The networking and problem solving that went on was really important.

At the meeting in November, it turned out that many teachers had similar questions in regards to data collection. A couple of teachers had elaborate plans to have students keep problem-solving journals, but the plans needed refinement. They did not really work in practice as teachers had anticipated. I liked the idea of a problem-solving journal. If students could write about the problems they solved, I would have a record of their progress. Problem-solving journals would also help students develop communication skills, an important NCTM Standard. The discussions we had during this meeting about how to use problem-solving journals were very helpful. I was able to learn from the experiences of the other teachers. They provided me with lots of options for implementing problem-solving journals. One teacher had photocopied pages that students used. The problems were typed at the top of the page and there was plenty of space below for students to solve the problem and explain how they solved it. The students worked on one problem a week. Another teacher just had the problems typed and students glued them in to spiral notebooks. Still another teacher had her students copy problems in to their spiral notebooks. Some teachers collected the problem-solving journals after every class; others let the students keep them in their desks. I did not think spiral notebooks would work for me. Many of my students came to school without supplies. In addition, the school year had already started. If I wanted to use spiral notebooks, I would have to supply them. I also did not feel like a photocopied packet was an option. My students were really making progress with the problem-solving process and I did not want to slow the process down while I put together a packet of problems. Plus, I wanted the flexibility to use problems that applied to what I was teaching. I did not think a photocopied packet of problems could do this. Another issue was the mobility of my student population. Students were constantly coming and going. I would have to constantly furnish students with packets. With the amount of students in my classroom with special needs, copying problems from another source such as the overhead or blackboard was also not an option. I decided that I would have students do problems on notebook paper and collect them to put in a portfolio. This seemed to be my best option.

The next issue was how to collect data on the problem-solving journals. It was not enough to just collect the problems without evaluating them in some way. This was another issue we discussed at length at our November meeting. I decided to use the following key. Students who got the problem correct would receive a plus. If students had a good start but made a mistake they would receive a circle. Students who were not on the right track received a minus. In future years as I continued to implement this action plan, I refined the evaluation process to include a more holistic scoring process based on a four-point rubric. Students were given a four when I looked at their solution and thought, "Yes!" They had the right answer and a good explanation for how they solved the problem. Students were given a three, when I looked at their solution and thought, "Yes, but..." They either had the right answer but not a very good explanation or a great explanation but made a careless mistake. Students were given a two, when I looked at their solution and thought, "No, but..." They didn't have the correct answer or made too many careless mistakes, but they did have a start. Students received a one, when I looked at their solution and thought, "No!" These students had no clue as to how to solve the problem. In this scoring method more emphasis was placed on the explanation and how to communicate a solution strategy.

Analyzing the Data

Analyzing problem-solving data was a constant process. First of all, I had the persistence scores to analyze. My strategy for improving persistence was indirect. I was counting on the fact that as students worked in small groups and we debriefed as a large group they would learn more strategies and skills for attacking problems. My hope was that a variety of strategies and skills would increase their persistence scores. Therefore, I didn't look at the persistence scores more than once a month. When I did look at them, I looked for patterns and trends. For example: Were the scores of the class as a whole increasing? Whose scores were improving, whose were not? As I determined new problem-solving groupings I took this data into consideration. I certainly did not want a group of students who had no persistence skills working together. Another way I used the persistence scores involved the students. Midway through the year I shared the scores with the students and had them reflect on them. We discussed a variety of questions: Did they feel like they were trying their hardest in problem solving? What does persistence look like? What did students who had high persistence scores do to help them be more persistent? As the year progressed and we talked about persistence scores, I had to change my persistence anecdotal checklist. Once students knew I was taking scores on persistence they wanted to get a good "grade." By March all students worked for at least ten minutes. However, not all of it was productive work. Some just tried to look busy! In order to document this, I had to change my anecdotal checklist key. Students received a star if they came up with a correct answer during individual work time. An okay was given to students who persisted the whole time with a strategy that would get them to a correct solution. Students received a circle if I could not tell what they were doing. The record was left blank if students did not persist.

The information on the anecdotal notes was analyzed formally three times during the year when it was time to do conferences and progress reports. I looked at the notes and grouped them by students. What patterns and trends did I see? Did the anecdotal notes document changes in student behavior? I was very glad that I had the notes. It was amazing that the incidences that were so significant when they happened were so easily forgotten. The notes brought them all back. The anecdotal notes gave me specific incidences to relate to families. They also documented incidences where students had breakthroughs in knowledge. Events like the first time Frank used something other than the *draw a picture* strategy or when Manuel found another way to solve the problem. It was also easy to pick up trends and patterns in student behavior. Martin was one of my students with special needs. However, when examining my anecdotal notes he emerged as a very creative problem solver. His creative solutions were mentioned several times.

Anecdotal notes were analyzed informally on a more frequent basis. Information from the notes was used to determine student problem-solving groups, which I varied periodically throughout the year. Sometimes the groups were totally heterogeneous, with one strong problem solver, two average problem solvers, and one struggling problem solver. Other times the groups were more homogeneous. I might put a couple of strong problem solvers together to give them a chance to work together and stretch themselves. Sometimes struggling problem solvers worked together to see what they would do. Using the anecdotal notes gave me the documentation I needed to determine these kinds of groupings. For example, without the anecdotal notes I never would have identified Martin as a strong problem solver nor would I have had him work with other strong problem solvers in a group.

The problem-solving journal data were analyzed each week because they had a more direct impact on my daily teaching. Scores were recorded in my grade book. Patterns and trends were identified. For example: How many people got the correct answer? How many had a correct method, but made a small mistake? How many were totally off base? What type of strategy was used most? How many people solved the problem by drawing a picture? How many used a chart? How many used a number sentence? When I looked at the answers to these questions I determined whether the problems were challenging enough. I also used the data to help me decide on the problem to give the following week. The key to problem selection was to find a problem that was not too hard and not too easy. If most students were getting the problem correct, I needed to choose a more challenging problem for the next week. Problems also had to have multiple entry points to meet the needs of a variety of learners. Looking at the journals helped me to decide if the students were using a variety of solution methods. I also used the problem-solving data in conjunction with my anecdotal notes to place students in groups. As mentioned above, in order to support all learners, sometimes the groups needed to be heterogeneous and sometimes they needed to be homogeneous. I tried to change groups so students got a chance to work with a variety of students.

The student attitude surveys (Table 7.1) were analyzed at the end of the year. My plan was to analyze the data more often, however as I got into my research plan, analyzing the journals and the anecdotal notes became much more important. Whether or not a student liked mathematics and thought they were good at it was not as important as whether they used a variety of strategies, persisted, or were able to communicate their thinking. My hope had been that students would have a more positive attitude at the end of the school year than at the beginning. My hypothesis was that if students felt more successful in math then they would have a better attitude. However, my data in this area was inconclusive. First of all, only 12 students who completed the survey at the beginning of the year completed it at the end. The average score on the nine-item assessment in the fall was 14.81. Nine would be a perfect score where the students strongly agreed with all of the questions. Thirty-six would be the opposite score with the students strongly disagreeing with all of the questions. At the end of the year the average score was 15.45. When comparing averages it seemed that students had a more positive attitude about mathematics in the beginning of the year than at the end. However, when examining individual student data, ten out of twelve students improved their scores. There were two students whose scores were significantly higher (i.e., less positive) than they were in the fall. Because I wanted the surveys to be anonymous so students would feel comfortable sharing their feelings I was not able to identify the two students who had the elevated scores. Maybe that would have given me an indication as to why their scores were so high. I tried to analyze the data by looking at each individual question. However, that did not provide any interesting information either. Essentially, there were no patterns or trends and collecting data on student attitudes was not very helpful in the long run.

Student journals were another way I was able to examine growth over time. In the beginning of the year, many students just wrote a number or answer with no explanation on their journal page. Sometimes pages were left completely blank because students had no strategy for solving the problem. However, by the end of the year all students attempted the problem; no pages were left blank. Drawing a picture was the most prevalent strategy students used. It seemed that even if students were unable to solve the problem correctly, they could at least draw a picture. It was also evident in the journals that students were learning a variety of strategies. Different problems called for different strategies. Though some students tended to favor drawing a picture, others were adept at making a table, working backwards, solving a simpler problem, and other more sophisticated strategies. Towards the end of the year, students began to give more of an explanation of how they solved the problem as well. After looking at the journals I realized I needed to focus more on the communication aspect of problem solving.

The ITBS data the next year was very promising. Most of the students in my class gained at least one year on the problem-solving subtest of the Iowa Test of Basic Skills. Many grew more than that.

Reflections

My participation in the ARC project had many benefits beyond the impact it had on the group of students in my class that year. First of all, I used the discussion on research and best practice to design a one-page handout summarizing what current research said about best practice in mathematics education. I have used this handout countless times in the years since my participation in this project. I have given it to new teachers I have mentored in my school district's New Professional Mentoring Program. Pre-service teachers in the class that I teach at the local college, *Curriculum and*

Instruction in Mathematics, get the handout every year. I have held staff meetings across the district to discuss the implications of the summary as well.

Secondly, the ARC project has affected my teaching today. No more do I try random suggestions from journals without collecting data so that decisions about best practice can be made based on the collection and analysis of data. My teaching tends to center around challenging problems with students working in small groups and a large group discussion as a follow up. My goal is for students to learn concepts through problem solving like the research states.

Conducting action research in the classroom is now a way of life in our district. As a team we gather data, plan instruction, and collect data on the instruction. Because I was involved in a project like this, I was a step ahead of the game. I had an idea of the type of data to collect and how to use the data in my instruction. Learning about the process in the safe supportive environment I experienced through the FINE Foundation's ARC project made the process much easier.

I truly enjoyed my participation in this project. The collaboration with other teachers from across the state was meaningful. It was very obvious that mathematics educational researchers truly cared about what I did in my classroom. I would encourage other teachers to use action research in their classrooms. My advice to teachers who want to conduct action research is to form a group and do it together. Conducting action research as a group provides a support network. The group helps to keep you motivated. It also helps to have others to share ideas with as you formulate and carry out your plans. A group also provides a fresh set of eyes as you look at the data. Read some research, formulate a plan to use it in your classroom, collect data, and use the data to inform your instruction! Good luck!

NOTE

1.   The FINE Foundation stands for First In the Nation in Education. It is a private, nonprofit educational research organization in Iowa, governed by a board of directors including faculty members from Iowa colleges and universities, legislators, and business leaders. The focus of the group is on improving teaching and learning in elementary and secondary schools in Iowa with an emphasis on the use of educational research. More information on the FINE Foundation can be found on the web at www.finefoundation.org.

REFERENCES

Moretti, Gloria. (1987). *The problem solver 5*. Mountain View, CA: Creative Publications.

Barton, M. L., & Heideman, C. (2002). Teaching reading in mathematics (2nd ed.). Alexandria, VA: Association for Supervision and Curriculum Development.

Cawelti, G. (Ed.). (1999). Handbook of research on improving student achievement (2nd ed.). Arlington, VA: Educational Research Service.

Hiebert, J., Gallimore, R., Garnier, H., Bogard Givvin, K., Hollingsworth, H., Jacobs, J. et al. (2003). Teaching mathematics in seven countries: Results from the TIMSS 1999 video study. Washington, DC: National Center for Educational Statistics.

National Council of Teachers of Mathematics. (1989). *Curriculum and evaluation standards for school mathematics*. Reston, VA: Author.

National Council of Teachers of Mathematics. (2000). *Principles and standards for school mathematics*. Reston, VA: Author.

Sutton, J., & Krueger, A. (2002). *EdThoughts: What we know about mathematics teaching and learning*. Aurora, CO: Mid-continent Research for Education and Learning.

Zaccaro, E. (2000). *Challenge math*. Bellevue, IA: Hickory Grove Press.

CHAPTER 8

TEACHER AS RESEARCHER

Researcher As Learner

Jennifer Segebart

Johnston Community School District, Johnston, Iowa

A teacher needs a multitude of qualities to meet the day's demands. Because students are ever changing and the teaching context is ever changing, teachers must change. Change evolves from curiosity and close observation of students, dialogue with colleagues, interaction with current ideas, and constant reflection to integrate these sources of information. As stated in the National Council of Teachers of Mathematics (NCTM, 2000) *Principles and Standards for School Mathematics*:

> Effective teaching requires continuing efforts to learn and improve. These efforts include learning about mathematics and pedagogy, benefiting from interactions with students and colleagues, and engaging in ongoing professional development and self-reflection. (p. 19)

Becoming a better teacher may be as complex as teaching itself, but ultimately it is a personal process of continual transformation.

Teachers Engaged in Research
Inquiry Into Mathematics Classrooms, Grades 3–5, pages 129–144
Copyright © 2006 by Information Age Publishing
All rights of reproduction in any form reserved.

I have taught for 17 years in three different Midwestern states in 2nd, 4th, and 5th grades. After teaching in an inner city, 2-way bilingual school, I moved to a rural area and studied for my Master's Degree in Curriculum and Instruction. My Master's Project involved researching the theory of what was then called "whole language" and the process teachers used when changing this theory into practice. I also studied different types of research and completed a classroom Action Research Project. After completing my Master's degree, I moved to my current school district, which is in a suburban community very near where I first student-taught. We have relatively ample resources, involved parents, and a community interested in education. Currently I am a "looping" teacher, keeping the same class of students in 4th and 5th grades.

One striking inner transformation has been my increased interest in mathematics. Piloting a standards-based series closely following NCTM's recommendations of utilizing inquiry and deductive reasoning awakened this interest. I also took a class, Elementary Math Leadership Academy II, lead by Dr. Larry Leutzinger from the University of Northern Iowa that cultivated my new thinking. From a teacher immersed in reading and language instruction, I have emerged as a teacher intrigued by the power of mathematical thinking and the best way to teach students to think mathematically. Essentially, I have considered ideas advanced in reading and language study and transferred these principals to mathematics. Connecting materials with students, emphasizing interconnectedness within the discipline, and looking at a wide view of the content is often part of reading, but it is not always apparent in mathematics.

THE ARRC PROJECT

Along this personal journey, I was fortunate to participate in a project, Applying Research Results in Classrooms (ARRC), through Iowa's First in the Nation in Education (FINE), Foundation.[1] The ARRC project targets the late elementary grades and supports teachers in conducting action research in mathematics. The project staff guides teachers in reviewing research, modifying their teaching based on research findings, and evaluating the results of instruction. In the spring of 2004, I was invited to participate in the project, along with seven other teachers from across Iowa. As a group, we had diverse background experiences and faced varied challenges in our school settings. We represented both rural and suburban, and high and low socio-economic districts from around the state. Yet we all shared a passion for teaching, a concern for our students, and a special interest in mathematics.

We began our action research study under the guidance of Dean Fre-richs from the FINE foundation and educational consultant Douglass Grouws from the University of Missouri. During our first meetings in late spring, we reviewed current research. We were given the *Handbook of Research on Mathematics Teaching and Learning* (Grouws, 1992) as a basis for reading and discussion. Among the chapters we read, "Mathematics Teaching Practices and Their Effects" (Koehler & Grouws, 1992) was of particular interest. The authors emphasized students' *opportunity to learn* and its impact on student achievement. I found it striking that opportunity not only encompassed the quantity of time devoted to mathematics study, but what is taught and how it is taught. We were encouraged to continue our research by exploring a variety of resources which I pursued with interest (e.g., Bohan & Vogel, 1995; Chapin, Koziol, MacPherson, & Rezba, 2002; Edwards & Hensien, 2000; Good, Multyan, & McCaslin, 2002; Mokos & Russell, 1995; Shaughnessy, 2003; Smith, 2004; Strong, Perini, & Silver, 2004; Weis & Pasley, 2004).

As a group, we discussed the importance of making instruction mean-ingful and student attitudes toward mathematics. An integral part of the process was sharing personal connections with the research presented. We talked at length about our specific teaching environments. We discussed the materials we used, challenges we faced, and the direction we would like to take in our action research project. We offered suggestions, support, and a fresh perspective to one another. We were encouraged to consider the design of our project over the summer.

In the fall we met to continue our discussion and to develop action plans for our research. Our action plans focused on two common themes showing the potential for decisive student achievement gains in mathemat-ics—opportunity to learn and positive attitudes toward mathematics. We followed a format which included documentation of background research used to formulate our plans, a set of implementation steps, plans for pre- and post- assessment, and suggestions for final reflection and data analysis which would be completed the following summer.

Periodically during the school year, we met to discuss our progress and setbacks, and throughout the year Dean Frerichs conducted site visits to our schools and was available for questions and consultation. In February, as a group, we presented our action plans at the Iowa Council of Teachers of Mathematics convention and shared with other teachers our experi-ences working on the ARRC project. This was a wonderful chance to meet other educators in the state and gain insight from them. It translated into renewed enthusiasm for our work back in the classroom.

In May, we gave final project presentations to our group and shared our experiences as action researchers to new teacher participants just begin-ning. We completed evaluations and said good-bye to our fellow action researchers, though we were not yet finished analyzing data and writing our individual project reports. This, however, was far into the future as I began a new school year as a teacher researcher.

DEVELOPING AND IMPLEMENTING MY ACTION PLAN

At the beginning of the school year, my focus turned from a review of research to practical applications of my newfound knowledge. My district had adopted a new edition of our traditional mathematics textbook series that emphasized algorithms and computation. Although my administrator had given me the freedom to de-emphasize our textbook, I was expected to teach to district standards and benchmarks. I also needed to address aspects of our school improvement plan required by the *No Child Left Behind Act*.

In order to increase my students' opportunity to learn, I strongly felt they needed to engage in mathematics beyond what their textbooks offered. I wanted to broaden their conceptual understandings and develop depth in their mathematical thinking; not only increase computational fluency and strengthen simple skills. According to the *Principles and Standards in Teaching School Mathematics* (NCTM, 2000):

> In recent decades, psychological and educational research on the learning of complex subjects such as mathematics has solidly established the important role of conceptual understanding in the knowledge and activity of persons who are proficient. Being proficient in a complex domain such as mathematics entails the ability to use knowledge flexibly, applying what is learned in one setting appropriately in another. One of the most robust findings of research is that conceptual understanding is an important component of proficiency, along with factual knowledge and procedural facility (Bransford, Brown, & Cocking 1999). (p. 20).

A strong conceptual basis, like the base of a pyramid, facilitates future building. I determined that the content we explored must be challenging and engaging in order to increase my students' opportunity to learn. Furthermore, like current thought in teaching reading, I wanted students to make connections between mathematics and themselves. With these ideas in mind, I developed an action plan that detailed significant changes in my instructional practice aimed at improving the teaching and learning of mathematics in my classroom. They are described in Table 8.1.

Table 8.1.   Changes in instructional practice outlined in my Action Plan

Change	*Purpose*
• In addition to a minimum of 300 minutes of scheduled math time per week, encourage extra school time engaged in mathematics. This could occur during recess and free time with motivating math games.	• To improve attitudes and add time on math tasks without negatively effecting time spent on other subject areas.
• Assign a "family" math project once every two weeks to be completed as math homework.	• To help students interact positively with parents, influencing attitude as well as deepening understanding. It would also utilize the strength of parent and community support.
• Condense/eliminate repetitive content in the district textbook. Instead, include mental math exercises and short, daily reviews in scheduled class routines. Use supplemental materials to explore concepts in depth.	• To expand inquiry-based opportunities, to improve attitudes and to correspond with our school improvement plan.
• Differentiate instruction, allowing students to work at their optimal level and minimizing instructional time spent on review. This would include small group work and open-ended assignments structured to accommodate differing ability levels.	• To increase opportunity to learn by matching activities to learners and to correspond with our school improvement plan.
• Integrate mathematics instruction in other content areas by using science problems of the week; charts, graphs, and data in socials studies; and math-related literature.	• To help students transfer math skills to other content areas, increase the mathematical concept base of the learner, and help them understand the relevance of math.

The needs of my students were paramount and dictated my teaching. As a looping teacher in the second year of my loop, I knew my students well. They had diverse needs, including two students with Individual Education Plans that required instructional modifications, and several students with identified areas of strength in mathematics. I was confident my students had a strong background in number sense and related concepts from 4th grade. However, in examining my students' Iowa Test of Basic Skill scores and Mid-west Iowa Achievement scores, I identified two weaker areas: measurement and data analysis, statistics and probability. Thus, I incorporated specific units on these two topics into my action plan. In this chapter, I focus on the data and probability unit and the effects it had on student learning. An outline of the unit I developed from various resources is presented in Table 8.2.

Table 8.2.   Outline of data and probability unit

Topic/Day	Lesson Activities	Notes/Resources
Ongoing (During the approximately 4 weeks of instructional time.)	Family Math Assignments Games related to data analysis, statistics, and probability Small group extensions with parent volunteer (while teacher works remedially with students showing need for clarification).	Family Math web site: www.figurethis.org • *25 Super Fun Math Spinner Games* (Aronson, 1997) • *From Your Friends at Mailbox: Games Galore* (The Education Center, 2002) Activities from web site: (www.balancedassessment.concord.org)
Pre-assessment (1 day)	Students individually take pretest for unit	The pretest will provide a baseline for future assessment.
Mean (3 days)	Exploring the mean with unifix cubes: • Students manipulate data (cubes) to find the mean and create data sets to represent a given mean.	From *Navigating Through Probability,* "Exploring the Mean" (Chapin, Koziol, MacPherson, & Rezba, 2002)

Table 8.2.   Outline of data and probability unit

Topic/Day	Lesson Activities	Notes/Resources
Probability (3–4 days)	Vocabulary development and landmark skills:	*Everyday Mathematics. Grade 5* (Bell et. al., 2002)
	• Certain, extremely likely… impossible with chart.	*The Mailbox Series: Probability, statistics, and graphing.* (Blackwood, 1999
	• Partners collect and record data, finding mean, medium and mode. They then predict.	
Data and Graphing (3 days)	Students read and discuss information from the Census Bureau.	*The Census and America's People* (Wilson, 2004)
Data and Graphing (3 days)	After a class discussion, students graph and predict using school data on class sizes by grade level and gender.	Data compilation from school office
Sampling (2 days)	Students randomly sample "sneabs" (beans spelled backwards) from paper bag then predict the sneab population.	Adapted from "Daily Activities for Data Analysis" (Hitch & Armstrong, 1994)
Fairness (3–4 days)	Students play game with different rules, determining if game is fair.	From *Navigating Through Probability*, "Is It Fair?" (Chapin, Koziol, MacPherson, & Rezba, 2002)
Post-assessment (1 day)	Students take parallel form of textbook unit posttest.	Scores will be entered and analyzed by ARRC consultants.

I took two detours when implementing the data and probability unit. First, I realized that graphing was integral to many of the concepts, and since it was also a district expectation, I took some time to specifically address the district graphing benchmarks and administer their corresponding assessments. As we progressed into the probability activities on fairness, we hit a barrier I had not anticipated. Students lacked background experiences with connections among fractions, decimals, and percents. Therefore, I took a break from the unit activities to focus on the rational number concepts necessary for more advanced work with probability. These detours, combined with student enthusiasm and desire to delve deeply into the topic, made the unit extend 2 weeks longer than I had initially planned, for a total of 6 weeks.

TEACHER AS RESEARCHER

I asked parents, administrators, and, of course, my students, for support in implementing my action research project. I wrote a parent note explaining my project and its goals of increasing student achievement and improving student attitudes. I invited parents to look more closely at my action plan if they were interested and requested they fill out a parent attitude survey. I explained I would be supplementing the newly adopted textbook to enrich student understanding. I introduced "family" math homework and wrote to parents about using the assignments to promote math conversations at home. To my administrator I provided copies of my action research plan and all parent correspondence. I also kept my administrator informed during my goal setting conferences, part of the district evaluation process. My students filled out an attitude survey, and, when told about my project, expressed a willingness to help. It made them feel special, and they were always ready to try something different than the regular routine.

Data Sources

To assess the effectiveness of the data and probability unit on students' learning, I collected data from several sources. I used a pretest from our mathematics textbook, the "Yearly Annual Progress" test, and administered a parallel form of the test at the end of the year. These 40-item tests (32 multiple-choice and 8 short-answer items) reflected district benchmarks and gave a general indication of a student's achievement level. To focus more specifically on data and probability, I used the pre- and post- tests from the related chapter in the textbook. These tests were comprised of 20 short-answer items, and I felt they were representative of my end goals, were objectively written, and provided two parallel exams for pre- and post-comparison. I collected samples of student work, noted class discussion and cooperative group work, and kept comments from parents related to "family" math and other math assignments. This collection would become important later to reflect upon and refine my teaching.

Findings

I found two aspects of my action plan effective and motivating from the beginning. Students clamored for games and materials that reinforced mathematics concepts in the unit. Another immediate success was the "family math" problems. These were challenging problems integrating unit concepts with real-world problems. I explained that the homework assignments were to promote math discussion, much the way reading books promotes literature discussion. The family math problems included hints for parents to help their child, explanations of why the concepts were important in real life, and possible solutions. In classroom follow-up, students raised their hands wildly to share different methods to solve the problems.

One segment of the unit especially effective in deepening students' concept of average was from *Navigating Through Probability*, "Exploring the Mean" (Chapin, Koziol, MacPherson, & Rezba, 2002). In this inquiry-based lesson, students rearranged cubes to represent different scenarios involving the landmarks of mean, median, and mode. While the traditional textbook had 4 pages on the topic and included pictures of cubes, this lesson took students deeper by giving them several different scenarios to investigate in small groups using the cubes. Students found that different data sets can be balanced, or distributed, around the same mean. After experience with finding this landmark, students created different sets of data to represent a given mean. This helped students understand that different data sets can produce the same mean. While students worked, I noted that when prompted many were able to create data sets where the mean was not found in the data, showing greater conceptual understanding than the traditional textbook could develop.

The students' most memorable lesson involved "snaebs," actually beans spelled backwards. The lesson, from "Daily Activities for Data Analysis" (Hitch & Armstong, 1994), was creative and addressed the idea of sampling, a concept absent from the district text. In the lesson, students were invited to randomly sample different colored "snaebs" from a paper sack and as a class use the samples to make predictions about the "snaeb" population in the sack. Students came surprisingly close in their predictions, and it is seldom I've seen students so excited about dried beans. This experience with sampling helped students develop the idea of using a representative of the group to make predictions.

My last segment of instruction from *Navigating Through Probability*, "Is It Fair" (Chapin, Koziol, MacPherson, & Rezba, 2002) effectively synthesized student learning. The textbook had a two-page explanation about fairness, but this activity was far more expansive. Students experimented playing a math game several times, each time changing the rules and examining outcomes. While playing they used mathematical vocabulary, collected and analyzed data, and, as a bonus, practiced computation skills. As they played, students were able to use fractions and decimals to explain their probability of winning. After several trials, they were able to identify game rules that gave students an equally likely chance of winning. After informal observation of my students' mathematical conversations and their work from the games, I felt students were ready for their posttest.

With the help of a consultant from the FINE foundation, I statistically analyzed the pre- and posttest scores for the data and probability unit. I was anxious to see if this test data would verify my informal assessment data. From my observations of student discussions and samples of class work, I believed that students had gained a deeper understanding of data and probability. The analysis did indicate that students had made significant gains, $t(20)=10.75$, $p < .0001$, between the pretest ($M = 6.10$, $SD = 2.02$) and the posttest ($M = 16.14$, $SD = 3.65$), with a mean growth of 10.05 ($SD = 4.28$). Both the statistics and students' responses demonstrated evidence of deeper conceptual understanding of the landmarks of mean, median, and mode, as well as line plots, data interpretation, and probability.

By way of example, the work of Rosie is presented below. When initially asked to find measures of center on the pretest (Figure 8.1), Rosie was confused with the vocabulary and how to approach the line graph. Although

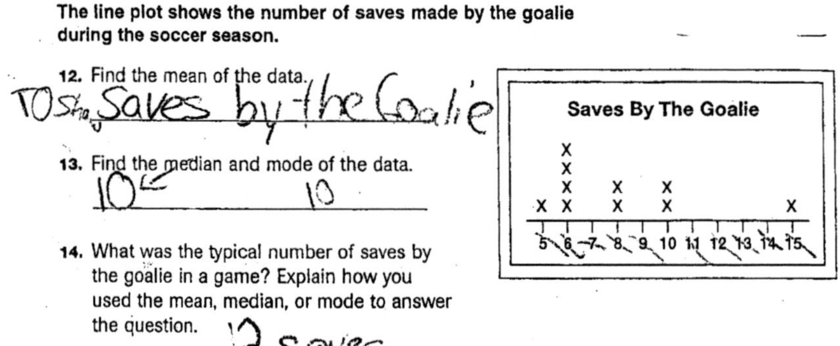

The line plot shows the number of saves made by the goalie during the soccer season.

12. Find the mean of the data.

13. Find the median and mode of the data.

14. What was the typical number of saves by the goalie in a game? Explain how you used the mean, median, or mode to answer the question.

Figure 8.1.   Sample pretest item and student response.

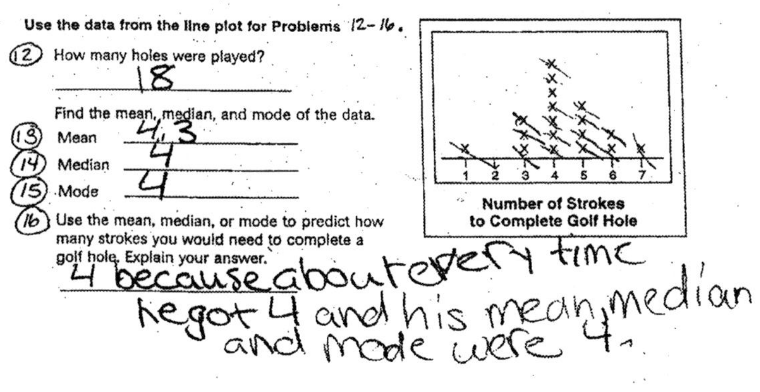

Use the data from the line plot for Problems 12-16.

12 How many holes were played?
    18

Find the mean, median, and mode of the data.
13 Mean   4.3
14 Median   4
15 Mode   4

16 Use the mean, median, or mode to predict how many strokes you would need to complete a golf hole. Explain your answer.
    4 because about every time he got 4 and his mean, median and mode were 4.

Figure 8.2.   Sample posttest item and student response.

she does systematically cross off numbers to find the median, she does this with the scale rather than the distribution. She does not refer to landmarks representative of the data to justify a generalization.

When asked a similar question on the posttest (Figure 8.2), Rosie has not only demonstrated she can read a line plot, but she has also used landmark data to explain a reasonable prediction. She used the distribution rather than the scale to find the median because she had multiple experiences manipulating data in the previous weeks. She had the opportunity to learn and use vocabulary while playing games, participating in class activities, and working with her parents at home. For Rosie, a deeper understanding of data and probability is reflected on the posttest item.

Data from the annual progress test was also analyzed to measure student growth. This test assessed a variety of concepts and skills, and students showed significant growth (t (20) = 5.69, p < .0001) between the pretest at the beginning of the school year ($M = 23.7$, $SD = 5.6$) and the posttest at the end of the school year ($M = 32.3$, $SD = 5.6$). Furthermore, students' responses to items pertaining to data analysis and probability indicated long-term retention of concepts and skills addressed in the data and probability unit completed several months prior to administration of the posttest.

To illustrate the kind of growth exhibited by students on this assessment, samples from John's pre- and posttest are presented below. John's response to the pretest item (Figure 8.3) demonstrated little understanding of probability concepts. He relied on subjective reasoning and selected "B" as the letter most likely to be picked because that is a letter he "uses a lot." Also, he neglected to respond to the second part of the item pertaining

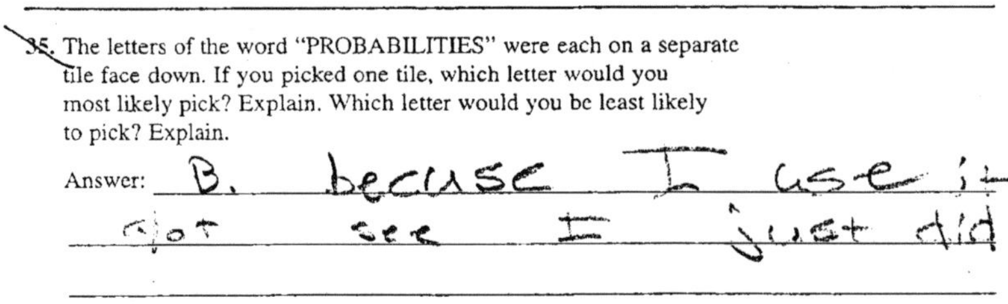

---

35. The letters of the word "PROBABILITIES" were each on a separate
tile face down. If you picked one tile, which letter would you
most likely pick? Explain. Which letter would you be least likely
to pick? Explain.

Answer: B.   becuse   I   use it
not   see   I   just did.

Figure 8.3.   Sample pretest item and student response from the
Yearly Annual Progress Test.

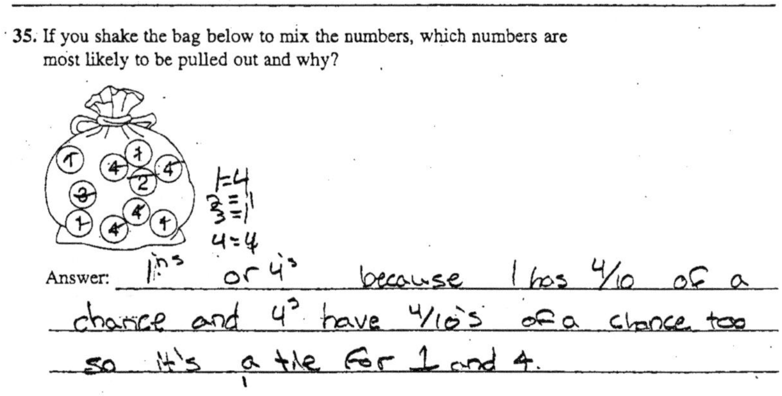

35. If you shake the bag below to mix the numbers, which numbers are
most likely to be pulled out and why?

Answer: 1's   or 4's   because   1 has 4/10 of a
chance and   4's have 4/10's of a chance too
so it's a tie for 1 and 4.

Figure 8.4.   Sample posttest item and student response from the
Yearly Annual Progress Test.

to the letter *least* likely to be drawn and did not provide any explanation
for his answer.

However, on the posttest (Figure 8.4), John's response indicated an
understanding of several probability concepts. For example, he appeared to
recognize the need to identify the sample space by listing how many of each
number were included in the bag. He also presented the probabilities
(represented as fractions) of drawing either a "4" or a "1" as a justification
for his response.

Opportunity to learn, both time spent on the unit and instruction made
meaningful, impacted John's understanding. Learning from multiple,
engaging activities such as sampling "snaebs" and playing probability
games allowed him to make connections between processes and skills, and
expand his vocabulary. The extra time spent on these activities may have
contributed to John's long-term retention well after the unit was over.

Engaging instruction, expansion beyond the textbook, and multiple experiences helped students developed a broad conceptual framework. Inquiry lessons, such as using cubes to create a data set, led to statistically significant growth and a demonstration of deep understanding of related concepts. But along with math skill achievement, solving challenging tasks helped students develop perseverance, confidence, and a positive attitude. Said Rosie on a year-end reflection, "(My teacher) was fun and believed in me in math, and now I like it."

REFLECTIONS

Creating an instructional unit to ensure a progression of concepts and skills that would both advance understanding *and* lead to higher performance on traditional achievement tests was challenging. I often felt I was balancing traditional test skills with genuine understanding and love of mathematics, thereby weakening the effectiveness of both. By choosing not to follow the textbook, I was enriching students' experiences, but I was also making more work and uncertainty for myself. I found myself short on the time and energy it takes to organize quality instruction. To compensate for this time shortage, I found myself up late many nights.

It was also difficult being different. I would sometimes panic seeing other teachers "ahead" of me in the textbook and watching students from other classes in the bus line completing worksheets from textbook pages we had not yet reached. I looked to my students' progress for confirmation as I stepped out of the textbook comfort zone. As students worked, they gave me indications of new conceptual understandings in their comments and daily work. I trusted these new concepts would be reflected in test scores.

The support of the ARRC program was important. Listening to other teachers facing similar challenges gave me new views, and, as we confirmed the importance of math to our students, gave me a sense of purpose. I gained a new respect for the importance of collecting data in a systematic manner, and I learned that goals and deadlines kept me more focused. I felt immense satisfaction as I gave an oral summary of my project to our group, and it became apparent that I had refined and developed my teaching of mathematics.

From my role as an action researcher, I better understand my role as a teacher. I'm an information processor. I filter the information, deciding its relevance and application. From this I have gained a greater understanding of the mathematics I teach, a more studied glimpse in the minds of my students, and the confidence that grows from greater understanding. I have also experienced the value of systematic monitoring and analysis of data to help direct and refine instruction. Interestingly, the more I learn, the more complex the process becomes.

The more we learn about the human mind and the way it works, the more apparent the influence of the teacher becomes. The teacher has the role of making objective ideas relevant and personal. New ideas and research inspire me, but they do not translate directly to success. The ideas must be transformed. I am the transformer. I am a buffer between "expert advice" and the vulnerability of my students. Research from experts is not personal, nor is the data I collect in my own classroom. It is meant to be objective. I make it subjective again.

NOTE

1. The FINE Foundation is a private, nonprofit organization dedicated to improving Iowa's education through research. The organization supports exemplary programs with recognition and grants, provides a forum for professional dialogue, and works toward helping Iowa's teachers improve their knowledge base and instruction.

REFERENCES

Aronson, J. (1997). *25 super-fun math spinner games*. New York: Scholastic.

Bell, M., Bretzlauf, J., Dillard, A., Hartfield, R., Isaacs, A., McBride, J. et al. (2002). *Everyday mathematics: Grade 5*. Chicago, IL: Everyday Learning Corp.

Blackwood, A. (1999). *The mailbox math series: Probability, statistics, and graphing*. Greensboro, NC: The Education Center, Inc.

Bohan, H., Irby, B., & Vogel, D. (1995). Problem solving: Dealing with data in the elementary school. *Teaching Children Mathematics, 256-60.*

Chapin, S., Koziol, A., MacPherson, J., & Rezba, C. (2002). *Navigating through data analysis and probability in grades 3-5*. Reston, VA: National Council of Teachers of Mathematics.

Edwards, T. G., & Hensien, S. M. (2000). Using probability experiments to foster discourse. *Teaching Children Mathematics, 524-29.*

Good, T. L., Multyan, C., & McCaslin, M. (2002). Grouping for instruction in mathematics: A call for programmatic research on small-group processes. In D. A. Grouws (Ed.), *Handbook of research on mathematics teaching and learning* (pp. 165-196). New York: Macmillan.

Grouws. D. A. (Ed.), *Handbook of research on mathematics teaching and learning*. New York: Macmillan.

Hitch, C., &Armstrong, G. (1994). Daily activities for data analysis. *Arithmetic Teacher, 41*, 242-45.

Koehler, M., & Grouws, D. A. (1992). Mathematics teaching practices and their effects. In D. A. Grouws (Ed.), *Handbook of research on mathematics teaching and learning* (pp. 115-126). New York: Macmillan.

Mokos, J., & Russell, S. J. (1995). Children's concepts of average and representativeness. *Journal for Research in Mathematics Education, 26.* 20-39.

National Council of Teachers of Mathematics. (2000). *Principles and standards for school mathematics.* Reston, VA: Author.

Shaughnessy, J. M. (2003). Research in probability and statistics: Reflections and directions. In D. A. Grouws (Ed.), *Handbook of research on mathematics teaching and learning* (pp. 115-126). New York: Macmillan.

Smith, W. H. (2004). A vision for mathematics. *Educational Leadership, 61,* 6-11.

Strong, R. S., Thomas, E., Perini, M., & Silver, H. (2004). Creating a differentiated mathematics classroom. *Educational Leadership, 61,* 73-78.

The Education Center, Inc. (2002). *From your friends at the mailbox: Games galore math grades 4-6.* Greensboro, NC: I. P. Crump, Project Manager.

Weis, I. R., & Pasley, J. D. (2004). What is high-quality instruction? *Educational Leadership, 61,* 24-28.

Wilson, N. (2004). *The census and America's people.* New York: The Rosen Publishing Company, Inc.

CHAPTER 9

THE IMPORTANCE OF STUDENT SHARING SESSIONS

Analyzing and Comparing Subtraction Strategies

Meghan B. Steinmeyer
University of Wisconsin Milwaukee

The National Council of Teachers of Mathematics (NCTM) *Principles and Standards for School Mathematics* (2000) identifies communication as one of the five Process Standards and an integral part of achieving the goals of the Content Standards. Communication is not solely defined as the discourse between teacher and student, it also includes students listening to each other and sharing in groups to clarify, question, and extend conjectures (NCTM). The goal is to use communication and discourse as a vehicle by which students can make sense of mathematical ideas and use them to solve problems. According to NCTM, "If students are to learn to make conjectures, experiment with various approaches to solving problems, construct mathematical arguments, and respond to others' arguments, then creating an environment that fosters these kinds of activities is essential"

Teachers Engaged in Research
Inquiry Into Mathematics Classrooms, Grades 3–5, pages 145–154
Copyright © 2006 by Information Age Publishing
All rights of reproduction in any form reserved.

(p.18). Establishing this kind of environment doesn't occur overnight; rather it is a process that is established as a part of the classroom routine.

In my third-grade classroom, students are expected to share, ask questions, and explain and justify ideas during mathematics. The foundations for these expectations are put into place at the beginning of the school year. As the teacher, I play a big role in creating this type of environment. It is my job to help establish the standards for explaining and justifying answers. I model good listening and then expect that students listen to each other. Students are required to ask questions as well as explain, clarify, and justify their own thinking (Whitenack & Yackel, 2002). Part of establishing this environment involves giving students the time to problem solve, formulate questions, prepare justifications of their strategies, reason through their work, and communicate both verbally and non verbally. By allowing students this time, I place an emphasis on understanding the mathematical process, not just the correct answer. By encouraging students to share their thinking, the importance of the process is stressed and value is given to students' mathematical ideas. This also provides me the opportunity to observe students while they are working to analyze the depth of their understanding of the mathematical content.

One of the mathematics content goals in the Number and Operations strand in Grade 3 is for students to develop computational fluency with larger numbers. Fluency is comprised of three main elements: flexibility, accuracy, and efficiency (NCTM, 2000). Flexibility means that students have more than one approach for solving a problem. Accuracy involves students carefully documenting their steps, as well as a strong understanding of number relationships. Efficiency is when a student has a strategy that makes sense, can be carried out easily, and does not involve excessive steps (Russell, 2000). Giving students the opportunity to invent their own strategies and examine various strategies through whole-class discussion is essential when trying to move students toward fluency in mathematics (Huinker, Freckmann, & Steinmeyer, 2003).

THE CONTEXT OF MY RESEARCH

I work in a large urban school district and my students come from a variety of cultural and ethnic backgrounds. We use the standards-based mathematics program, *Investigations in Number, Data, and Space*. Because of the learning environment I have established in my mathematics classroom, specifically the emphasis on students sharing of strategies to develop computational fluency, I was asked to participate in a professional development project aimed at introducing teachers to student-invented algorithms for addition and subtraction. A mathematics teaching specialist from my school district visited my classroom and videotaped typical mathematics lessons. The videotape was shown to teachers in my school district as part of a professional development workshop emphasizing computational fluency. After viewing the videotapes, teachers analyzed student work samples and worked through the various addition and subtraction strategies highlighted in the video.

My participation in this project not only helped other teachers, but it also provided me an opportunity to reflect on my teaching and to evaluate the effectiveness of my instructional practices with regard to student sharing sessions. I consistently devoted a large chunk of my mathematics instructional time to sharing student strategies. Although I knew students were learning from each other, I wanted to examine the ways in which I facilitated sharing sessions and validate the amount of time students spent sharing strategies in my mathematics lessons. What was my role in the sharing session? How did my students go about sharing their mathematical thinking? Were they just telling step-by-step how they solved the problem? Or were they grasping important concepts like number sense, place value, and the decomposition of numbers?

In this chapter I share what I have learned by taking a reflective stance and looking critically at my teaching (Mills, 2000). I begin with an explanation of my data gathering techniques using the videotape that was made for the professional development project. Then I share the findings of my analysis including examples of student sharing sessions. Finally, I examine how this research has impacted my teaching and how through effective and purposeful communication I have helped to deepen my students' understanding of mathematics.

METHODS AND FINDINGS

I used a qualitative approach (Mills, 2000) in my research whereby I observed my teaching and recorded teacher and student interactions using the videotapes of mathematics lessons in which students were adding and subtracting multidigit numbers using multiple approaches. The videotapes of eleven student sharing sessions were transcribed and I read through each transcription, paying close attention to my interactions with the students, and the interactions among the students. In order to reduce the data, I coded the transcripts (Mills) and made note of all the questions and statements that I made while I was teaching. I focused on the prompts I used to elicit student sharing and made a list of all the prompts to see what types of questions and statements I was making. I analyzed the prompts and found that my questions and statements fell into two main categories based upon the way students responded to them. These categories were *prompts that supported the analysis of student strategies* and *prompts that supported the comparison of student strategies* (Huinker, 2003). I found that in some sharing sessions I used only prompts to help analyze student thinking, while in other sessions I used a combination of both types of prompts. Examples of these different prompts are presented inTable 9.1. Some of these examples are prompts that I found myself frequently asking as I reviewed the video transcripts, others are ones that I have since found in other sources (e.g., NCTM, 1991, Rowan & Robles, 1998).

I did not fully realize the impact of these different prompts until I examined the data further. I found that the richest part of my mathematics lesson was when I facilitated the sharing session with my students. Prior to analyzing the videotapes, I had viewed the time students spent problem solving individually or in small groups as the time when most of the learning occurred. However, my analysis revealed that my interactions with the whole class during the sharing sessions were critical because they allowed students to not only share their own knowledge but also to deepen each other's thinking. In the sections that follow, I present excerpts from a lesson transcript to illustrate my use of prompts to encourage students' analysis and comparison of strategies.

Analysis of Strategies

I posed the question "What is the difference between 328 and 674?" and gave my third graders time to solve the problem individually and in small groups. After the opportunity to investigate and problem solve,

Table 9.1.   Questions to promote mathematical thinking

Prompts Supporting the Analysis of Student Strategies	Prompts Supporting the Comparison of Student Strategies
• How did you get your answer? • What are other numbers that this strategy would work well for? • Tell me (or the class) how you _____. • Would your strategy work the same if we used different numbers? Why or why not? • Tell me (or the class) what you were thinking.	• How does this strategy relate to _____? • What did _____ do differently? • What was similar about _____'s strategy? • How are _____'s and _____'s strategies alike/different? • When looking at these two strategies, what do you notice?

the students were ready to share. Two different solution strategies are illustrated by the work of Callie and Shawn, presented in Figures 9.1 and 9.2.

Callie (C) solved the problem by subtracting the number in parts. She explained her strategy to the class and me (T) as follows:

T: Tell us how you solved 674 - 328.

C: I broke this number apart (student points to 328) and this number (3) stands for 300. This number (2) stands for 20. And this one (8) stands for 8.

T: What did you do next?

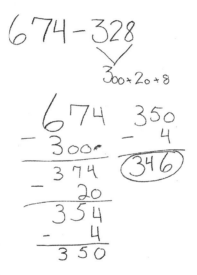

Figure 9.1.   Callie's strategy

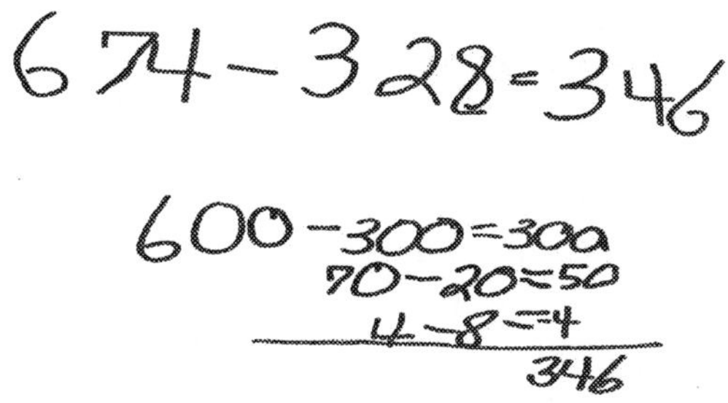

674 – 328 = 346

600 – 300 = 300
70 – 20 = 50
4 – 8 = 4
346

Figure 9.2.   Shawn's strategy.

   C: I subtracted 300 from 674, and that equals 374. Then I subtracted 20 from that number, and that equals 354. Then I subtracted four instead of eight.

   T: Why did you subtract four instead of eight?

   C: Because it would be too hard to count from eight. So I subtracted four and that equals 350.

   T: Were you done then?

   C: No. So I only subtracted four, but I was supposed to subtract eight. So then I had to subtract another four from 350 and that equals 346.

In the following excerpt Shawn (S) explained how he solved the same problem by subtracting each place.

   T: Tell us how you solved 674 – 328.

   S: I had 674 take away 328. So what I did is I took the 600 and the 300 and subtracted them to get 300. Then I subtracted the 70 and the 20 to get 50.

   T: Tell us how you subtracted 8 from 4.

   S: I subtracted the four and the eight. So what I did is I have four dollars and eight dollars, and I give my four dollars and I still owe four - so it's a 4 minus. So what I did is I added 350 dollars all together I subtracted four (because it's a four minus) and I still owe four...that's how I got 346.

In both situations, I asked the students questions or prompted them to illustrate the steps they followed when solving the problem. By doing this, I hoped to achieve three main goals. I wanted the students to understand the mathematical concepts and strategies, learn new strategies from their classmates, and evaluate and become more efficient with their own strategies (Huinker, 2003). Giving the students the opportunity to share and analyze their strategies also allowed for me to "check in" to determine what concepts the children understood and to assess for accuracy.

Since adopting the *Investigations in Number, Data, and Space* mathematics program, most of my mathematics lessons have followed the same protocol. As a class, we engage in a mini-lesson of instruction. Then the students are given a task and time to problem solve. Lastly, we all come together for sharing time. In terms of my goals, I felt this "show and tell" provided students an opportunity to learn. What I didn't realize until after the videotape project, was that I could push my students' thinking even further during these sharing sessions. Questions and prompts were a part of my repertoire, but I didn't regularly emphasize the comparison of strategies as a part of the sharing sessions. Having my students tell how they solved a problem was important. However, through my analysis of the video-tapes and transcripts, I realized that having my students analyze how and why a strategy worked made them connect mathematics concepts in important ways. My students started to see the relationships among strategies, instead of seeing each strategy separately. To illustrate this point, I refer again to the lesson transcript of the sharing session with Callie and Shawn.

Comparison of Strategies

As I listened to my students explain their mathematical thinking and the process that went into solving the problem, some common ideas began to surface among the computational strategies. Connections were emerging. Some of my students noticed that both Callie and Shawn had broken up the numbers in their problems. I decided to have the class explore this further.

T: Several of you noticed something similar about both Callie and Shawn's strategies for solving 674 – 328. Let's look at their problems again. How are Callie's and Shawn's strategies alike?

R: They both broke up their numbers.

T: They both broke up their numbers – very good. In this problem, what number or numbers did Callie break up?

M: She broke up the 328 into 300, 20, and 8.

J: Then she subtracted each part of 328 from 674.

T: So Callie broke up 328 in this problem. What did Shawn do?

N: He broke up both the 674 and 328. He turned the 674 into 600, 70, and 4. Then he turned the 328 into 300, 20, and 8 like Callie.

T: What did he do differently?

L: Instead of subtracting the parts of one number, he subtracted both numbers in parts. He used place value to help him solve this problem.

T: Tell us more about this idea.

L: He subtracted the hundreds place, then the tens place, and then finally the ones place.

T: Looking at both problems, they both broke up 328 and used the places of the numbers to help them solve the problem. However, Shawn's strategy was different because he broke up both numbers. Whether they broke apart one number or both numbers, they wanted to help make the problem easier for them to solve.

As the class took a second look at Callie and Shawn's work, they examined the strategies more closely and began to see how they were related. In this situation I made statements that focused on the similarities and differences among the students' strategies. By comparing strategies, I realized I had the opportunity to push students to progress to more complex strategies, evaluate and adjust their current strategies, and move toward efficiency (Huinker 2003). By looking at the discussion surrounding Callie's and Shawn's strategies, the concepts of subtraction, place value, and decomposition of numbers were highlighted. I realized that by asking questions that highlighted these important concepts, I could help increase my students' awareness of the connectedness of concepts in mathematics.

DISCUSSION

After viewing the videotapes, reading and analyzing the transcriptions, and reflecting upon my teaching practices I learned a lot about facilitating meaningful sharing sessions. I found that I need to continue developing a repertoire of good questions to prompt student thinking, an important part of my role in the sharing sessions. I need to regularly ask questions that encourage students to both analyze their strategies and compare the mathematics of their strategies with the strategies of their classmates. Good questions help students to not only share their strategies, but also see how their strategies relate to other students' thinking. These types of questions can lead students to think deeper and make connections to enhance their understanding (Rowan & Robles 1998). I also found that by asking good mathematical questions, my students became more confident and self reliant. The following example of a dialogue between two students illustrates this point well.

S1:   Could you explain what you did to solve 581 + 397?

S2:   I added the three to 397 that equals 400. I added three because 400 is an easier number for me to work with. Then I added 400 and 581, and that's where I got 981 from. Then I subtracted the 3, and that equals 978.

S1:   Why did you take away the 3?

Without prompting, one student took the initiative to ask another student how he had solved the problem. He then took it a step further and asked that student to justify the steps in his strategy. This student asked virtually the same questions that I would have asked when analyzing a strategy.

Second, I realized how important it is to emphasize the connections of mathematical concepts. This connectedness is an important element in

Principles and Standards for School Mathematics and is a tool to help students see mathematics as a unified body of knowledge rather than a set of complex and disjointed concepts, procedures, and processes (NCTM 2000, p. 200). By giving students the opportunity to compare strategies, like Callie's and Shawn's, they were able to discuss different ways to decompose numbers and consider different problem-solving strategies. Seeing similarities within the subtraction strategies helped to emphasize this idea of connectedness.

Lastly, I wondered whether all the think time and work time I had given in class was a worthwhile experience for my students and a beneficial part of my daily mathematics lessons. As I watched my students explain strategies that highlighted their mathematical knowledge, justify their solution strategies to their classmates, and enhance their mathematical fluency, I knew the answer was yes. My students had become a community of young mathematicians.

On a final note, I realize that there are limitations to this study. This is a snapshot of one classroom and one grade level. By systematically analyzing transcriptions of the mathematics classes, I hoped to minimize my personal biases. My intent was to remain open and objective in order to conduct research that not only enhanced the learning of my students, but helped me to grow as a professional.

To reflect on your current questioning practices, I would encourage you to either invite a colleague into your classroom to transcribe the questions that you ask during a sharing session or videotape yourself as I did. I found that the key was to look at the questions that were currently a part of my repertoire and to analyze how those questions impacted student sharing. You may find that you need to further develop your questioning prompts or you may find that you already ask good questions and just need to use them purposefully. Either way, both you and your students will benefit.

NOTE

1.   This chapter reports my experiences as a classroom teacher working on a collaborative project with Dr. DeAnn Huinker from the University of Wisconsin Milwaukee and Mrs. Janis Freckmann from the Milwaukee Public Schools. It is based upon work supported by the National Science Foundation under Grant No. EHR-0314898. Any opinions, findings and conclusions or recommendations expressed in this material are those of the author(s) and do not necessarily reflect the views of the National Science Foundation (NSF).

REFERENCES

Huinker, D. (2003, May). Subtraction strategies from children's thinking: Moving toward fluency with larger numbers. Paper presented at Green Lake Conference, Green Lake, WI.

Huinker, D., Freckmann, J., & Steinmeyer, M. (2003). Subtraction strategies from children's thinking: Moving toward fluency with greater numbers. *Teaching Children Mathematics, 9,* 347–353.

Mills, G. (2000). *Action research: A guide for the teacher researcher.* Upper Saddle River, NJ: Prentice Hall.

National Council of Teachers of Mathematics. (2000). *Principles and standards for school mathematics.* Reston, VA: author.

National Council of Teachers of Mathematics. (1991). *Professional standards for teaching mathematics.* Reston, VA: author.

Rowan, T., & Robles, J. (1998). Using questions to help children build mathematical power. *Teaching Children Mathematics, 4,* 504–509.

Russell, S. J. (2000). Developing computational fluency with whole numbers. *Teaching Children Mathematics, 7,* 154–158

Whitenack, J., & Yackel E. (2002). Making mathematical arguments in the primary grades: The importance of explaining and justifying ideas. *Teaching Children Mathematics, 8,* 524–527.

CHAPTER 10

EXAMINING TEACHER QUESTIONING THROUGH A PROBABILITY UNIT

Keri Valentine
Clark County School District, Athens, Georgia

Dorothy Y. White
University of Georgia

Teaching probability in the elementary grades is like a two-sided coin. On one side, it is an enjoyable experience because students are enthusiastic about playing games of chance, thinking about notions of fairness, and gathering data to analyze. On the flip side, teaching probability can be challenging because students often have intuitive misconceptions about the likelihood of events that can be difficult to correct, have trouble thinking about the sample space with all the possible outcomes for an experiment, and are often confused when representing probabilities as ratios. The *Principles and Standards for School Mathematics* (PSSM, National Council of Teachers of Mathematics, 2000) recommends that students need to engage in and understand the ideas of data collection, data analysis, chance, and probability. More specifically, according to the PSSM in grades

Teachers Engaged in Research
Inquiry Into Mathematics Classrooms, Grades 3–5, pages 155–178
Copyright © 2006 by Information Age Publishing

155

3–5, students should consider the likelihood of events and explore probability through experiments that have only a few outcomes. Students should also be encouraged "to develop conjectures, show how these are based on the data, consider alternative explanations, and design further studies to examine their conjectures" (p. 180). In order to effectively teach students about probability, it is necessary to understand how students think about and learn concepts of probability.

Several studies have described how students learn probability concepts. Shaughnessy (2003) reviewed the research literature on students' understanding of probability and found that children have some intuitions about probability and chance before they are taught these concepts and that many students have misconceptions about them. Students, for example, have notions about "fairness" when they enter school. They know that if they get one cookie and their sister gets two cookies, it's not fair. These intuitive notions of fairness form the foundation for their beliefs of the likelihood of events. Although these notions work when a game is fair or when there is an equal chance of an event occurring, they do not apply to all probability situations. If, for example, I have two red balls and one green ball in a bag, it is more likely that I will pull out a red ball than a green one. However, many students have a notion of *equiprobability bias* that suggests that all outcomes have the same chance of happening regardless of the sample. Jones, Langrall, Thornton, and Mogill (1999) studied the thinking of third-grade students and proposed that there are four levels of children's probabilistic thinking: subjective, transitional, informal quantitative, and numerical. Shaughnessy described their findings:

> For example, when asked what color a spinner would come up, some students responded, "Blue, it's my favorite color" (subjective) or "Blue because there's more blue on the spinner" (transitional). Other students used quantitative expressions in their reasoning: "Blue, there's three blue pieces on the spinner and one green piece" (informal quantitative) and "The chance of blue is three out of four and green is one out of four" (numerical). (p. 217)

Knowing how students think about probability is useful when planning how these concepts should be taught.

Van de Walle (2004) suggested that probability instruction should move toward providing students with experiences that lead to "intuitive understanding and conceptual knowledge" (p. 386). Students need a wealth of classroom experiences with probability ideas to build their understanding (Aspinwall & Shaw, 2000; Edwards & Hensien, 2000; Friedlander, 1997). For example, engaging students in experiments about chance that builds on their natural curiosity helps students explore the mathematics embedded in the experiments. Asking students to record and explain the results from these experiments in a systematic way such as a table or chart enables them to observe patterns in the data and to reflect on their intuitive notions of probability. These activities provide students with opportunities to confront and reflect on their intuitions and to begin to shift their thinking to recognize what one would expect to happen when a given event takes place (Frykholm, 2001).

Central to any meaningful mathematics instruction is the type of discourse teachers foster in the classroom. In particular, asking good questions and encouraging students to share their answers and solutions promotes students' thinking and enables them to learn mathematics (Rowan & Robles, 1998; Sullivan & Lilburn, 2002; White, 2003). According to Sullivan and Lilburn, good questions have three main features: (1) they require more than remembering a fact or procedure; (2) students and teachers can learn about the students' thinking from the answers; and (3) there may be several acceptable answers. Good questions are often referred to as higher-level questions. Such questions ask students to think about and share their mathematical thoughts and confusions. They are excellent ways to assess what students know, what they do not know, and where further work is needed. For probability lessons, asking children to make and explain predictions about the outcomes of an experiment allows the teacher to gain insight into the students' thinking and helps students gain greater ownership of the problem and the possible solutions (Mason & Jones, 1994). Higher-level questions help create a classroom environment where thinking and learning is encouraged and enhanced.

This chapter describes an action research project that explored the use of questioning to teach probability concepts in an inclusive fifth-grade classroom. A special education teacher and a university teacher educator were involved with me on this project. Together, we examined what students learned in a seven-lesson unit on probability. Our mathematical focus was the PSSM content standards of data analysis and probability. Throughout the unit, we focused on all five of the PSSM process standards: Problem Solving, Connections, Communication, Representation, and Reasoning and Proof. The main focus of this project was to examine how the questions I asked while teaching a unit on probability elicited students' ideas and promoted their learning. We begin the chapter with a description of the context for the study that includes the project's rationale, a description of the school and students, the components of the probability unit, and our data sources and analysis. Next, we present the types of questions that we believe helped students talk about and learn probability concepts. We also show a progression of how these questions emerged and how they improved. Students' verbal and written comments are used to illustrate our findings. We conclude with what we learned about student's probabilistic thinking from our work and what others might learn and attempt in their respective schools.

THE CONTEXT

We began the project in the spring of 2004. I was reading the book, *Good Questions For Math Teaching* (Sullivan & Lilburn, 2002) and was eager to try some of these questions. I was curious about how I ask questions in my class and wanted to learn ways to improve. I asked a teacher educator, Dorothy White, whom I had worked with previously to assist me in this endeavor. She was one of the directors of a three-year professional development project, (Project SIPS: Support and Ideas for Sharing and Planning in Mathematics Education) focused on building a mathematics learning community with the entire school staff. This action research project was my way of studying and owning the ideas espoused in the project. In particular, I wanted to create a classroom climate that was conducive to increasing students' mathematics understandings and explore the role of discourse in putting it all together in my classroom.

The School and Students

Adams Elementary (pseudonym) is a PreK–5 school in the Southeast that enrolls approximately 300 children. The students are predominately African American (51%) and Latino (39%) and 90% of the children qualify for free or reduced lunch. The school staff consists of 18 regular classroom teachers and 9 resource teachers. At the time of this study I was one of two fifth-grade teachers at the school.

I had the unique opportunity to teach a small group of eight students for mathematics. This inclusive fifth-grade mathematics class consisted of special education and general-education students from various ethnic and gender backgrounds. Of the eight students, there were 4 Latino/as (2 females and 2 males), 3 African Americans (2 females, 1 male) and 1 White male. Five of the eight were special education students identified as having Emotional Behavior Disorder (EBD), Mild Intellectual Disability (MID), and/or Learning Disability (LD). All of these students scored in the lower 20% lower on the Criterion Reference Competency Test (CRCT). The CRCT is a district-wide test administered annually each spring to assess students' understanding of the State's curriculum in reading, language arts, mathematics, science, and social studies. Students fall into 3 broad categories: exceeds expectations, meets expectations, and does not meet expectations. Compared to the rest of the 5th graders in the school, my students were the eight lowest scoring students in the school. None of them met expectations in mathematics on the CRCT. However, their test scores were *not* an indication of how they could think about mathematical ideas.

The Unit

From the beginning of the school year, the special education teacher, Donna Wilkins, and I planned and taught mathematics. For this study, we collaborated with Dorothy White, the university teacher educator, and designed a probability unit to challenge the students and to help them deepen their thinking. The goal of the unit was to provide students with some concrete experiences to expand their study of probability. The students were first introduced to probability earlier in the year when they explored the textbook chapter on the likelihood of events and representing probabilities as ratios. We wrote our predictions for picking marbles out of a bag, made spinners and predicted and wrote how the spinner would land. We also engaged in data analysis where we collected data, graphed it, and discussed our findings. However, I was not sure how well my students understood these concepts and wanted to build on them in this unit.

The unit was comprised of three activities that were adapted from the book, *In All Probability: Investigations in Probability and Statistics* (Lawrence Hall of Science, 1993). A detailed description of the activities—the Horse Race, Keeping Track/The Sum Game, and Native American Game Sticks—are found in Table 10.1. In this unit we spread the activities out over several days to provide a pacing that was not too overwhelming for the students. In Days 1 and 2 the students played the Horse Race and graphed the results. They completed the Keeping Track Activity and the Sum Game during days 3–5. The unit ended with students making Native American Game Sticks and completing related activities during days six and seven. In each lesson the students made predictions and observations, engaged in probability activities, and represented their solutions. These activities engaged students in experiments, investigations and problem-solving situations as I posed higher order thinking questions. Activities described in the unit may be used in earlier elementary grades and may seem inappropriate for fifth graders. However, these activities served as a springboard for us to examine the students' knowledge of probability and for me to practice my questioning techniques.

Overall we wanted to engage the class in activities that would reinforce the topics of chance, likelihood, and sample space; help them build on their intuitive notions of probability; and further develop the classroom discourse among me and my students. One strategy that I used throughout the unit was to ask students, at various points within each lesson, to write about their thinking as a way of encouraging them to reflect on what they were learning and to provide a record for them to use when they were called on to share their thoughts. I had used this strategy in previous mathematics lessons and found it helped students to process new information in chunks instead of asking them to reflect on an entire lesson after it was completed. I gave the students open-ended prompts in which the sentence was started for them and written on the active board[1], an interactive whiteboard that projects my computer screen onto a large magnetized screen. The prompts asked students to make predictions and conjectures and to share the various patterns they noticed.

Table 10.1.   Description of Probability Unit Lessons

Lesson	Description
Lessons 1–2: *The Horse Race*	The Horse Race was played by rolling two dice, summing the amounts and placing a marker to show that a numbered horse had moved closer to the finish line. Essentially 12 horses compete to cross the finish line first. The horses are numbered one through twelve and students are given 12 markers to move a horse when the sum of two dice equals its number. See Figure 1 for a copy of the horse race playing sheet. In this unit, students played the game three times to generate data. Before each game we asked the students to predict which horse they thought would win (1–12). After each game, students grappled with ideas about why the horses do not win an equal number of times. Students also discussed their ideas about the probability of certain horses winning more. We also created a graph of students' wins to represent the data (see Figure 10.2)

Table 10.1.   Description of Probability Unit Lessons

Lessons 3–5: *Keeping Track/* *The Sum Game*	Students completed a chart showing all the possible ways that two dice can land, and used this information to help explain the results of the Horse Race. We asked students to color the dice on the Keeping Track sheet two different colors to help them show that they are not the same dice (see Figure 10.3 for a completed chart). After we completed the investigation sheet, where students recorded the possible combinations of 2 dice, (see Figure 10.4) we played several rounds of the Sum Game and recorded the wins on a large graph (see Figure 10.5). The Sum Game started by students placing their 10 markers on the numbers 1–12. They could place them all on one number or distribute them in any fashion. I rolled the dice and students could take a marker off the board if the combination of the dice equaled a number in which a marker was placed. The first one to remove all the markers won. Students started to make connections with the horse race as they looked at the various combinations (i.e., only one way to get 2) and shared their thoughts.
Lessons 6–7: *Native American* *Game Sticks*	First the students designed their 6 craft sticks and played the game. Each person or team used two-sided sticks (one side was blank [B] and the other had a design [D]). Counters were awarded based on the type of combination that landed. For example, having all the sticks land design-side up or all blank-side up won the most counters. Having the sticks land with 3 design sides up and 3 blank sides up did not win any counters. When the game is played, it is the combinations that are important. When examining the probability for Game Sticks, one must look at the permutations, or all the possible ways the sticks can land. We modified the game to use only 3 sticks so we could talk about the sample space. Our whole class discussion began with recording the sample space for 2 sticks and moving up to 3 sticks. Students had to really think about what it means to be design side up or blank side up.

Data Sources and Analysis

The project was designed to answer two questions: (1) How do my classroom questioning techniques elicit students' mathematical thinking and learning about probability? and (2) In what way do my questioning techniques improve throughout the unit? We collected data from various sources: audiotaped classroom lessons and debriefing sessions, student journals, electronic classroom artifacts, and fieldnotes. Each lesson was audiotaped and transcribed for review. The data analysis for this project was carried out in two phases. In the first phase, Dorothy and I (and Donna occasionally) met after each lesson to debrief the lesson, review the student journals, and plan for the next lesson. We used the time to specifically highlight questions that seemed to elicit more students' thinking and to examine how my responses were used to assess student ideas. The second phase of analysis involved reading the transcriptions, searching for specific types of questions and student responses, and determining whether these instances improved over the course of this seven-day unit. The next section presents our interpretation of the data we gathered during the unit and from our debriefing/planning sessions. In this paper, pseudonyms are used for students' names.

TEACHING THE UNIT

There were two types of questions that I wanted to focus on during the unit: Clarifying questions and Consensus Building questions. *Clarifying questions* are questions that ask a student to clarify his/her thinking after he/she has answered a question. Questions such as *"How did you know that?"* and *"What do you mean when you say that?"* are examples of clarifying questions. I wanted to work on these types of questions so I could assess my students' thinking, move them forward in their mathematical understandings, and let them know that I valued their thoughts and ideas. I also wanted to build a community of learners in my classroom by asking students to listen to and respond to their classmates. *"What do you guys think about what he said?"* *"Do you agree with that answer?"* and *"Does anyone have a different solution?"* are examples of *Consensus Building questions*. Although I asked other questions, these were the two types of questions that I wanted to focus on for this project. Therefore, my collaborators, Dorothy and Donna, took notes and shared their observations in our debriefing sessions. Our analysis follows and is presented in three sections: (1) Asking Clarifying Questions, (2) Asking Consensus Building Questions and (3) Growing into my Questions.

Asking Clarifying Questions

When I started the unit the students were excited about playing new games and using manipulatives. I was excited because I was going to test my use of questions, and I had the help of my colleagues who were observing and taking notes. I wanted to focus on asking more clarifying questions because they seemed to be the easiest questions to add to my teaching. I already included clarifying questions in some of my lessons prior to this project; however, I never studied the use of these questions on students' thinking and learning.

My use of clarifying questions can be seen in the following excerpt from the first lesson in the unit, the Horse Race Game (see Figure 10.1). I asked the students to write their thoughts in their journals and then share them with the class. I used the following journal prompt to elicit their thinking, *I predict that horse # ___ is going to win the race because____*. As the students wrote, I walked around the room to note their responses. Most students predicted their favorite number or a lucky number would win. In particular, two students, Monica and Felix (pseudonyms), had interesting answers that I tried to understand as they shared their journal entries with the class. My clarifying questions are presented in bold font.

1.	T:	Monica what horse do you think will win and why?
2.	Monica:	I think10 because it is an even number and 5
3.		because it is my lucky number.
4.	T:	**Is ten the only even number?**
5.	Monica:	No. Two, four, six, eight, ten, and twelve.
6.	T:	**Why did you pick 10?**
7.	Monica:	[No answer]
8.	Rita:	I say 12, because it has the most dots (on the dice).
9.	Felix:	Eight, because it has a one out of 12 chance of
10.		winning.
11.	Monica:	All of them have a 50/50 chance.
12.	T:	**What does that mean?**
13.	Monica:	Ten has a 50/50 and 5 has a 50/50 chance.
14.	T:	**So it's like when you flip a coin, and it lands on**
15.		**heads or tails?**
16.	Monica:	All have a 50/50 chance of winning.

17.	T:	Felix said one in 12. **Why did you say 12?**
18.	Felix:	There's 12 horses and 8 is one of them, so one out
19.		of 12.
20.	T:	We talked about this with marbles. **So if there are**
21.		**six marbles and three are yellow?**
22.	Felix:	It's 3 out of 6
23.	Monica:	50/50.
24.	T:	Did anyone think of it another way?
25.	Ciara:	6 out of 3
26.	Monica:	I don't know, but it's not the same.

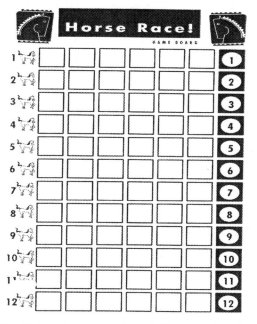

Figure 10.1.   The Horse Race game board. Each student has a sheet with 12 markers placed on the horses on the left hand side of the sheet. After each roll of two dice the player moves her/his marker one space until a horse reaches the finish line numbered down the right hand column. Student sheet reprinted with permission from *In All Probability*, Great Explorations in Math and Science (GEMS), Lawrence Hall of Science, copyright Regents of the University of California.

In the above exchange, I tried to ask clarifying questions for students to elaborate on their answers. I was trying to assess what they knew about probability but did not know how to respond to their answers. In the exchange with Monica (lines 1–6) I asked her why she chose ten but my question did not help her think more deeply about her response. Felix's response in his journal implied that he was trying to connect what he knew about probability to this situation. His response of eight having a one in twelve chance of winning showed that he knew that we sometimes speak of probabilities in terms like "one out of something." I wanted to ask clarifying questions (lines 17 and 20–21) to help him connect his prior knowledge but my questions failed to prompt this kind of connection. Monica's comments of everything having a 50/50 chance (lines 11, 13, and 16) showed that she was listening to Felix and also trying to make a connection. By asking her what that meant (line 12) and if it was like flipping a coin (line 14) I was able to assess her *equiprobability bias* but not able to help her see her misconception. Unfortunately, I did not know how to respond to either of these students with a question to guide their thinking. Instead, I moved the lesson along. I realized that asking higher-order questions is not an easy task. Asking the question is the first step, knowing how to respond is the second and most important step.

During our debriefing sessions from the first two lessons we talked about what the students were able to do and where they had confusion. Most of the students were operating from a subjective level of probabilistic thinking and selected their favorite horses even after several games. However, they were surprised with the outcomes and started to wonder why their numbers were not winning. We also noticed that all the students were counting the pips on the dice; some needed to count all the pips while others could count on from one die. For fifth graders this was a concern and so we decided that I should ask questions like, "*What number combination did you learn from playing this game?*" to help students think about using their addition facts as they played the games.

Our last observation was that my questions were not helping students reflect on their answers. Students were just repeating what they had written or answering my questions with what they thought was right. I needed to focus more on the mathematics embedded in the games, use more probability terms, and ask questions that were clear to the students in order to help them think more deeply. One strategy we used was to prepare some probability questions before the lessons based on student responses and misconceptions.

Asking Consensus Building Questions

As the unit progressed, I learned to prepare my questions in advance and to ask more questions focused on the mathematics. For example, *What sum is more likely to occur? What number combination did you learn from playing this game?* and *Is this game fair?* I also began to ask the class what they thought about a classmate's answer. In the following excerpt from Lesson 2, the students shared what they noticed about the Horse Race Graph (Figure 10.2).

Felix wrote that he noticed that five was winning and that six numbers had bars and six did not. In this example the Consensus Building questions are presented in bold.

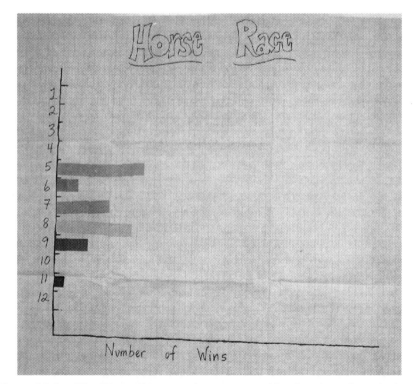

Figure 10.2.   The Horse Race graph constructed by the class after playing 3 rounds of the game. Each win was recorded on the graph horizontally with a one-inch square. We used a different color for each horse to help the students distinguish the different horses. Horse 5 won the most followed by horses 8 and 7.

1. 2.	T:	You want to share first, ok. Go ahead. Is everybody listening?
3.	Felix:	I guess so.
4. 5.	T:	All right it looks like it. Go ahead and tell us what you wrote.
6. 7.	Felix:	Uhm, from the horse race I notice that 5 is winning and the colors.
8. 9.	T:	**Did anyone else say that 5 was winning? How many of you wrote that in your journal?**
10.	Students:	Some students raise their hands.
11. 12.	T:	Ok, there's one. I saw a couple of other people too. Ok
13.	Felix:	Oh and that there's 6 numbers.
14.	T:	Oh, there's 6 numbers, well six of those horses.
15.	Felix:	Yeah six horses with the bar.
16.	T:	What does that mean about those horses?
17.	Felix:	They, they have been winning.
18.	T:	They have been winning ok. Very good.
19.	Felix:	[Inaudible]
20. 21. 22. 23. 24.	T:	There are 6 horses that don't have anything at all. What does that mean about those horses?.. What about horse, the horses with nothing beside them? What about horse 1, 2, 3, 4, 10, and 12? What does that say about those horses?
25.	Felix:	They haven't won anything.
26.	T:	They haven't won anything.
27.	Monica:	People haven't been rolling their numbers.
28. 29.	T:	**So what do you guys think [about what Felix said]? Thumbs up or thumbs down or not sure?**
30. 31. 32.	Class:	[All students raise their thumbs up to signal their agreement with Felix's statement that some horses have not won any races]

In this exchange, I asked consensus-building questions (lines 8–9 and 28–29) to encourage the students to listen to Felix and to see if they had the same answer of five. Some of the students raised their hands, and at the end all showed a thumbs up sign that they agreed with Felix's observation. Notice that Monica rephrased his comment in her own words (line 27) that suggested she was listening to Felix. I also wanted Felix to think deeper about the graph and to interpret what the bars represented. In lines 16 and 20–24, I wanted him to share with the class and me so I asked him clarifying questions but this time my questions were more probing in nature. Building on my questions that asked students to clarify their answers, I began to probe students so they could reflect on the mathematics in their answers.

We noticed that students were making connections across the different probability experiences during Lessons 3–5, as they played the Sum Game (Table 10.1). Students first completed and discussed the Keeping Track sheet (Figure 10.3) and the Sum Game Investigation sheet (Figure 10.4), recording all possible sums for two dice. Following these activities they played several rounds of the Sum Game and recorded the "wins" on a graph (Figure 10.5).

The journal entries for George and Monica suggested that they were starting to notice a pattern and to make some inferences about the numbers, 6, 7, and 8. This is shown in Figure 10.6 as they recorded where they placed their chips before each round of the sum game. For the first game,

Figure 10.3.   A student's completed sheet for keeping track of various sums when two dice are rolled. We completed the sheet as a class and students could use two dice if they needed to find the sums by counting. Student sheet reprinted with permission from *In All Probability*, Great Explorations in Math and Science (GEMS), Lawrence Hall of Science, copyright Regents of the University of California.

SUM GAME INVESTIGATION
POSSIBLE OUTCOMES TABLE

SUM	COMBINATIONS	FRACTION
2	1 + 1 = 2	
3	2 + 1 = 3 / 1 + 2 = 3	
4	2 + 2 = 4 / 1 + 3 = 4 / 3 + 1 = 4	
5	3 + 2 = 5 / 2 + 3 = 5 / 4 + 1 = 5	1 + 4 = 5
6	3 + 3 = 6 / 5 + 1 = 6 / 2 + 4 = 6	4 + 2 = 6 / 1 + 5 = 6
7	6 + 1 = 7 / 5 + 2 = 7 / 4 + 3 = 7	3 + 4 = 7 / 1 + 6 = 7
8	5 + 3 = 8 / 2 + 6 = 8 / 4 + 4 = 8	3 + 5 = 8 / 6 + 2 = 8
9	6 + 3 = 9 / 5 + 4 = 9 / 4 + 5 = 9	3 + 6 = 9
10	6 + 4 = 10 / 5 + 5 = 10 / 4 + 6 = 10	
11	6 + 5 = 11 / 5 + 6 = 11	
12	6 + 6 = 12	

Based on the results of this investigation, please write a
description of a possible winning strategy for the Sum Game
explaining your choices. Please use the following vocabulary
words: probable, more or most likely, less or least likely.

Kate Poole Math Resource Teacher Cherokee Lane Elementary PGCPS

Figure 10.4.   A student's completed Sum Game Investigation Sheet. This
sheet followed the keeping track sheet to provide another
way for students to examine the various combinations for
rolling two dice. We talked about the probabilities for each
number as the number of possible combinations/the total

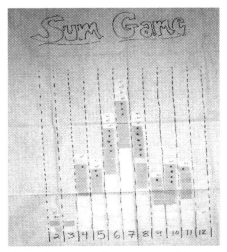

Figure 10.5.   The Sum Game graph constructed by the class over three
days. A sticky note was placed on the graph after each roll of
two dice. The bottom lighter rows were the rolls from Day 1,
the darker shaded rows from Day 2 and the rows with dots
were from Day 3.

Monica placed four chips on number 7, two chips on each of the numbers 6 and 8, and one chip each on 9 and 10. George placed his chips in a similar fashion. The work of these two students typified the thinking of the class and illustrated their emerging understanding that the sums "in the middle" were more likely to occur. Nevertheless, there were still some students who held onto their hunches and spread their chips across the board.

I also tried to incorporate more probability terminology in my questions to focus on the concept of the likelihood of an event. Consider the following exchange from Lesson 4 with Hector about his observation of the combinations he recorded on the Sum Game Investigation Sheet (Figure 10.4).

Monica's Journal

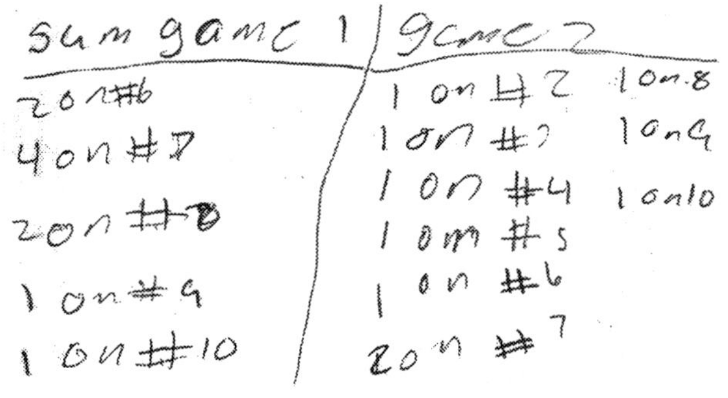

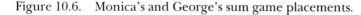

George's Journal

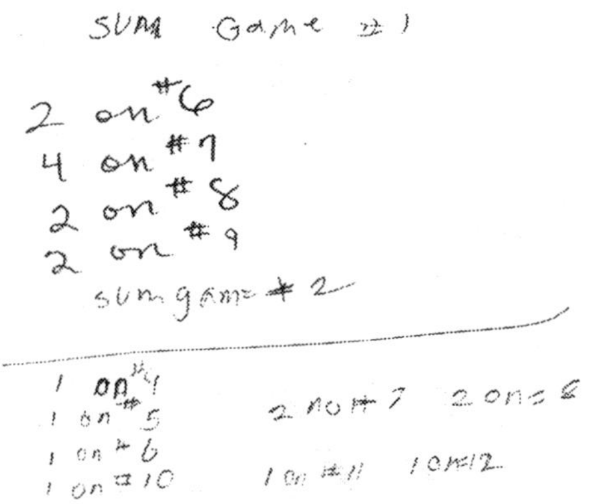

Figure 10.6.   Monica's and George's sum game placements.

1. 2. 3. 4. 5. 6.	T:	[Reads Hector's journal] "I learned to pick 7 when I am playing a number cube game. I learned that 7 has a lot of combinations. Six combinations. Seven is a common number." Ok, and what does that mean, seven is a common number? Now that you know what it means.
7.	Hector:	Seven is uhm, a lucky number.
8.	T:	It's what?
9.	Hector:	It's a more likely to pop up number.
10. 11.	T:	It's more likely to pop up, good. **Why is it more likely to pop up?**
12.	Hector:	Cause it's, in the middle.
13. 14. 15.	T:	It's in the middle ok, and **what do you notice about the numbers in the middle? What do you notice about the numbers toward the middle?**
16. 17.	Hector:	Uhm, they have more [Points to numbers in middle of the sheet].
18. 19.	T:	You pointed out that seven has more combinations.
20. 21.	Hector:	[Starts to count the different number combinations on the Sheet] 1, 2, 3, 4, 5, 6.
22.	T:	Ok, so you see 1, 2, 3, 4, 5, 6 in the middle.
23.	Hector:	So it's six chance
24.	T:	**Six out of how many?**
25.	Hector:	Six out of 12.
26. 27. 28.	T:	**Six out of 12, you think that's all? If the seven comes up 6 times, how many different combinations are there?**
29.	Hector:	[Counts some of the combinations] 14.
30.	T:	**So what do you mean by combinations?**
31. 32.	Hector:	These [Points to the different number sentences. Then counts them.] I got 36.

33.	T:	**So how many chances does the seven have**
34.		**to pop up?**
35.	Hector:	Six out of 36.
36.	T:	**Ok, write that in your journal.**

The exchange with Hector shows that he was developing a sense of the likelihood of events but was still struggling with thinking of the entire sample space. He, like many of the students, could count the combinations or number sentences but was still not making the connection to thinking of the probability of rolling a sum of seven as six out of 36 possible outcomes. However, the game experiences and discussions were moving him forward. I felt that in the above exchange, I probed more with my questions and started to find ways to help Hector answer questions for himself.

By the end of the unit, I was asking more questions. I felt more confident in my ability to ask questions and to listen to students. Although I was making strides, I wanted my students to become better listeners to each other and to converse about mathematics. In the following exchange during Lesson 7, I asked the students to determine the probability of two Native American Game Sticks landing design side up. The sticks, which are decorated with a design on one side and blank on the other side, are pictured in Figure 10.7.

We decided to record the four outcomes on the board with a picture and the letters B for blank side and D for design side. We wrote the four possible outcomes for the two sticks as: Blank, Blank (BB); Blank, Design (BD); Design, Blank (DB); and Design, Design (DD). One student Elsa believed there were two ways for the two sticks to land design side up (DD).

Figure 10.7.   Students' Native American game sticks.

1. 2. 3.	T:	Oh so you're counting all these [Points to the two recordings with a blank side and design side (DB and BD)]? These aren't all designs though, are they?
4.	Elsa:	No.
5.	Felix:	I see what she means.
6. 7.	T:	Oh, you're looking at this one? [Points to the sticks DD]
8.	Felix:	I know what she means but it's not correct.
9.	T:	Ok, what does she mean?
10.	Elsa:	[Student comes to the front]
11.	Felix:	She'll show you.
12.	T:	She'll show me, ok.
13.	Felix:	I still think there's just one.
14. 15. 16.	Elsa:	These two. [She points to the two different designs on the two sticks to show the DD outcome]
17. 18. 19.	T:	Oh you see the two different designs, but I'm talking about when our sticks land, both land design side up. How many ways are there to do that?
20.	Some:	Two.
21.	T:	Look at, look at the board you guys
22.	Ciara:	One.
23.	Felix:	I say one.
24. 25.	T:	So what is the probability of it [the pair of sticks] landing on design sides?
26.	Hector:	One out of two.
27.	Rita:	No, one out of four.
28.	T:	Ok?
29.	Hector:	[Nods yes]

In this exchange, Felix understood what Elsa was trying to say even though he disagreed (lines 5–13) and Rita was very comfortable disagreeing with Hector (lines 26–27). While I would have liked to see more discussion among the students I realized in this short seven-lesson unit, it was not possible. I did not move the students to talk with each other, but I believe I was off to a good start.

Growing into my Questions

As I reflected on my questioning during the unit, I could see growth. I began to notice when my questions did not achieve what I was hoping for, namely, getting students to think and learn. I also noticed when I asked questions that really probed the students and provided me with a glimpse into their thinking. Asking students to think about the mathematics they were engaged in helped them become active learners instead of passively accepting what a classmate or I told them. I believe that the students were beginning to make sense of the probability concepts as I asked them to reflect on their learning. My questions helped them think about how the probability activities were tied together as they investigated the likelihood of events.

As I grew in my questioning, I began to feel comfortable asking more questions and switching between the different types of questions. My clarifying questions evolved as I started to probe more. As I listened more intently to the students I began to realize the difference between asking a student to explain their answer and helping them think more about the mathematics embedded in the activities. I am still growing and learning to incorporate more and better questions.

WHAT WE LEARNED

There were so many things that we learned about the students, I realize how powerful good questions can be. Not only can you accurately assess what students are thinking, but good questions can also lead students to investigate a problem further and to look for evidence to support their conclusions. In a mathematics class where students are problem solving, one answer is not the goal; rather, the process of thinking, predicting, reflecting, and investigating become the focus. The students seemed to enjoy this style of learning mathematics so much that they would look forward to class. We wanted the students to make sense of representations of data, to explore various contexts to think about probability concepts, to understand what was important, and to develop a community of sharing through classroom discourse. We learned that the students needed the various contexts to grapple with probability ideas and that my questioning helped them make connections. Most students started the lesson with notions about probability and games of chance with dice (i.e., lucky numbers and snake eyes) and some knowledge of how probabilities could be named (i.e. one out of two, or a fifty-fifty chance). They learned that probability is about chance and sometimes what is less likely to happen can happen but with more trials you get closer to the number that is most likely to occur. For example in the horse race the students saw that some numbers like 5 or 8 could win more races even though 7 was most likely. In contrast, in the sum game with more rolls, they saw the 7 win most often and how it matched the probabilities. Through this unit they began to understand that a sum of seven was most likely to occur when rolling two dice because there are more combinations or ways to make that sum.

Visual representations of data (e.g., graphs) helped the students to predict, summarize, and question their hunches. I learned that students love mathematics when they feel they are the ones creating the data. However, in order for students to talk about mathematics, they must develop knowledge and use of math vocabulary. I also realized that students need each other. In the beginning students would share their own thoughts without any attention to what their classmate had just shared. As I continued to ask them what they thought about the comments made by classmates, they began to listen to each other. Talking in the mathematics classroom aids everyone in advancing further. Writing in mathematics also helps students think for themselves before they share with the group.

I realize that I am constantly learning as a teacher. Even when I see a line of incorrect mathematical reasoning, I still do not always know what task or question to present to lead students toward correct thinking. However, I do know that if I try to ask questions and listen, I will learn what the student is thinking.

WHAT OTHERS MIGHT LEARN FROM US

This action research project enabled us to collectively listen to the students' mathematical thinking. The project also created a vehicle for a classroom teacher, a special education teacher, and a university teacher educator to collaborate and learn from each other. In this project, we were fortunate to have three sets of eyes attending to the students' thinking. Given that this was an inclusive mathematics class, having a special education teacher in the room was key. She was there to help students that needed extra support and to make modifications to the lessons, such as using different colors in the graphs and asking students to think about the sum combinations. In this project we debriefed together and included the special education teacher whenever she was available. She provided insight into the special learning needs of some of the students and how we should modify certain tasks. The key however, was that the special education teacher and I saw this classroom as a collective.

The ideas learned in this project are not limited to inclusive education classes. These ideas can be implemented in any mathematics classroom where the teacher is open to exploring and using various questioning techniques. We found by incorporating one type of question at a time, it made the process a little less frustrating. The important part was thinking about which questions worked well and which questions did not. Then I gradually added different types of questions, as I felt more informed and comfortable.

We also found that the use of journal prompts allowed the students to think about what they wanted to say before sharing with the class. Asking students to write in their journals throughout the lesson let them reflect on chunks of information instead of the whole lesson. It allowed me time to think about the questions I wanted to ask as I noted what students were writing in their journals. Having students read their entries was a comfortable vehicle for my students to communicate their thoughts and for me to ask questions. A similar strategy is think-pair-share. In this strategy, students first think independently about the question or prompt, next they pair with another student to think and talk about their ideas, and then share with the whole class. This gives everyone a chance to think about and talk before presenting to the class. Although it does not allow me to know what they will say, it does give the students a chance to "think before they speak."

In closing, this experience gave us an opportunity to work, plan, and learn together. Developing questioning techniques like the ones described in this probability unit can be used with any mathematical topic. It is definitely worth trying.

ACKNOWLEDGMENT

We wish to thank Ms. Donna Wilkins, Special Education teacher, for participating in this project and sharing her time, insights, and thoughtful reflections

NOTE

1. An active board is an interactive whiteboard that projects a computer screen onto a large magnetized screen. A teacher can write on the board or control computer programs with a pointer or her finger. The active board also allows the teacher to save any written work onto the computer. In this study, we used the board to project copies of the game sheets so the class could see them as we practiced how the games are played. We also saved the completed sheets from the active board onto the computer for future reference.

REFERENCES

Aspinwall, L., & Shaw, K. L. (2000). Enriching students' mathematical intuitions with probability games and tree diagrams. *Mathematics Teaching in the Middle School, 6,* 214–220.

Edwards, T. G., & Hensien, S, M. (2000). Using probability experiments to foster discourse. *Teaching Children Mathematics, 6,* 524–529.

Evitts, T. A. (2004). Action research: A tool for exploring change. *Mathematics Teacher 97,* 366–370.

Friedlander, A. (1997). Young students investigate number cubes. *Teaching Children Mathematics, 4,* 6–11.

Frykholm, J. A. (2001). Eenie, meenie, minie, moe… Building on intuitive notions of chance. *Teaching Children Mathematics, 8,* 112–118.

Jones, G. A., Langrall, C. W., Thorton, C. A., & Mogill, A. T. (1999). Students' probabilistic thinking in instruction. *Journal for Research in Mathematics Education, 30,* 497–519.

Lawrence Hall of Science. (1993). *In all probability: Investigations in probability and statistics grades 3–6 – Teacher's Guide.* Berkeley, CA: Author.

Mason, J, A., & Jones, G. A. (1994). The Lunch-wheel spin. *Arithmetic Teacher, 41,* 404–408.

National Council of Teachers of Mathematics. (2000). *Principles and standards for school mathematics.* Reston, VA: Author.

Rowan, T. E., & Robles, J. (1998). Using questions to help children build mathematical power. *Teaching Children Mathematics, 4,* 504–509.

Shaughnessy, J. M. (2003). Research on students understanding of probability. In J. Kilpatrick, W. G. Martin, & S. Schifter (Eds.), *A research companion to principles and standards for school mathematics,* (pp. 216–226). Reston, VA: NCTM.

Sullivan, P., & Lilburn, P. (2002). *Good questions for mathematics teaching: Why ask them and what to ask [K–6].* Sausalito, CA: Math Solutions Publications.

Van de Walle, J. (2004). *Elementary and middle school mathematics: Teaching developmentally,* (5th ed.). Boston, MA: Pearson Education, Inc.

White, D. Y. (2003). Promoting productive mathematical classroom discourse with diverse students. *Journal of Mathematical Behavior, 22,* 37–53.

CHAPTER 11

GWEN'S STORY

Researching Teaching With Others in a Lesson Study Transforms a Beginning Teacher's Understanding

Ann R. Taylor and Laurel D. Puchner
Southern Illinois University Edwardsville

Gwen Scheibel
Millstadt Consolidated School, Millstadt, Illinois

INTRODUCTION

Gwen Teaches Problem Solving in Her Fourth-Grade Class–October 2001

I stepped into my fourth grade classroom in August 2001 as a first-year teacher, fairly confident of my teaching skills, and not questioning the curriculum I was to teach. However, I soon became involved in a professional development program provided by our County Regional Office of Education. This program focused on problem solving, and through its activities I learned that reform math educators advocated

Teachers Engaged in Research
Inquiry Into Mathematics Classrooms, Grades 3–5, pages 179–200
Copyright © 2006 by Information Age Publishing

179

using a problem solving approach to teaching mathematics. So, even though I didn't recall hearing anything about problem solving in my teacher education program, and my rural elementary school of 550 students used the scripted Saxon mathematics curriculum, I decided to supplement the curriculum by teaching a problem solving lesson every Wednesday.

I picked out one of the lessons (a problem with possible solutions) that had been provided in the grant workshops, and decided to teach it to my students. It didn't seem like a difficult task. I had received excellent reviews from my professors during my teacher preparation program. I had also worked in Millstadt School as an aide for a year before being hired as a teacher with my own classroom, and so had seen a wide range of teaching styles. In addition, the workshops made teaching problem solving look easy, and the "lesson" was all ready to go.

I taught the lesson on a Wednesday in October. I approached it determined to let my students come up with solutions on their own. I handed out a photocopied math problem with some working space at the bottom, and told them to come up with as many ways to find the answer as they could. I didn't want to give them too much of a lead because this is what I thought problem solving was all about – doing it on your own. To my horror, the lesson was a total flop. After about five to ten minutes over half the class still sat there blank-faced with nothing on their papers. The ones who did have writing on their papers were just using the numbers in the problem and trying to either multiply, divide, add, or subtract them. Finally I did guide them a little, but even then I could see the frustration on their faces.

What had gone wrong? I thought I had done everything the way it was supposed to be done, so I blamed the class. It was clear to me that these children could not think independently and problem solve like the question expected them to. Apparently this kind of problem was for older children, or maybe even brighter children. I knew that my large class had about seven or eight children with IEPs related to disabilities and behavioral problems. With a class this low, there was no way to do open-ended problems: shorter activities were what they really needed. So I decided the "bombed lesson" made sense – after all. Never again, I told myself, would I attempt this type of problem-solving lesson with this group of students. Fortunately, the grant program coordinators never asked any of us how our lessons went, so I didn't have to talk about my disaster.[1] From then on, I still set Wednesdays aside for more thought provoking mathematics, but we worked on shorter activities involving manipulatives.

Little did I know that seven months later not only would I attempt the disastrous lesson again, but that three colleagues, a university professor, the county math coordinator, and a first-grade teacher I'd never met before would be watching the lesson and taking notes.

Stories like Gwen's problem-solving "disaster" are probably repeatedly occurring in schools all over the country as bright graduates emerge from teacher preparation programs, enter their own classrooms, and encounter the kind of complex challenges of practice Gwen faced. Teachers such as Gwen can react to such challenges in different ways. One possibility is the

response Gwen had – deciding that her students were not up to the challenge. In light of the realities of the new teacher's job situation, this
response is understandable. Apart from the short prelude of pre-service
education, and an even shorter interlude of inservice professional development, the bulk of teachers' time is spent working individually in their classrooms. Most schools have an isolationist culture, in which teachers attempt
to solve problems in their classroom on their own, and in which asking for
help might be perceived as a sign of incompetence (Joyce, Bennett, &
Rolheiser-Bennett, 1990; Short, 1992). Under these conditions it is very
difficult to become skilled at any aspect of teaching; in the area of math,
this makes it very difficult to develop teaching practice that embodies the
vision of "mathematical proficiency" (National Research Council, 2001)
recommended by the mathematics education community.

Teacher research can help teachers take a different approach to such
challenges. Teacher research is a form of research in which classroom
teachers develop a problem, and then design a project, collect data, and
analyze their own findings (Dana & Yendol-Silva, 2003). Because teacher
research involves teachers investigating their own problems, they are more
likely to change their practice in response to research findings. The most
common example of teacher research is action research. However, there
are other forms, one of which is lesson study. Like action research and
other forms of teacher inquiry, lesson study involves "systematic, intentional study of one's own professional practice" (Dana & Yendol-Silva, p.
5). Unlike action research, lesson study is necessarily collaborative in
nature, as teachers work together to plan a research lesson.[2]

Gwen is a fourth-grade teacher, and the lesson study was initiated as part
of a research grant directed by Laurie and Ann, university professors in a
School of Education in southwest Illinois. Laurie specializes in educational
psychology and Ann in elementary mathematics methods. They met Gwen
when she joined a grant-funded lesson study group five months after her
problem-solving lesson had flopped. For the lesson study, the group
revised the lesson that had been such a flop for Gwen, and then Gwen herself retaught it. This chapter describes the lesson study research process
that Gwen and her colleagues undertook, and the way in which this process led Gwen to understand her initial disastrous problem-solving lesson
in a different way.

Two Research Projects

This chapter focuses on two research projects that occurred simultaneously and that were closely linked. The first is Gwen's research into her
own teaching as she engaged in lesson study with three other teachers at

Millstadt School, a small rural school enrolling primarily white, middle-class children. In addition to Gwen, who taught fourth grade, the Millstadt group comprised Cinde, who also taught fourth grade, and Sandi and Marilyn, who taught 3rd grade. Ann and Laurie invited Gloria Oggero, a county mathematics coordinator who was interested in and knowledgeable about lesson study to become the group's mathematics advisor. Gloria knew the four teachers, and as advisor she played a strong role, attending all the planning meetings, as well as the teaching of the lesson, and the debriefing.

The purpose of the lesson study was for the teachers to improve their thinking about mathematics and enhance their teaching of mathematics by closely collaborating to develop one detailed mathematics lesson plan. The research questions for the teachers' project were:

- What important overarching mathematics goal do we want to focus on in our research lesson?
- What lesson plan best meets this goal?
- How will planning and teaching one lesson help us teach mathematics?

The data sources for the lesson study included the teachers' joint knowledge of mathematics and mathematics teaching; the knowledge of their advisor, Gloria Oggero; and lesson plan and mathematics books that were at their disposal. The methods used in the study were in-depth discussion of the goals and procedure for the lesson.

The second research project was undertaken by Laurie and Ann, as they examined the lesson study process of Gwen and her colleagues as part of a larger study to examine lesson study in several different schools in southern Illinois. The main purpose of the larger study was to assess the challenges, benefits, and barriers to the use of lesson study as a means of improving the teaching and learning of mathematics (Taylor & Puchner, 2002, 2003).

Laurie and Ann collected data and simultaneously facilitated the lesson studies, taking a relatively hands-off approach in terms of the latter. Drawing on their experience working cooperatively with teachers, and mindful of the inevitable power differences in such relationships (Fu & Shelton, 2002), they tried to use their expertise and time to focus on collecting data to understand the larger picture of the value of lesson study for improving the teaching of mathematics, tasks the teachers did not have time or resources for. This chapter focuses on a subset of the findings from Gwen's group only, with the specific question emerging in this case as: How did lesson study help one first-year teacher reinterpret one bad experience with problem solving? Data collection related to Gwen's lesson study group involved Ann attending one teacher planning meeting and the teaching of the lesson and debriefing. In the end, the data comprised the following: fieldnotes taken by Ann during and after her participation in the planning meeting, during the observation of the lesson, and during the debriefing session; a report prepared by the group and by their advisor after the lesson study; an audio transcript of the debriefing session; and transcripts of individual interviews with Gwen and one other teacher from the Millstadt group carried out in June 2002 (following the completion of the lesson study).[3]

The rest of the chapter is divided into two parts. The first part is the report of Gwen's research project, and describes the lesson study process and results from Gwen and her teacher colleagues' perspective. The second part is Laurie and Ann's analysis of the project, as they try to see the bigger picture of how lesson study interacted with Gwen's first year teaching experience.

GWEN'S STORY: THE LESSON STUDY

The Five Planning Meetings

We held five planning meetings for our lesson study. At the first meeting, we were optimistic about our ability to complete the lesson quickly, and somewhat skeptical about the lesson study process. We simply didn't see why planning one lesson should take very long. At the first planning session we identified our general research theme: "Students will use critical and higher-level thinking skills to solve open-ended problems." After the first meeting we all felt pretty confident and doubted we would even need all four of our remaining sessions to complete our lesson study.

At our second meeting we really began working, and that is when we realized that lesson study was going to be much more difficult and time-consuming than we had originally believed. In our final report we described the second meeting as follows:

> **April 5th 2002**—Boy were we wrong! We spent this entire session discussing what problem we were going to use and how to introduce it. Gwen brought in a sample of an open-ended problem she taught in her class, without success. We analyzed this problem in order to determine why it had not been successful. This took a substantial amount of time. We decided to write a similar problem, changing the language in order to simplify it. This also took a substantial amount of time. Once we finalized the problem, we began working on the introduction. Again, this took a substantial amount of time! Finally, Gloria [advisor] put our misery to an end by suggesting that we stop

here and go home. Now, we were doubting that we would have enough time to complete the lesson study, let alone survive it! (Report, June 2002)

However, from the second meeting on things just flowed really well and went very fast. Even though we were surprised at how long it was taking us to create the research lesson plan, we felt good about the process. My own attitude underwent an amazing transformation, from a mind set of being skeptical about this whole thing, to learning more about exactly what it was, to then thinking that it would be amazing if all four of us could come up with a lesson. I began to believe that with four people working on it together and sharing ideas, we would create a great lesson, even though none of us had more than 5 years' teaching experience. Our final report tells this story of transformation over our last three meetings:

April 12, 2002—After a week of personal reflection, we came back refreshed but a little apprehensive. We were now aware of how time-consuming the process could be, and we were not expecting much progress tonight. However, we surprised ourselves. By the end of this session, our lesson was completed! We agreed that Gwen would teach the lesson to her class, and we would use her previous attempt as a baseline for comparison. We left with a renewed sense of accomplishment.

April 30, 2002—At this session we had hard copies of our lesson to edit and revise. Gloria formatted our lesson on the computer to include a Teacher Comment column [to use during the observation]. We also made the necessary corrections and revisions. Everyone left with a revised hard copy to look over before our next meeting. We could now see the light at the end of the tunnel. Gwen, however, perceived the light to be the headlight of the train that was about to run her down. We assured her that we would only evaluate the *lesson*, not her. We also decided that she would practice teaching the lesson to us at the next session. Now she not only saw headlights, she could hear the train whistle, as well.

May 8, 2002—After Gwen's practice run, we found a few flaws. We made those corrections, and called it a night. We were now ready for the much-anticipated final presentation. (June 2002, Final Report)

One of the helpful forces that kept us on track during our planning meetings was the advisor who had been assigned to our lesson study group. We knew Gloria Oggero already, as many of us had worked with her before in problem-solving workshops hosted by the Regional Office of Education.

She basically volunteered to guide us through the lesson study because it was a totally new experience for all of us and she is the expert when it comes to problem solving.[4] She was also an organizer, in that she helped us through the steps and kept us on track with what needed to be done. She gave us goals to accomplish by the end of our meetings. At the same time, although she provided us with ideas and examples of problems, she allowed us to make our own choices and decisions, and she went where we said we wanted to go. She guided us, but we teachers still came up with all the ideas on our own. We could have done it without her, but her facilitation and mathematics expertise were very helpful.

The Teaching of the Problem Solving Lesson – May 2002

Finally the big day came. I taught the lesson study research lesson to my fourth-grade class on May 14, 2002, seven months after my first attempt at problem solving. Observing the lesson were my three fellow group members, Gloria Oggero, Ann (as researcher), and Carol (a university instructor and first-grade teacher in a neighboring district). I was surprised how closely I was able to follow the specific details in our plan. I began with an introduction focusing on the idea that there may be multiple ways of solving a single problem. Then we read the problem together from an overhead transparency: "Farmer Brown saw 40 heads in the barnyard, some were chickens and some were pigs. He counted 100 feet. How many of each animal did Farmer Brown see?" I asked questions so the children could identify the important information in the problem; I marked their responses on an overhead transparency. Next, I provided some examples on the board of how a particular number of animals could be used to find a number of feet. During the next phase of the lesson, children worked on their own, and I moved around the room helping. Some children wanted me to tell them what to do, and I followed our plan by asking them questions and guiding them to think about the ideas. The final section of the lesson provided time for the students to share their solutions on the board. After the sharing session, the lesson was over. (See Appendix for complete lesson plan.)

Amazingly, the students were engaged, busy, and well-behaved during the entire lesson. During the introduction, the children were very attentive and answered all of my questions; I noticed that at one point, all but two had their hands up. When they were supposed to work on their own, they all did, some of them coming up with mathematics solutions and ideas I never would have thought they could do. I can't describe how thrilled we four teachers were. Although we knew we had spent a lot of time and thought on our lesson plan, we still had low expectations for this class going in. The lesson went so well, however, that we almost couldn't contain ourselves when it was over.

Following the lesson we all walked down the corridor to the library for the official debriefing and the atmosphere was almost electric, we were bursting to talk. However, because we wanted to wait until we were all gathered and could follow the lesson study debriefing protocol Ann had given us, we tried not to converse about the extraordinary experience we had just had in the research lesson. Soon, everyone was gathered, and the debriefing began. Although we were all thrilled and surprised that the class was so engaged throughout the lesson, I shared my thoughts first.

Frankly, I was completely surprised. I thought that we had come up with a lesson that was good and I had felt confident that I would be able to teach it the way we had planned even though I was nervous about teaching it in front of others. But I was never confidant that my children were going to get the mathematical thinking. Prior to the lesson, I still had a huge doubt that my students just might not understand this type of problem being a low, low class like they were. Then when it went so well I was just amazed. I actually said in the debriefing:

> That was not my class! I don't know who those people were! I was so happy, I couldn't quit smiling when I walked around and I saw some of their [responses]. I just had to smile and say, Oh, they are doing it....Normally I have a very needy class: they just want you to tell them what to do. (Debriefing, May 2002)

In any classroom, but especially in my class you can just figure on a couple of students sitting there with nothing on their paper no matter what, but there wasn't a single student with nothing on their paper. One girl even used the sample problem I had put on the board at the beginning and developed a pattern from that. I just could not believe it – I never imagined the children would engage with the mathematics like they did. I had done so little with problem solving strategies. I had not told them that using a chart was one way you can solve a problem, yet one boy came up with a different chart all by himself. My colleagues' comments show that they shared my perspective:

> I think all of us just about fell over.... Because we have all had some of those kids at some point in the last couple of years ....[Their] being quiet didn't surprise me as much, ...but they were all on task...most of them worked the entire time. Even the kids that I know don't do well with thinking on their own without specific directions, were trying. I didn't see if they got the correct [answer]... but they were trying, they did not shut down, they did not give up. (Cinde).

I think that because we were prepared for them to just be their normal selves and...in the lesson we tried to remember that they are going to ask this question and they are going to ask this question, they are going to do this, and so we tried to waylay that...and it worked. I am just amazed. (Marilyn)

After the lesson, I went back and compared the students' work with their work from the lesson that bombed. In this second lesson, all the writing was mathematical – there were no drawings of animals. All the children wrote more, and some children even had time to add sentences and words to explain their strategies. In the first lesson Jenna just used symbols representing the standard algorithm. The second time, however, she explained her strategy step-by-step referring to her own diagram (see Figures 11.1 & 11.2).

Altogether, there are 20 cranes-and-tortoises.
The sum of the number of their feet is 52.
How many cranes and how many tortoises are there
respectively?

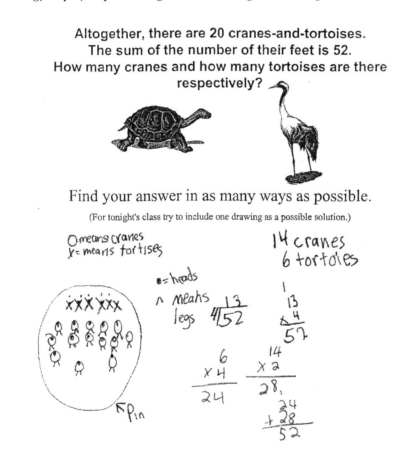

Find your answer in as many ways as possible.

(For tonight's class try to include one drawing as a possible solution.)

Figure 11.1.   Jenna's paper from the first problem-solving lesson.

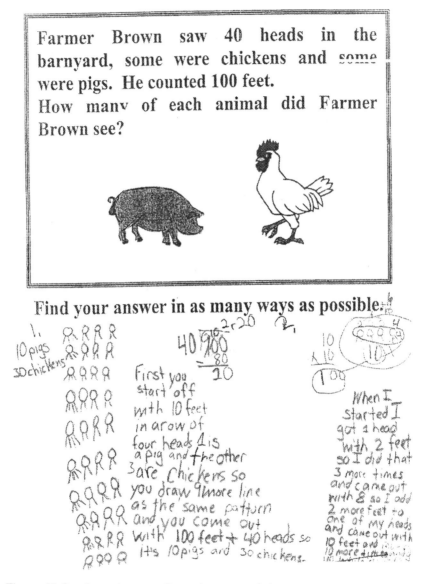

Figure 11.2.   Jenna's paper from the research lesson.

Many children tried new strategies; for example, Brad developed a table to organize his thinking. After drawing a diagram with rows of heads with either two or four feet, he then organized his ideas into a chart (see Figure 11.3). His chart indicated how many feet an increasing number of chickens

Figure 11.3. Brad's paper from the research lesson.

would have. For example he started with 20 chickens and recognized they would have 42 feet and then he went up incrementally to 30 chickens having 60 feet. Interestingly, on his chart he started with 20 chickens and 20 pigs, then he increased the number of chickens each time by one and decreased the number of pigs until he reached the appropriate number. Importantly, the writing came from the students, it wasn't because I was doing it for them on the chalkboard.

The lesson study experience was very valuable, and I would say the two most important things that I learned are the importance of planning and the benefits of collaboration. In terms of planning, one initial misconception I had was that open-ended problem solving had to be a completely "on your own" mathematics lesson. I thought if I gave students examples it took away the idea of them coming up with their own ideas and their own solutions. I also thought I didn't need to plan anything or even think about it because I had the lesson/problem right there. In fact, I learned that a clear introduction accompanied by some examples just helps their brains start working and thinking up their own ideas. Also, now I am much more careful to make sure that problems are worded appropriately for the grade level, rather than just photocopying whatever I find and using it that way. I can see the difference when we did take the time to really think about each aspect of the lesson. In terms of collaboration, I am so quick to go to my colleagues with questions now after realizing the value of working so closely with them. Sometimes all it takes to get through a problem or tough time is to get a couple more brains involved, especially those that I worked with on lesson study. There is no fear that I'm stealing Marilyn's ideas, for example, because we know that's the best thing to do. We formed a bond and a respect for each other that may never have come about without our lesson study experience.

UNIVERSITY RESEARCHERS' REFLECTIONS: LAURIE AND ANN

Gwen's story is particularly interesting for two reasons. First, Gwen taught a mathematics problem to her fourth-grade class in October 2001 with minimal direction from others. Six months later she worked with a lesson study group to plan, teach, and debrief a version of this same lesson. This teacher research project allowed for an interesting comparison of the same lesson under these two very different conditions. Second, the fact that Gwen had taught as an aide in Millstadt School during the previous year makes it easier to separate her learning to teach mathematics from her learning to deal with other issues. Specifically, most first-year teachers are learning to teach mathematics while simultaneously learning to deal with classroom discipline, a new school setting, and other issues. Such new teacher issues can compound a beginning teachers' learning of "pedagogic content knowledge" (Shulman, 1986) of mathematics into an undifferentiated tangle of teaching dilemmas. With fewer new teacher issues to worry about than most first-year teachers, Gwen's story presents us with an unusual window into a beginning teacher's learning about one method, problem solving in mathematics, in the complex situation of her own fourth-grade classroom.

Gwen knew from her inservice program that problem solving was important for effective mathematics learning, and that it was seen by many as a central plank in efforts to reform mathematics teaching (Bransford, Brown, & Cocking, 1999; Kamii, 1994; Stein, Smith, Henningsen, & Silver, 2000). The workshops had also provided her with some good sample problems. What Gwen didn't have the first time she taught a challenging problem was a good understanding of how to teach such problems to her particular students. It appears that lesson study provided Gwen with the type of support she needed in order to face this challenge. Through engaging in this form of teacher research, Gwen changed her beliefs about problem-solving lessons and about her students, in two major ways. First, the lesson study research work and subsequent lesson led Gwen to recognize that detailed planning can result in lessons that have much better results than she had believed possible, especially with her somewhat challenging group of students. Second, Gwen recognized how useful collaboration is, and although the lesson study support ended after two rounds, she has continued to regularly consult members of the lesson study group about teaching problems. When Gwen taught the problem-solving lesson for the first time at the beginning of the year, she came away believing that that type of problem solving was too hard for her students. The lesson study experience led Gwen to unlearn what she had convinced herself of in her isolated, trial and error, first-year teacher experience. One aspect of this unlearning was realizing that her students were not the ones to blame. This realization is reflected in the following comment from her interview following the lesson study, when she talked about her change in thinking:

> *I'd had rave reviews by my professors in college and my cooperating teachers. You know and so I guess that was one huge surprise for me, because I was like "Yikes I've failed, it was me not the students".... And what I thought they were, was more of a reflection of what I was. And when I turned myself around, it turned them around.* (Interview, June 2002)

In her initial lesson, although she had a vision of wanting students to think mathematically, she was not able to manage the details of her particular context, her students' apparent abilities, changing from her usual curriculum, and her own beginning pedagogical content knowledge of teaching through problem solving. As Gwen stated in a recent conversation: "*I thought I didn't need to plan anything or think about it because I had the lesson/problem right there.*"

When she joined the lesson study group, and she and her fellow teachers decided to examine how to teach mathematics through problem solving, they began to adapt and think specifically about the challenges they may face. These challenges included their children's passive dependency on the teacher. The teachers adapted the lesson plan to engage students and also to scaffold them through their first experience of problem solving. Although teachers with more experience in teaching through problem solving might choose different strategies for this lesson plan, for these teachers their plan fit the particular context and their level of teacher knowledge. In addition, in the lesson study planning the teachers predicted the kind of responses children would have, and then imagined how they might respond. They asked questions and sought the advice of their mathematics advisor. They thought of every detail. The reward was that they experienced their students thinking in a way they did not believe they were capable of.

"They truly amazed me, and it just shows that when you have such good planning and thought process going into your lessons, how much it can affect your students and what you get from them, and even what you think of them."
(Gwen interview, June 2002).

IMPLICATIONS

Just as one teaching disaster can be reified into a lifetime of practice, so too one success can be. However, we believe the lessons from this teacher research go deeper. What this experience illustrates is the benefit to teachers of collaborating and of thinking deeply and carefully about the details of a lesson. What emerged was not "The Perfect Lesson," but something much richer —an opportunity to work on a real problem of practice, to think deeply about the small daily issues of teaching, like question wording, timing, how much to say, likely student response, materials to use, and then exploring fully what happened and following through those predictions to reality. The mathematics *Principles and Standards* (National Council of Teachers of Mathematics, 2000, p.19) indicate that "worthwhile tasks alone are not sufficient for effective teaching. Teachers must also decide what aspects of a task to highlight, how to organize and orchestrate the work of students, what questions to ask students having varied levels of expertise, and how to support students without taking over the process of thinking for them." These standards also state that teachers must have high expectations for all learners. The teachers in Gwen's lesson study group realized that when they planned in detail, they were capable of engaging their students in mathematical thinking that they had not thought the students were capable of. This is something the teachers figured out for themselves, when they began to inquire carefully and to re-form their practice in small ways, at a pace that they set and in a process that was driven by their own thinking and discussion, albeit with the benefit of a mathematics advisor's support.

Teacher reflection is an important part of learning. However, many teachers reflect on their practice and draw incorrect conclusions that do not lead them to better mathematics teaching (Taylor & O'Donnell, 2004). Reflecting immediately on her "bombed" lesson in October, Gwen had concluded that her children were not capable of problem solving. The lesson study research process slowed down and deepened teachers' thinking as they spent 20 hours exploring, planning, and teaching a lesson in the best way imaginable. The lesson study process also provided them with an opportunity for careful and detailed observations of their students' mathematical responses because their detailed planning provided them with predictions against which to observe children's responses. This is consistent with the development of what Fernandez (Fernandez et al., 2003) has described as a student lens, through which teachers begin to consider lessons through the experience of the learner, rather than from the teachers' perspective (Fernandez, Cannon, & Chokshi, 2003). Finally, the discussions before and after the teaching provided multiple viewpoints and interpretations of teaching and learning. This detailed discussion and sharing of different viewpoints throughout led the teachers' reflection to be more effective as they concluded that their students were more mathematically able than they had previously thought.

The report *Before It's Too Late: A Report to the Nation* from the Glenn Commission, identifies the solution to the problem of students' low achievement in mathematics as "better mathematics and science teaching" (National Commission on Mathematics and Science Teaching for the 21st Century, 2000, p.7). To achieve this goal they advocate stronger initial teacher preparation and "sustained, high quality professional development" (p.5), which they believe can be facilitated by, among other strategies, "building- and district-level Inquiry Groups …for teachers to engage in common study to enrich their subject knowledge and teaching skills"(p. 8). Lesson study provides the possibility of such a structure within which teachers can study and improve their own teaching. In addition, professional developers, teacher educators, and county and district administrators privileged to join with teachers in part of the lesson study process gain an important window through which they can understand more deeply some of the issues of teacher learning, and therefore improve their own practice. Gwen's experience of problem solving within a lesson study context was highly successful, affecting not only her understanding of the teaching method, but transforming her understanding of her children's abilities and the impact of her role as a teacher of mathematics.

NOTES

1. The grant was designed as a two-year program with instruction in problem solving and follow-up sessions. However, due to cuts in state funding, the grant was terminated early.

2. School-level lesson study involves a group of 3-5 teachers meeting regularly to collaboratively set an educational goal and then produce a detailed written plan for one "research lesson" which embodies this goal. One teacher teaches the "research lesson" while other teachers observe and take notes. Immediately following the lesson, all teachers meet to share feedback. Sometimes the group then revises the lesson and reteaches it. An outside expert, or advisor is sometimes included as part of the process. With lesson study, improvement of teaching is assumed to happen gradually over long periods of time as teachers inquire and think together.

3. The voices of several participants are included in this chapter. Ann and Laurie analyzed their data independently of one another. After recognizing the compelling nature of Gwen's story, they discussed the possibility of a joint writing project with Gwen. They then synthesized their analyses, and wrote an initial sketchy draft of this paper based on the joint analysis. They circulated the draft to Gwen for the addition of her voice into the narrative, her response, perspective and revision. Gwen's additions and revisions led to a reworking of the draft, which was followed by a meeting among the three of them to carefully discuss the chapter. This discussion and revision process was repeated several times.

4. Gloria was paid a stipend by the grant to attend two of the group's lesson planning meetings as well as the teaching of the lesson and the debriefing. Gloria went above and beyond that as she attended all of the planning meetings.

REFERENCES

Bransford, J., Brown, A. L., & Cocking, R. (Eds.). (1999). *How people learn: Brain, mind, experience, and school. Washington,* D.C.: National Academy Press.

Dana, N. F., & Yendol-Silva, D. (2003). *The Reflective Educator's Guide to Classroom Research.* Thousand Oaks, CA: Corwin Press.

Fernandez, C., Cannon, J., & Chokshi, S. (2003). A U.S. – Japan lesson study collaboration reveals critical lenses for examining practice. *Teaching and Teacher Education, 19*(2), 171-185.

Fu, D., & Shelton, N. R. (2002). Teaching collaboration between a university professor and a classroom teacher. *Teaching Education, 13*(1), 91-102.

Joyce, B., Bennett, B., & Rolheiser-Bennett, C. (1990). The Self-Educating Teacher: Empowering teachers through research. In B. Joyce (Ed.), *Changing School Culture Through Staff Development.* Alexandria, VA: Association for Supervision and and Curriculum Development.

Kamii, C. (1994). *Young children continue to reinvent arithmetic, 3ʳᵈ grade: Implications of Piaget's theory.* New York: Teachers College Press.

National Commission on Mathematics and Science Teaching for the 21st Century. (2000). *Before It's Too Late: A Report to the Nation from The National Commission on Mathematics and Science Teaching for the 21ˢᵗ Century.* Washington, D.C.

National Council of Teachers of Mathematics. (2000). *Principles and standards for school mathematics.* Reston, VA: National Council of Teachers of Mathematics.

National Research Council. (2001). *Adding it up: Helping children learn mathematics.* Washington D.C.: National Academy Press.

Short, P. (1992). *Dimensions of teacher empowerment.* State College, PA: Pennsylvania State University.

Shulman, L. (1986). Those who understand: Knowledge growth in teaching. *Educational Researcher, 15*(2), 4-14.

Stein, M. K., Smith, M. S., Henningsen, M., & Silver, E. (2000). *Implementing standards-based mathematics instruction.* New York: Teachers College Press.

Taylor, A., & O'Donnell, B. (2004). Revealing Current Practice Through Audio-Analysis Promotes Reflection and Change. In D. Thompson (Ed.), *The Work of Mathematics Teacher Educators: Exchanging Ideas for Effective Practice* (pp. 158-174). San Diego: AMTE.

Taylor, A., & Puchner, L. (2002). *Lesson Study and the Teaching of Elementary Math.* Paper presented at the AERA proposal.

Taylor, A., & Puchner, L. (2003). Learning from Lesson Study in Southern Illinois. *Illinois Mathematics Teacher, 54*(1), 20-25.

APPENDIX: RESEARCH LESSON PLAN

CHICKENS AND PIGS

TIME: 60 minutes

PROBLEM: Farmer Brown saw 40 heads in the barnyard, some were chickens and some were pigs.

He counted 100 feet.

How many of each animal did Farmer Brown see?

GOAL OF THE STUDY LESSON: Individuals use critical and higher-level thinking skills to solve open-ended problems.

PROCESS OF THE STUDY LESSON

Introduction (5 minutes)

Teacher:	I am going to collect some data from you in a very unusual way. You cannot make a sound. (Whisper) Stand up. If you rode the bus to school today, sit down, quietly. (Teacher writes "bus" on the board). If you rode your bike to

school today, sit down, quietly. (Teacher writes "bike" on the board) If you walked to school today, sit down, quietly. (Teacher writes "walked" on the board). If someone drove you to school today, sit down, quietly. (Teacher writes "car/ truck" on the board).

If any students now remain standing, teacher will ask them how they got to school today, and write it on the board.

Teacher: We all had the same problem this morning. We needed to get to school. We all solved our problem in many ways. Some of us rode the bus. Some of us rode bikes. Some of us walked. Some of us came by car or truck. (Also mention any additional ways that students may have brought up.) We solved our problem of getting to school in many ways. We're going to look at another problem today that can be solved in many ways.

Teacher puts transparency with problem on it on overhead.

Teacher: Listen while I read this problem to you.

Teacher reads problem aloud, while students track words with their fingers.

Teacher: Now, as I point to each word, read the problem aloud with me.

Teacher and students read the problem aloud as teacher tracks with her finger.

Understanding the problem (5 minutes)

Teacher: What information do we need to know to solve this problem?

Bracket important information as students respond.

Possible Student Response:

A pig has 4 legs.

A chicken has 2 legs.

Teacher should clarify that the chicken's toes are not feet.

Some are chickens and some are pigs.

There are 40 heads.

There are 100 feet.

Teacher: This one head (circle the chicken's head) has 2 feet attached to it. This one head (circle the pig's head) has 4 feet attached to it. So here we have 2 heads and how many feet?

Possible Student Response: 6 feet.

Possible Student Response:

They could all be chickens.

They could all be pigs.

Teacher: No, the problem says, "some were chickens and some were pigs." (Point to the words) If they are all chickens, he would have to have 50 chickens to have 100 feet. That would be 50 heads, and we know there are only 40 heads.

If they were all pigs, pigs have 4 feet. 40 heads x 4 feet = 160 feet. We know he only has 100 feet.

Teacher: If I have two chickens, how many heads and feet do I have?

Possible Student Response: 2 heads, 4 feet.

Teacher: If I have two pigs, how many heads and feet do I have?

Possible Student Response: 2 heads, 8 feet.

Teacher: What would happen if you came up with a solution that had 100 feet, but not 40 heads?

Possible Student Response: It's wrong, it wouldn't work.

Teacher: Would you have to start all over?

Possible Student Response: Yes.

Teacher: Actually, you don't. Once you have 40 heads, if you have too many feet, you can turn a pig into a chicken.

Let's say I have 4 heads and 10 feet. What animals can be created with these numbers?

Use drawing here to illustrate.

4 heads and 10 feet

You have used 4 heads and 8 feet.

You now have 4 chickens, but you still have 2 feet left. By adding them on to a chicken you will use all ten feet and change a chicken into a pig.

	If you don't have enough feet, you can turn a chicken into a pig.
Possible student response:	4 chickens
Teacher:	OK, but how many feet would these 4 chickens have altogether?
Possible student response:	8 feet, because 2 x 4 is 8.
Teacher:	But I said we have 10 feet. What can I do to change these 8 feet into 10 feet?
Possible student response:	Add two more feet to one of the chickens.
Teacher:	Now what kind of animals do I have?

Use P and C to denote chickens and pigs.

Problem solving by students (20 minutes)

Teacher hands out Chicken and Pig Problem.

| | |
| *Teacher:* | You will have 20 minutes to find as many solutions to this problem as you can. So once you find one solution, don't stop. Try to find another way to solve the problem. |

As students work individually, teacher will circulate around the room keeping students on-task and looking for examples of student work that can be placed on the board at the end of class.

Possible Student Response:	Are we going to work with a partner?
Teacher:	No, I want you to try to solve the problem on your own.

Teacher may choose to pair students up at her own discretion.

| | |
| *Teacher:* | I'm going to come around and put a line below your current work, but don't stop. I just want to see how much more you learned after seeing some students' solutions on the board. |

After about 10-12 minutes, as other students continue working, teacher will send some students to the board to share their solutions. They need to show all their work. (It's ok if other students begin copying this down.)

Comparing and discussing (30 minutes)

| | |
| *Teacher:* | Let's listen now to these students as they explain their solutions. |

As students explain work at the board, the teacher will allow the class to ask questions.

> *Teacher.*   Is there anyone else who would like to share a different way to solve the problem?

Teacher will look at the solutions of any volunteers to make sure they used a different method of solving the problem than the other students. Students with different solutions will be allowed to share their ideas on the overhead. (These may be incorrect, but we can still learn from them.)

> *Teacher.*   Which solution did you like the best? Why?

If students choose one that is a picture, then:

> *Teacher.*   What if the problem said that there are 1,000 feet and 200 heads? Would you want to draw all of them?

> *Teacher.*   People use many different ways to solve problems. One way may work for you that does not work for others. So just as we all came to school in many different ways, we all solve other problems in many ways, too.

CHAPTER 12

WHAT'S A LITERATURE PERSON LIKE YOU DOING, TEACHING AND RESEARCHING IN ELEMENTARY LEVEL MATHEMATICS?[1]

Vicki Zack

St. George's School, Montreal, Quebec, Canada

I have been thinking a great deal about teacher research, as it has been an integral part of my life for the past twelve years.[2] I will share with you some of the joys as well as the constraints. You will see that my connection to teacher-research is intense. Some have spoken of the uniqueness of teacher research, the insider status, and the intimate relationship between practice and research (Anderson & Herr, 1999, p. 12). For me, researching from the "inside" has been transformative and generative. There have been numerous instances, including the episodes I describe in this paper, in which I have learned something significant about the mathematics due to the children's questions and this has changed my understanding

Teachers Engaged in Research
Inquiry Into Mathematics Classrooms, Grades 3–5, pages 201–224
Copyright © 2006 by Information Age Publishing
All rights of reproduction in any form reserved.

in fundamental ways (see for example, Zack, 2002; Zack & Graves, 2001). I learn more about the children as they do the mathematics work, and more about the mathematics from the way the children solve the non-routine assignments.[3] In regard to generativity, I will show how during the course of one investigation new questions emerge and are pursued, and in turn generate other investigations. There is recursiveness in the process, in that the questions are continuously reformulated, extended and revisited, and analysis is ongoing. Some insist that teacher research is about change, that as educators we must be committed to improving our practice. However, it might just as likely involve a deliberate attempt to make more visible what is going on (Cochran Smith & Lytle, 1993, p. 52). As I try to make more visible what is going on, I come to better understand the mathematics and the children's thinking, and this in turn affects my practice. It has been a stimulating journey for me, a "literature person," to engage with mathematics and to learn to love it with a passion.

MY BACKGROUND

I returned to the elementary classroom in 1989 after completing my doctoral work, and after working at the university level in a faculty of education for a number of years, in order to research from the inside, in the changing ecologies of reform-oriented classrooms (literature-based approaches in reading and problem-solving approaches in mathematics). In the case of the task I have chosen for this paper, we, teacher and students, explored some of the surprises and puzzlements together. My background in formal mathematics is weak and in regards to personal identity I have seen myself as a "literature" person for much of my life; I came to a love of mathematics in my late 30's. What I desired for my students in their encounters with mathematics differed from what I myself knew as a student, or as a teacher of fifth graders in the late 60's. Ball has noted that teachers who are "themselves products of the very system they now aim to change" (in Schifter & Fosnot, 1993, pp. xi–xii) are also revisiting and reconstructing their understandings of mathematics. It has been a challenging and stimulating journey for me, working with reform-oriented approaches, and the sustained, systematic observation and analysis that I have been doing, namely my research, has been instrumental to my learning and teaching.

I have worked for the most part alone, always following my own agenda, posing and pursuing questions of import to me. At various points when the need arose I enlisted the involvement of others whose knowledge was more extensive than mine.[4] I will show here for example how the help of a mathematician/mathematics educator, David Reid, was invaluable. I can well attest to the importance of connectedness in research relationships. The insights we have been able to gain due to our work together underlines the value of collaborative engagement between colleagues who have a deep familiarity with the children and the data. However, I do emphasize that I am in charge of the agenda. Stating my position as the initiator of the investigations is important, since in reports about teacher-research, there is often talk of issues of power, of who's in charge (i.e., whose agenda); teachers involved in classroom research are at times obliged to investigate topics of another person's choosing when working with university faculty (Breen, 2003).

THE SCHOOL AND CLASSROOM SETTING

Our school in Montreal, Quebec, Canada is private and non-denominational, with a population that is ethnically, religiously, and linguistically mixed. Most students come from English-speaking, middle-class backgrounds. Non-routine problem solving is central to the mathematics curriculum at all grade levels. Our school curriculum is based upon the reform-oriented Quebec curriculum entitled *Défi mathématique/Challenging Mathematics* (Lyons & Lyons, 1991, 1996) and has also been heavily influenced by the initiatives envisioned by the National Council of Teachers of Mathematics *Standards* (NCTM, 1989, 1991) in the United States.

The school is a problem-solving culture in which the students are expected to support their positions and present arguments for their point of view in most areas of the curriculum. In my fifth-grade classroom (10 to 11 year-olds) we use an inquiry-based approach in which we—students and teacher alike—often pursue questions of interest to us (see for example our inquiries in the literature and social studies areas, Zack 1991, 1999b, as well as in the mathematics area, Zack & Graves, 2001).

Mathematics periods are officially scheduled for 45 minutes each day, five days per week but twice a week I have lengthened the time to 90 minutes. Each year's cohort is usually about 25 students, but mathematics in done as a heterogeneously grouped half class of 12 or 13. While I am working with one group of 12 or 13, the other group is with another teacher (in French, physical education, science, music, or art class). From September to end of March, I assign the partners and team members (heterogeneous groupings), and change the group structure every three weeks. In April to June, the children choose their partners and teams.

Extended investigations of non-routine problems take up the entire mathematics lesson three times a week. The children are given time to experiment with, think through, discuss and refine their understandings. The problem-solving tasks with which the children engage always include discussion in pairs and small groups, as my goal has been to study how learning is interactively accomplished. One particular task, the Problem of the Week, differs from the other non-routine problem-solving tasks I assign in that the children are asked to write a detailed explanation of their work. Thus, when working on a Problem of the Week, the children first tackle the problem alone, and write a detailed description in their Math Log. I read all the Math Logs prior to any discussion, and see what each child can do independently. The Math Log serves as an initial basis of the children's discussions, which are conducted by the children themselves. They work first in pairs (or a group of three), then come together in a group of four or five to compare solutions and discuss further, and then report to the half-class, with more discussion ensuing. The amount of time spent problem-solving is three, often four days each week. During the week there is time spent dealing with cultural conventions; I seek to link the children's inventions with the conventions of the culture and we do work with traditional algorithms and deal with the language of the mathematics textbook as well, so that the students will be familiar with the "formal school textbook" language of mathematics.

DATA COLLECTION ROUTINES

I will elaborate more fully now upon the classroom routines, and my data collection routines over the school week and year, with an emphasis upon those related to the Problem of the Week tasks as that is the focus in this chapter. Once a week every week throughout the school year, on Monday, I assign a Problem of the Week task. Over the school year, I assign approximately 20 Problem of the Week tasks. The students work independently on the problem during class time (a 90 minute class period); I ask them to write in detail in their Math Log about what they are doing, encouraging them to "speak" to me in writing as if I were standing at their side. On Monday night, I read the Math Log entries and take note of the strategies used, any difficulties and strengths and unique approaches, etc. On Tuesday, I allow time for the students to review their Logs if they choose to do so and at times nudge some students to deliberate upon their explanation (for example, clarify their thinking, elaborate on a diagram or add one). Wednesday is the day the discussions take place, again a 90-minute session. I select the pair (which later becomes a group of four) I will observe and stay with that group only. I set up two cameras for the Wednesday session and can thus capture the discussion going on at two tables, but I maintain my position at one station, as I find that if I move away I lose the thread of the children's thinking. An aspect in a Math Log which has aroused my interest, such as a novel strategy in a child's work for example, will at times play a role in my decision in regard to which group I choose to observe while videotaping. I take turns over a month and throughout the year to observe all the children on a rotating basis; that is, I observe a different pair/group of four every Wednesday. In accordance with ethical considerations of course, any child who does not wish to be videotaped can opt out for any specific session, or for a longer stretch of time, or for the year. I videotape the discussion of the Problem of the Week every Wednesday throughout the school year, and write observation notes throughout the year. For seven sessions in the second semester (January to May), I set up six videocameras, one for each pair of students. It is an ambitious undertaking; however, in a number of cases, having the data of all the children's work has enabled me to trace the trajectory of the discussion, and the evolution of the children's thinking. I analyze only select aspects from among all the videotape data available. However, even though in the end I look closely at very few of the videotapes and spend a great deal of time analyzing small segments of these videotapes, a wealth of data is there should I wish to return to it. I emphasize that this way of working is one I chose for my needs, and I do not wish to suggest it as a model to follow!

A number of researchers have spoken of the importance of discussion for individual and collective knowledge and of discussion-based approaches for in-depth understanding (Applebee, Langer, Nystrand, & Gamoran, 2003; Ball, 1991; Hicks, 1995; O'Connor; 1995; Pimm, 1987). My role is to offer rich mathematical tasks (although admittedly at times I only become aware of the richness in the doing, as in the instance of the Count the Squares task which I will describe below), observe to see how the thinking processes unfold, and build upon the students' ideas. As I mentioned above, during the small group discussions I observe first one pair, then that pair's group of four throughout their interaction, and write observation notes as they work together; I very rarely intervene. When the groups of four then come together as a class, I continue to listen to their discussion, writing notes as the videocamera continues to record. At the end of the class discussion, I highlight salient ideas which have been put forth, and introduce to the children other relevant ideas appropriated, with their permission, from cohorts of previous years. At the close of each session, I distribute a sheet I have titled the "Helpful explanations/Helpful ideas" sheet and ask the children to note any ideas or explanations they found helpful and tell why, and to credit the peer(s) who helped. I have found that the children become increasingly aware of the contribution others have made to their understanding, and at times can indicate how they have reshaped others' ideas to make them their own (See Zack & Graves, 2001 for an elaboration of how these Bakhtinian ideas are seen in practice in this classroom).

The structure of seeing what the child can do independently (as reflected for example in the child's work in the Math Log), and then seeing what develops as a result of the interaction corresponds with Vygotsky's (1978) view of the *zone of proximal development.* Vygotsky contended that, in order to observe a child's level of potential development, we need to examine their understanding in the course of working with others. The zone is defined as the difference between a child's performance in two situations, without assistance first, then with assistance. Vygotsky's (1978) theory that the thoughts and practices of others become integrated in our own has been fundamental to my thinking.

With time I have come to appreciate more and more the pivotal role that theory and other research studies play in my own practice and research. My questions emanate from neither theory nor practice alone but from the mingling of the two. In my life experience now, sometimes theory, at other times practice, is in the foreground, but both are always present. I have elaborated elsewhere on the role played by theorists such as Vygotsky, Bakhtin, Bruner, and Dewey in my teaching and research work (Zack & Graves, 2001).

I rely on a number of data sources, and when an episode intrigues me I return to the sources in order to learn more. These sources include my observational notes, videotape records, the children's artifacts (Math Logs), and the children's written responses to my focused questions. Also, when the need arises, I explore the children's thinking further via retrospective interviews with individual students and/or small groups. The children's unique perspectives add new dimensions to my interpretations.

THE COUNT THE SQUARES TASK AND
THE INQUIRIES THAT EMERGED

The Task and Overview of the Trajectory

Over the twelve years in which I worked with the students, I have become intrigued by various aspects in regard to a number of Problem of the Week tasks and their extensions. I have chosen as my focus a Problem of the Week task which as we engaged with it over the years offered surprise after surprise. I discovered later that it is at times called the Chessboard Task (see Mason, Burton & Stacey, 1982). I am still learning. The investigation has deepened my understanding as the findings were richer and more complex than I had anticipated. Perhaps a few of the ideas will resonate with some readers who might use them as a springboard for their own explorations. As teachers, and researchers, we all draw on the work of

	Find all the squares in the figure on the left. Can you prove that you have found them all?

Figure 12.1.   Count the Squares task.

others for generative frameworks. The task as I presented it to the class in the first year (May, 1994) is shown in Figure 12.1.

The children discerned patterns (Zack, 1997). There were two patterns which emerged at times, albeit infrequently, and these proved fruitful (see Figure 12.2). I expanded the process each year, adding extensions in order to see whether and how the children could see and generalize various patterns, primarily the sum of squares. In May 1995 I asked, "What if it were a 5-by-5 [grid]?" And in May 1996 I asked, "What if it were a 10-by-10? A 60-by-60?"

Originally, my thinking was that some children might see the pattern of the sum of the squares, and express their hypothesis that the pattern would continue (i.e., $1 \times 1 + 2 \times 2 + 3 \times 3 + 4 \times 4 + 5 \times 5 \ldots$, or $1^2 + 2^2 + 3^2 + 4^2 + 5^2 \ldots$). When I posed the "What if it were a 60-by-60 square?" question in 1996, what I expected the children to say was that "the pattern just continues." I did not expect the children to work out the actual numerical answer. They ignored me. This unanticipated response in actuality led to a number of interesting developments. Some children insisted that there must of course be an "easier way" than working through to the 60-by-60, and tried to construct an expression. However, I was not aware in 1995/6 that it was not possible for the children to construct an algebraic expression for this generalization. Nor could I, which pushed me to seek out other resources, people as well as book sources. I found in a journal,

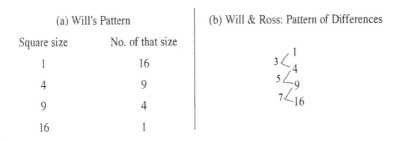

Figure 12.2.   Two patterns for the Count the Squares task.

and brought to the children, the formula Johnston Anderson (1996) reported—n(n + 1)(2n + 1) ÷ 6—one which Anderson himself called a "non-obvious expression." My expectation was that all would use it and see that it fit all of the examples, which the children had calculated concretely. I knew *that* it worked. However, the students wanted to know *why* it worked as it did (Zack, 1997). They also wanted to know how anyone could come up with that expression. It did not fit the kind of algebraic expression which some of them had been able to construct in other instances, where there was a meaningful connection and transition between the concrete examples, and the general algebraic expression (Zack & Graves, 2001). When I sought an explanation to bring back to the students, I was told by one member of a university mathematics education department that fifth graders could not construct or understand the mathematical approach to the construction of Anderson's algebraic expression given the state of their current mathematical knowledge. It seemed at that time a dead end. But perhaps due to the emphasis in our classroom environment that had been put upon explaining oneself, the children pushed to know the whys, and hows. I therefore enlisted David Reid's help, and he in turn worked to construct an explanation that made sense to fifth graders (see Zack & Reid, 2003). Thus, over the past eight years, inquiries generated by the students' work on the Count the Squares task dealt with: (a) the children's talk about proving and disproving; (b) everyday and mathematical language in the children's talk and arguments; (c) the diversity and robustness of the children's counterarguments; (d) teacher efforts to explain a non-obvious expression; and in line with the last-mentioned component, (e) thinking/theorizing about how one comes to understand complex ideas.

Fifth Graders' Talk About Proving and Disproving

You will note that in the wording of the task, the children are asked to "prove that they have all the squares." I assigned the task as it had been written, but was not intending to provoke discussion on proof. Indeed, the very word *proof* has been intimidating to me. I was not aware then that the children's work and questions would lead me to begin to explore children's notions of proof and *proving*, and would demand that I determine for myself and make explicit my definition of proof as it pertains to fifth graders. However, with hindsight I can say that I cannot be too surprised that inquiries ensued. The groundwork laid for our classroom work generally includes an expectation that the children would be looking for interesting mathematical patterns, that they would support and debate their moves, and that they could then be nudged to think about the mathematical structure underlying the pattern. It was thus not so great a leap to go from explaining and arguing to trying to convince, and to notions of proving. And because I was still a bit in awe of the term proof, thinking about proving rather than proof kept it manageable.

The children's work led me to reflect and explore. As you will see below, the team of fifth graders (Will, Lew and Gord) featured in this chapter and whose work is elaborated elsewhere (Zack, 1997, 1999a), are convinced *that* their patterns work, and they use what they know of the patterns to refute a proposal presented by their peers. Prompted by some of what arose during the children's discussions, I searched to see what mathematics education researchers had said about proof (see Zack, 1999a for examples) and then thought about what proof might mean at the elementary level. My personal definition, which evolved in response to what I was seeing, is that in order for an argument to be considered a proof the students' reasoning has to be general (i.e., they are contending that the pattern will always work) and convincing. I feel that at the elementary level, the students need not only to convince but also to explain. As I will show, this aspect of explanation was a greater challenge in the instance of the non-obvious expression than in regard to other work the children had done.

Hanna (1995) has spoken of "assumption, conjecture, example, counterexample, refutation and generalization" as elements of proof (p. 48). In the 1996 school year, I saw evidence of conjecture, generalization, and refutation, and will now speak briefly about them. Two patterns were focal in the work of the children. In relation to the first of the patterns (Figure 2a), one of the students, Will, was heard to conjecture, check the hypothesis, and once he felt sure the pattern worked, he was prepared to generalize it as a rule. To start, Will told his partners, Lew and Ross, about his conjecture, referring to his pattern: "I was pretty sure there would be a pattern, so I was keeping my eyes open and I found one." He then said he had not tested it on a different size square yet, but "the chances are if it works for those it works for others." Will then checked his answer for the next size square, and assumed that the pattern which had worked for up to 5 would continue to work in the same way. I saw other instances as well of students learning "to describe relationships that hold across many instances and to develop and defend arguments about why those relationships can be generalized and to what cases they apply" (NCTM, 2000, p. 190).

Other interesting aspects about proving and disproving arose in 1996 in regard to refutation. Will, Lew, and Gord were working toward calculating the answer for the number of different size squares in the 60-by-60 square by using the pattern of differences strategy (Figure 2b) and felt that they still had a long way to go, when the team members were asked to meet and discuss their answers. Their partners Ross and Ted joined them, and stated that 2310 would be the answer for the sum of the squares for a 60-by-60. In actuality, their ideas were not worded as explicitly as that. Ted stated, "We figured out a ten by ten is three hundred and eighty-five– . . . and a sixty times sixty is six times greater." Will, Lew, and Gord immediately disagreed vigorously, and Ross challenged them to prove that his and Ted's answer was wrong (Zack, 1997). Will, Gord and Lew used what they knew of the mathematical structure underlying the patterns to present three counter-arguments (CA), shown in Figure 12.3.

Everyday and Mathematical Language in the Children's Talk

What intrigued me was not only the solid mathematical thinking which Lew, Will and Gord used to try to convince Ted and Ross that their answer was wrong, but also the nature of their talk. Although the talk sounds like everyday conversation, it at the same time reveals an intricate mathematical structure. It was only upon close examination that I saw certain elements. I have written about the everyday and mathematical ideas, the ways in which the children could and could not articulate their thinking, and have noted the logical terms they used in their arguments, such as *because, but, if . . . then* (Zack, 1999a). In considering spontaneous and scientific concepts (Vygotsky, 1934/1986) as seen in the children's work, I have seen how the children invent procedures, have a tacit but not conscious awareness, and work ahead of formal instruction. They are able to present robust arguments when the mathematics is meaningful to them. One of my enduring questions is in regard to the role the teacher should play in making more explicit what the children are doing naturally. Richard Pallascio has suggested

First Counterargument	The answer for the [number of squares in the] 8 by 8 (which is 204) is not double the answer for the [number of squares in the] 4 by 4 (which is 30). (CA #2a in Figure 12.4)
Second Counterargument	The pattern does not stop at 385 and then *restart* itself. It keeps growing. (CA #2b in Figure 12.4)
Third Counterargument	60-by-60 gives you 3600 squares of the smallest size the 1 by 1 squares (not counting the others) and 3600 is already larger than 2310. (CA #1 in Figure 12.4)

Figure 12.3.   Lew, Will and Gord's three counterarguments (paraphrased).

that the teacher is instrumental in making certain elements visible (Gordon Calvert, Zack, & Mura, 2001, p. 45). The students use sophisticated reasoning, but may not see the power in the reasoning they are doing. The teacher can make explicit some of the components. She/he can point out the mathematical concepts the students have used perhaps without being conscious of them, and the types of arguments they have used. The teacher can re-visit what the students have said, and connect their talk with the ways in which a mathematician would express those ideas.[5] However, I am concerned about the tyranny of the formal, as formal ways are highly valued, and colloquial ways far less so (for more, see Zack, 1999a). Making the link between everyday and scientific ways of knowing is challenging, much more so than most researchers have appreciated when they speak of moving *from* spontaneous *to* scientific ways of knowing (Zack, 1999a). I contend that the interaction between spontaneous and scientific must forever be in a back and forth movement, not unidirectional, as the students make connections between their inventions and the conventions of the culture. My personal goal as their teacher is to encourage them to always press for explanations, to always keep in touch with their personal ways of knowing. Indeed, conceptual knowledge means understanding ideas in such a way that one can express them in one's own words.

Eliciting Counterarguments

It has been said that "'wrong' ideas can be opportunities for important mathematical discussions and discoveries" (NCTM, 2000, p. 191). When I saw the Ted-Ross strategy appear in the work of a number of students over the subsequent years, and noted how attractive it was at first to their peers who heard it, I wondered what discussions, and perhaps new counterarguments, might be provoked if all were to hear it. I thus decided to offer the Ted-Ross idea to all of my fifth-grade students for consideration in the 1999–2000 and 2000–2001 years. Would they understand Ross and Ted's reasoning? Would anyone refute the idea; and if yes, when and how? The Ted-Ross question was posed as follows:

> Imagine that two of your classmates, Ted and Ross, came up with the following solution for the 60-by-60: The answer for the 10-by-10 grid is 385 squares. So take the answer for the 10-by-10 square (385) and 10 x 6 = 60 so multiply 385 x 6 = 2310 and you have the answer for the 60-by-60. What would you say?

The authors of the NCTM (2000) *Principles and Standards for School Mathematics* envision children constructing valid arguments and evaluating arguments of others, detecting fallacies and critiquing others, thinking, and reasoning about mathematical relationships, such as the structure of a pattern (p. 188). I saw all of these elements. I have listed in Figure 4 the diverse counterarguments which emerged, and included within these are the three offered by Lew, Will and Gord in 1996. Here again, in regard to some of the counterarguments I heard, the children's ways of doing changed my understanding in substantive ways. I see more due to my research, as I observe closely and examine carefully. This informs my work with future cohorts of children, in a continuing cycle of generative growth (Franke, Carpenter, Levi & Fennema, 2001).

CA #1	60-by-60 gives you 3600 squares of the smallest size, the 1by1 squares (not counting the others) and 3600 is already larger than 2310.
CA #2	The growth pattern is one in which the pattern of differences between the numbers grows as the numbers get bigger. There were a number of counterarguments which dealt in some way with the idea that the numbers increase in size, and are numbered 2a through 2d below.
(2a)	The answer for the [number of squares in the] 10-by-10 (which is 385) is not double the answer for the [number of squares in the] 5-by-5 (which is 55). If you could just double the answer for the 5-by-5 to get the answer for the 10-by-10, the answer for the 10-by-10 would be 110, and it is not. (There were variants on this as the children chose different pairs to present their arguments, for example, the 4by4 and the 8by8, the 3by3 and 6by6, but the reasoning was the same.) This counterargument proved hard to express. A few of the students (5 and 2 in the respective years) could not understand Ted and Ross's method. The majority however did understand Ted and Ross's method, and understood as well the connection between Ted and Ross multiplying by 6, and the presenters of the counterargument choosing to show that when one multiplied by two it did not work.
(2b)	The pattern does not stop at 385 and then *restart* itself. It keeps growing.
(2c)	Look at the string of numbers (1x1, + 2x2, + 3x3 . . .). By the time one reaches a certain point, for example, the 20 by 20 square, the answer for the total number of squares in the 20 by 20 was a number already greater than 2310.

(2d)	Refer back to a task previously done in class, one which had a similar growth pattern. For example, in the task "What is the number of diagonals in an n-sided polygon?" one could not take the answer for the number of diagonals in a 10-sided polygon, multiply that number by 2 and get the answer for the number of diagonals in a 20-sided polygon.
CA #3	If one takes a 10-by-10 grid and lays six of them side by side, representing what Ted and Ross are suggesting, one omits counting all the different-size squares within each grid, and the squares which overlap the (10-by-10) grids. (This counterargument was offered only twice, by Jake in 2000, and by Dora, in 2001)
CA #4	There are 51 times 51 10-by-10's in a 60-by-60. This statement was offered once only as a counterargument, by Jake in May 2000, immediately after he presented CA #3.
CA #5	If theirs (Ted and Ross) works, you should be able to take the answer for the 6 by 6 (91) and multiply it by 10 and it should give you 2310, but it does not. One student, Theo, presented this argument, in 2001.

Figure 12.4.   The five counterarguments which emerged
in 1999–2000, 2000–2001 (paraphrased).

PURSUING INTRIGUING DATA AND ANALYZING THEM

I would like to deal here with the aspects of *data* and *analysis* as the terms can sound sterile and alien, as they did to me when I was first learning about research. My aim as both a teacher and a researcher is to better understand the children's thinking. In order to do that I collect information (data), and look closely at it (analyze it) in order to make more visible what is going on.

Eileen Phillips, a friend who has also been a teacher-researcher for many years, recently addressed the question of what distinguishes teacher research from good practice by noting that framing questions, collecting data, keeping detailed notes, heightened awareness, and committed looking are some of the elements which distinguish a research stance from a teaching stance (see Glanfield, Poirier, & Zack, 2003). For me, research is sustained, systematic, intentional inquiry and differs from what I did when I was teaching but not researching.

I have been asked how I go about selecting what I will study closely, within the large corpus of data that I gather each year. I have always chosen incidents or ideas which made me pause and wonder. McCarthy (Fishman

& McCarthy, 2000) recently articulated what I do implicitly when in her advice for teacher researchers she said:

> [R]espect your intuitions, take seriously the moments in your teaching that touch you, make you want to cry or sing or shout. Pay close attention to events you feel you need to understand or which you want to memorialize in your writing. If the moment "refuses to go away" . . . I urge you to study it. . . . Try to figure out why you were so affected, which of your assumptions, your closely held beliefs, were challenged by the incident. (p. 270)

My search almost always begins with a question. My main overarching goal, from the outset when I was first became involved in research work in 1985, has been to study how learning is interactively accomplished, namely: How is mathematical meaning made, and shared? (See Bishop, 1984.) My focus when I began was on explanations—children's explanations to their peers—and I then extended my search to explore arguments, and the children's notions of convincing and proving. During the course of one investigation new questions emerge and in turn generate other investigations; the questions are continuously reformulated and extended; the data are revisited or new data are collected.

When I decided to return to look again at Lew, Will and Gord's three counterarguments, in order to look more closely at the language the students used, I relied primarily on the videotape segments and the transcriptions of the approximately 10 minutes of interaction of the group of five students—Will, Lew, and Gord with Ross and Ted—discussing the answer for the 60-by-60. Also, I had met with the students eight months after the class sessions for retrospective interviews and explored with them some of their thinking in regard to their reasoning and argumentation. I discovered the intertwined everyday and mathematical language, and was intrigued to find coherence of idea and language structure in their first two counterarguments (Zack, 1999a).

When I decided to explore the reasoning and counterarguments which might emerge when I presented all the fifth-grade students in my class with the Ted-Ross strategy (years 2000, 2001), my primary data sources were all the videotape records of the students' discussions of the Ted-Ross strategy. In 2000 and 2001 I scheduled a number of retrospective interviews with the children during the last part of May in instances when I noted something of interest in the videotapes or in my notes. The students' responses during the class sessions with their peers and during the interviews offered new insights and gave rise to new puzzles and new paths to study. I studied the videotapes with heightened awareness, listening for both previously-encountered and for novel counterarguments. You will note that in categorizing the arguments (Figure 12.4), I determined that there were four, which though they sounded different in actuality reflected the same general idea, that of a growth pattern; I numbered them 2a to 2d. This category includes Will, Lew and Gord's first and second counterarguments, ones which I had considered distinct when I first analyzed their counterarguments in 1996. All the counterarguments are robust in that they are deeply rooted in the children's grasp of various aspects of the mathematics of the task. The students formulated generalizations about observed regularities in regard to diverse patterns they detected (NCTM, 2000, p. 262),

I learned about an "array strategy" (my term), an idea which I had heard a number of students mention over the years but which I did not appreciate until I looked closely at the children's explanations of their strategy for counting the number of squares in a n-sized grid (in the year 2000) and at one student's, Jake's, second counterargument refuting the Ted-Ross position. I had to work hard to understand the array strategy, which among others I have written about over the years, I felt was important to document and share with a larger audience. Jake's second counterargument (Figure 4, CA #4) came swiftly upon the heels of his presentation of his first counterargument (CA #3). He stated that there are 51 times 51 10-by-10s in a 60-by-60, without any elaboration. This took me by surprise. I recall wondering how he had arrived at those numbers. I had to sit down after the session and figure out by working down from 60 times 60 1-by-1's, to 59 times 59 2-by-2's, etc., to 51 times 51 10-by-10's that it was indeed so. I then viewed the videotapes to see whether he had at any point explained his thinking to any of his partners, in a pair or group of four, and found that he had not. When I interviewed Jake (May 23, 2000), and tried to probe, he at first could not explain his thinking. I asked two of his partners what they thought, and how was it that they knew he was correct. Dexter said: "I visualized (the) others would be off the grid." Another clue to Jake's approach might be found in his partner Ari's explanation of his/their way. In answer to the question "Why does it go down by one?" (i.e., from 60 x 60, to 59 x 59 etc.), Ari said: "The size goes up by one row of squares so there's one fewer." Ari's reasoning introduced to me a new perspective: First there are 60 x 60 little 1-by-1 squares with none going off the grid. The next size square, the 2-by-2, is one square larger than the 1-by-1 going up and across, and therefore only 59 x 59 2-by-2's fit on the grid. Jake quickly dropped 9 squares down to get 51 x 51 10-by-10's, while I had to work it out one step at a time.

Jake may possibly have worked out yet another generalization. He said the following later on during the interview as part of his response to how he arrived at the 51 x 51 10-by-10's: "I remember Jennine showed there are four 2-by-2's [in a 5-by-5]. The one itself plus 3. There are 50 rows plus the one at the bottom that's 51." I had to ask David Reid for help in understanding what Jake might have been doing. David felt that Jake might have made the following connections (illustrated in Figure 12.5), building upon Jennine's idea:

> In the 5-by-5, 5 minus 2 (the size of the square) gives you three more 2-by-2 squares which you can fit; three plus the first one gives you four 2-by-2's (along one dimension) in a 5-by-5. Hence there would be 4 times 4, or 16, 2-by-2's. In a 60-by-60, it would be 60 minus 10 (the size of the square) which gives you fifty more squares which you can fit on the grid; fifty plus the first one gives you fifty-one 10-by-10's in a 60-by-60. Hence there would be 51 times 51 10-by-10's in a 60-by-60. (David Reid, personal communication, January 5, 2002)

Jake found it difficult to articulate how he had arrived at his counter-argument of 51 times 51 10-by-10's. Doubtless, articulation of the idea is challenging because the procedure itself is complex.

For the past three years a number of students have "seen" what I have called the array strategy, and have attempted to explain in writing and in talk their strategy of how to figure out how many squares of different sizes are contained within a large square. These students develop and test conjectures about mathematical relationships. They work with generalizations they have made while doing their first tasks; they apply to the larger square, the 10-by-10, the generalizations about how many squares one can

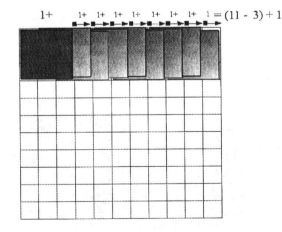

Figure 12.5.   A representation of the Jake-Jennine array strategy; 9x9 3-by-3 squares in an 11-by-11 grid (David Reid, personal communication, March 29, 2005)

fit along two dimensions; that is, both vertically and horizontally. For example, Clare, in discussing the 10-by-10, showed how she arrived at 64, or 8 times 8, squares of the 3-by-3 size, saying: "It would only be 8 [3-by-3's], 'cause you would go off the grid otherwise." Others also constructed and used this rule to arrive at their answer for how many there were of each size square. However, Jake was the only student seen to generalize this rule to an any-size square, and to use this rule to counter and refute.

My learning trajectory of the array strategy had its genesis in Lew's sliding of each size square across each row, from left to right (proof by cases) in 1996; was extended by students seeing the array as a way to arrive at the answer for the number of each-size square (Walt in 1999); and was further extended by Jennine, Jake, and Ari's knowing why it works that way (in 2000). As a result of the children's work and my commitment to inquiry when confronted with ideas that startle and stump me, I am constantly developing my own knowledge of children's thinking and my understanding of the mathematics in the task.

GOOD ENOUGH UNDERSTANDING: THEORIZING ABOUT HOW ONE COMES TO UNDERSTAND COMPLEX IDEAS

I spoke earlier of Anderson's (1996) non-obvious expression: $n(n+1)(2n+1) \div 6$, and some of the students' need to know why it worked. David Reid worked with the students for a number of years (1996, 1998–2001) trying diverse approaches as he searched for an explanation that would make sense to fifth graders. We have detailed elsewhere his attempts, the children's algebraic expressions, and the crucial ideas inherent in the diverse explanations (see Zack & Reid, 2003). Part of David's conversation with the children included telling them of his own coming to understand the explanation he had seen in a book (Nelsen, 1993) and of his working at ways to present an explanation to fifth graders. In telling this story David gave the children insight into the challenging and creative work a mathematician does. They and I had a glimpse of the mathematician's work as a human endeavor.

While David interacted with the students on the explanation of the non-obvious expression, I became increasingly aware of my own thought processes as I myself worked to make meaning of his explanation. I sometimes thought I understood the ideas, and proceeded as if I understood, only to realize later that it was not clear. Thinking about my own thinking led to a focus on the children's thinking. When David and I considered the children's work, we marveled that they seemed to grasp so much, as the ideas were complex. However, when we looked more closely our investigation revealed that much of what we had marveled at was in fact at times incomplete, tentative, and sometimes inconsistent. However, the students were able to continue to work on the problem, to explore, and even to explain things to each other that they seemed not to fully understand themselves. David and I began to explore the notion of "good enough" understanding, an idea about which I had read in an article by Mackey (1997) that dealt with the reading of complex literature; David had discussed the idea of "good enough" with colleagues at the University of Alberta in relation to enactivist theory and mathematics. Briefly put, whereas the learning of mathematics is often portrayed as sequential, and complete understanding of underlying concepts is assumed to be necessary before new concepts can be learned, we are suggesting otherwise. Under the pressure to progress and to try to get a picture of the whole, learners often resort to making good-enough decisions, which are temporary and based upon less than complete information (Mackey, 1997, p. 430). Opting for a temporary decision which is good enough for the time being is one which we make all the time in the midst of learning. The untidy and inevitably partial nature of the students' work perhaps indicates lack of understanding to some, but to us it is part and parcel of the process of coming to understand. We claim that the learner's disposition to proceed on the basis of an incomplete grasp is an essential component in complex problem solving. We have elaborated elsewhere about how the fifth grade students operate with good-enough understandings as they try to make meaning of David's explanations of Johnston Anderson's non-obvious expression (Zack & Reid, 2003, 2004).

When I read years ago that teachers who are researchers become theorists (Goswami & Stillman, 1987), I recall thinking that theorizing was done or disseminated by academics, handed down from above; it was my job to try to understand theoretical arguments, and see how they might apply, or not apply, to my life experience in the classroom. Thus, that I should be involved in theorizing astounds me.

SOME CONCLUDING THOUGHTS

I would like to touch here in closing upon a number of items, aspects of particular import to me, namely: Why do teacher research? Should all teachers be researchers in their classrooms? If involved in teacher research as a life-long commitment, how does one sustain the effort? How does a person whose identity has been tied into literature and language arts for half of her lifespan, such as myself, go forward and explore mathematics?

I know I have already dealt with the first point, Why do teacher research? but need to emphasize the reasons why I research in my classroom, as I will deal soon with the constraints. I am fulfilled in doing both the teaching and the research. I could find no better way to push my learning. Pursuing challenges has often exhilarated me, and at times rattled me. In this paper I have shared a few of the inquiries in which the children and I have been engaged. Each year I marvel at how much further the children and I go when working on the "same problem," which of course each year is in many ways not the same problem (Brown, Reid, & Zack, 1998), despite the fact that the written text with which we begin the problem-solving task remains constant. I have come a long way from the person who feared mathematics in elementary and high school and ran as far away from it as I could while in university. I now relish the joy I experience, almost all of the time, in engaging with the mathematics. Even when feeling vulnerable, my modus vivendi has been to push forward, going beyond the fear of sounding foolish, resolved to ask questions, admit ignorance or errors in thinking, and seek help when I find myself at a standstill. Other teachers have found it refreshing, or startling, that I would admit to gaps in knowing. I can do no other, one, because I am honest, and two, because when I am puzzled and I inquire and discuss my search with the students, I validate for them that it is human, and good policy, and exciting, to pursue answers to questions which intrigue us. This process serves as a model for them. Helping students pursue questions of urgent import to them, so that *they* can find the answers, is at the heart of teaching and learning, since after all they are citizens and key agents in shaping their own learning over their life span.

For me, teaching and research have become inseparable, and I cannot not be a teacher-researcher. However, I am *not* suggesting that all teachers should be researching as they teach. Requiring or suggesting that all teachers should do research implies that teaching is not enough, and perhaps reflects a lack of appreciation of the demands of teaching, let alone teaching and researching. *If* deciding to embark on some research endeavor, each individual would have to decide whether this might be a short-term involvement or done from time to time, or at the other end of the spectrum, a life-long commitment.

There are time constraints and task demands involved in doing teacher research across the professional life span. The nature of teacher research is such that even when the teaching and the research are tightly integrated and mutually constitutive as in my case, nevertheless we are speaking of two jobs. Each of the commitments–teaching and research–entails a range of discrete demands. The hyphen often seen between the two, teacher-research, may inadvertently suggest to some that the two have been collapsed into one. Very few have dealt with the issues of energy drain and time constraints in teacher research (for exceptions, see Baumann, 1996; Huberman, 1996; Zeni, 2001), and these elements need to be acknowledged. I say this not to discourage teachers but to be honest about the demands. The pace is draining, and I often have felt I have little life out-side of the work. I have never worked as hard, or had as much satisfaction from learning and teaching, as in the past twelve years spent teaching and researching. I would choose no other way, but the question of sustainability has been an essential one for me.

NOTES

1. This research was supported by Social Studies and Humanities Research grants from the Government of Canada #410-94-1627 and #410-98-0427.

2. Some of what I will say here I have already said elsewhere and in greater detail. I will indicate the sources where applicable. I have always found it challenging to write but have pushed myself to do so because writing papers and presenting at conferences has forced me to be explicit about my ideas and to explain them coherently. Attending conferences has served as a source of networking for me and has given me the opportunity to engage in discussion with others who pushed my thinking.

3. I am paraphrasing here Mikkelsen's (1989) observation in regard to chil-dren and books: "We learn more about readers from the way they read books and more about books from the way they are read" (p. 624).

4. Academics/colleagues to whom I owe a debt are Barbara Graves, Mary Maguire, and Laurinda Brown.

5. Here is David Reid's rendering, in mathematical language, of Will, Lew and Gord's first counterargument:

   1. You claim that the answer for the 60-by-60 is 6 times the answer for the 10-by-10 [because 60 is 6 times 10]
   2. We claim that if your method is valid in this case it should work for all other numbers [implicit generalization]
   The argument:
   3. We ask: Does it work for the numbers involved in the 4-by-4 and 8-by-8? [the answer for the 8-by-8 would then be 2 times the answer for the 4-by-4, because 8 is 2 times 4]
   4. We show that it does not.
   5. We reject the validity of your method. (Zack, 1999a, p. 138)

REFERENCES

Anderson, G. L., & Herr, K. (1999). The new paradigm wars: Is there room for rig-orous practitioner knowledge in schools and universities? *Educational Researcher, 28*(5), 12-21, 40.

Anderson, J. (1996). The place of proof in school mathematics. *Mathematics Teaching 155*, 33-39.

Applebee, A. N., Langer, J. A., Nystrand, M., & Gamoran, A. (2003). Discussion-based approaches to developing understanding: Classroom instruction and student performance in middle and high school English. *American Educational Research Journal, 40*(3), 685-730.

Ball, D. L. (1991). 'What's all this talk about "discourse"?', *Arithmetic Teacher 39*(3), 44-48.

Ball, D. L. (1993a). Introduction. In D. Schifter & C. Twomey Fosnot (Eds.), *Reconstructing mathematics education: Stories of teachers meeting the challenge of reform.* (pp. xi-xii). New York: Teachers College.

Baumann, J. F. (1996). Conflict or compatibility in classroom inquiry? One teacher's struggle to balance teaching and research. *Educational Researcher, 25(7)*, 29-36.

Bishop, A. (1984). Research problems in mathematics education – II, *For the learning of mathematics, 4*(2), 40-41.

Breen, C. (2003). Mathematics teachers as researchers: Living on the edge? In A. J. Bishop, M.A. Clements, C. Keitel, & J. Kilpatrick F.K.S. Leung (Eds.), *The Second International Handbook of Mathematics Education* (pp. 521-542). Dordrecht: Kluwer.

Brown, L., Reid, D., & Zack, V. (1998). On doing the 'same problem'. *Mathematics Teaching, 163*, 50-55.

Cochran-Smith, M., & Lytle, S. (1993). *Inside-outside: Teacher research and knowledge.* New York: Teachers College Press.

Fishman, S., & McCarthy, L. (2000). *Unplayed tapes: A personal history of collaborative teacher research.* Urbana , IL: National Council of Teachers of English, & New York, NY: Teachers College Press.

Franke, M. L., Carpenter, T. P., Levi, L., & Fennema, E. (2001). Capturing teachers' generative change: A follow-up study of professional development in mathematics. *American Educational Research Journal, 38*(3), 653-689.

Glanfield, F., Poirier, L., & Zack, V. (2003). Teacher research: An empowering practice? Report on the working group. In E. Simmt, B. Davis (Eds.), *Proceedings of the Canadian Mathematics Education Study Group (CMESG) Conference.* Acadia University (pp. 55-68), May 30–June 3, 2003.

Gordon Calvert, L., Zack, V., & Mura, R. (2001). Children's proving. Report on the working group. In E. Simmt, B. Davis (Eds.), *Proceedings of the Canadian Mathematics Education Study Group (CMESG) Conference.* University of Alberta (pp. 41-46), May 25-29, 2001.

Goswami, D., & Stillman, P. R. (1987). *Reclaiming the classroom: Teacher research as an agency for change.* New Jersey: Boynton.

Hanna, G. (1995). Challenges to the importance of proof. *For the learning of mathematics, 15*(3), 42-49.

Hicks, D. (1995). Discourse, learning and teaching. In M. Apple (Ed.), *Review of research in education 21, 1995-1996.* (pp. 49-95). Washington, D. C.: American Educational Research Association.

Huberman, M. (1996). Focus on research: Moving mainstream. Taking a closer look at teacher research. *Language Arts, 73*(2), 124-140.

Lyons, M., & Lyons, R. (1991). *Défi mathématique.* Montréal, Québec: Mondia éditeurs.

Lyons, M., & Lyons, R. (1996). *Challenging mathematics (Grade 1-6): Teaching and activity guide.* Trans. V. Tétrault.. Montréal, Québec: Mondia Editeurs.

Mackey, M. (1997). Good-enough reading: Momentum and accuracy in the reading of complex fiction. *Research in the Teaching of English, 31*(4), 428-458.

Mason, J., with Burton, L. & Stacey, K. (1982). *Thinking mathematically.* Toronto, Canada: Addison Wesley.

Mikkelsen, N. (1989). Remembering Ezra Jack Keats and The Snowy Day: What makes a children's book good? *Language Arts, 66*(6), 608-624.

National Council of Teachers of Mathematics. (1989). *Curriculum and evaluation standards for school mathematics.* Reston, VA: National Council of Teachers of Mathematics.

National Council of Teachers of Mathematics. (1991). *Professional standards for teaching mathematics.* Reston, VA: National Council of Teachers of Mathematics.

National Council of Teachers of Mathematics. (2000). *Principles and standards for school mathematics.* Reston, VA: NCTM.

Nelsen, R. (1993). *Proofs without words: Exercises in visual thinking.* Washington, D.C.: Mathematical Association of America.

O'Connor, M. C. (1995, draft). *The role of language and discourse in the emergence of mathematical understanding.* Boston University. <mco@bu.edu> or 617-353-3318.

Pimm, D. (1987). *Speaking mathematically: Communication in mathematics classrooms.* Routledge & Kegan.

Vygotsky, L. S. (1978). *Mind in society: The development of higher psychological processes.* M. Cole, V. John-Steiner, S. Scribner, & E. Souberman, (Eds.). Cambridge, MA: Harvard University Press.

Vygotsky, L. S. (1986 [1934]). *Thought and language.* A. Kozulin, (Ed.). Cambridge, MA: M.I.T. Press.

Zack, V. (1991). It was the worst of times: Learning about the Holocaust through literature. *Language Arts, 68* (1), 42-48.

Zack, V. (1997). "You have to prove us wrong": Proof at the elementary school level. In E. Pehkonen (Ed.), *Proceedings of the Twenty-First Conference of the International Group for the Psychology of Mathematics Education (PME 21)* (Vol. 4, pp. 291-298), Lahti, Finland, July 14-19, 1997.

Zack, V. (1999a). *Everyday and mathematical language in children's argumentation about proof. Educational Review, 51*(2). Special issue: The culture of the mathematics classroom. Guest editor: Leone Burton. 129-146.

Zack, V. (1999b). Nightmare issues: Children's responses to racism and genocide in literature. In J. P. Robertson (Ed.), *Teaching for a tolerant world.* (pp. 167-183). Urbana, IL: National Council of Teachers of English.

Zack, V. (2002). Learning from learners: Robust counterarguments in fifth graders' talk about reasoning and proving. In A. D. Cockburn & E. Nardi (Eds.), *Proceedings of the Twenty-Sixth International Conference for the Psychology of Mathematics Education (PME 26)* (Vol. 4, pp. 433-441), Norwich, United Kingdom, July 21-26, 2002.

Zack, V. and Graves, B. (2001). Making mathematical meaning through dialogue: "Once you think of it, the z minus three seems pretty weird." In C. Kieran, E. Forman, & A. Sfard (Eds.), Bridging the individual and the social: Discursive approaches to research in mathematics education. Special Issue, *Educational Studies in Mathematics, 46,* 1-3, 229-271.

Zack, V. & Reid, D. (2003). Good-enough understanding: Theorizing about the learning of complex ideas (Part 1). *For the learning of mathematics, 23*(3), 43-50.

Zack, V. & Reid, D. (2004). Good-enough understanding: Theorizing about the learning of complex ideas (Part 2). *For the learning of mathematics, 24*(1), 25-28.

Zeni, J. (2001). *Ethical issues in practitioner research.* New York: Teachers College Press.

Breinigsville, PA USA
11 May 2010
237807BV00003B/18/A

9 781593 114978